Plone 3 Products Development Cookbook

70 simple but incredibly effective recipes for creating your own feature rich, modern Plone add-on products by diving into its development framework

Juan Pablo Giménez

Marcos F. Romero

[PACKT] open source *
PUBLISHING   community experience distilled

BIRMINGHAM - MUMBAI

Plone 3 Products Development Cookbook

First published: May 2010

Production Reference: 1300410

Published by Packt Publishing Ltd.
32 Lincoln Road
Olton
Birmingham, B27 6PA, UK.

ISBN 978-1-847196-72-9

www.packtpub.com

Cover Image by Vinayak Chittar (vinayak.chittar@gmail.com)

Credits

Authors
Juan Pablo Giménez

Marcos F. Romero

Reviewers
Martin Aspeli

Alec Mitchell

Emanuel Sartor

Acquisition Editor
Rashmi Phadnis

Development Editor
Reshma Sundaresan

Technical Editor
Pallavi Kachare

Copy Editor
Lakshmi Menon

Indexer
Hemangini Bari

Editorial Team Leader
Akshara Aware

Project Team Leader
Priya Mukherji

Project Coordinator
Prasad Rai

Proofreader
Kevin McGowan

Graphics
Geetanjali Sawant

Production Coordinator
Shantanu Zagade

Cover Work
Shantanu Zagade

About the Authors

Juan Pablo Giménez's programming career started in 1996. He was a C/C++ programmer in real-time systems under the QNX OS, but quickly the philosophy of Linux and free software became more and more interesting for him as he became a sysadmin and a PHP programmer. In 2000 he began his own company, Rcom, through which he has provided IT services using FOSS tools to cover a wide range of languages and technologies. Despite having gone through abundant experience with other languages and CMS frameworks, today he focuses totally on developing products and sites under Plone.

I want to thank my family, my parents, my sister, and especially my grandmother Chola, for years of support and understanding while I sojourned in the-for them-incomprehensible world of programming.

Thanks to my best friends and associates in Rcom, Juan Pablo Noriega, Roman Mottino, Eugenio Oliveri, and Leandro Viani.

Thanks to Emanuel Sartor and the Plone community for always being there to help me in my learning process.

And thanks, Laura, for putting up with me and my crazy passions; without you, it would not have been possible for me to reach this far; thank you also for bringing to life Julieta and Sofia, the joy of my days.

Marcos F. Romero has been a software developer since 1997, working with Lotus Notes, both to develop applications, and as a trainer of users and other developers.

In 1999, he launched his first web site, after which he specialized in HTML, CSS, JavaScript, and DOM among other technologies.

Since then he has taken part in numerous other web sites and webapps—including a Lotus Notes CMS—and started working as a consultant to other professionals.

In 2007, he started to participate in Plone projects and became fascinated by the Open Source world.

For over 10 years he has been interested in Usability as a discipline applicable to everyday activities and, focused on the customer's and end user's needs, he aims to simplify and help their everyday tasks. Today he actively applies this concept in Inter-Cultura, a company that specializes in Usability and User Experience, where he has been working for several years.

All my appreciation to Gonzalo J. Auza, who ushered me into the world of Plone and who has supported me all along. A big thanks to Juan Pablo Giménez, who can't but continue to teach me; and to Martin Aspeli, Alec Mitchell, and Emanuel Sartor, who kindly agreed to share their knowledge by reviewing this book.

My gratitude to Rebeca Resnik, my English teacher, who has a lot to do with this endeavour.

A special thanks to my family and friends—especially to my parents—who phoned me continually for updates on my progress towards completion of this book.

But most of all, thanks to my wife, who lovingly did more than her share with our kids, buying me the time and quiet to complete this book.

About the Reviewers

Alec Mitchell is a Plone core developer and has been an active member of the Plone community since 2004. He was the release manager for Plone 2.5, a member of both the inaugural Plone 2.5 Framework Team, and the Plone 4.0 Framework Team. He is the co-maintainer of the Plone core content types (ATContentTypes), as well as the maintainer of Plone's default versioning system (CMFEditions) and a few popular add-on products for Plone.

Alec is an independent consultant based in Los Angeles, California. He specializes in Python, Zope and Plone development, high-performance website deployment and optimizations, and integration with web services. He has helped small and large organizations around the world to get the most from their content management systems.

Emanuel Sartor is an IT professional who has been involved in open source software since 1999. He is the cofounder and CTO at Menttes, an Argentinean company that provides custom Python, Plone and Zope based solutions.

As an active participant in the Open Source community, Emanuel has contributed many add-on products for Plone. He has conducted multiple talks and trainings at conferences such as The Jornadas Regionales de Software Libre and PyConAr. He also cofounded Plone Cono Sur, a regional Plone users group that continues to educate others about Plone.

A Laura, Julieta y Sofía

A Mercedes, Clara, Magui y Rosario

Table of Contents

Preface

The Plone Content Management System is one of the best open source CMS because, by using Plone's development framework, you can extend its functionality according to the specific requirements of your website. The Plone framework has lots of components that can be used to create add-ons or extensions called Plone Products. You can optimize your site for improved usability, accessibility, and security, by creating custom Plone products.

This book covers recipes that will help you create custom Plone Products and implement them on your website. Every topic covered in this book is accompanied by essential fundamentals and step-by-step explanations that will help you understand it better. With the help of this book you will be able to create custom Plone products that are well suited to your website.

What this book covers

Chapter 1, *Getting Started* will introduce the reader to the project that will be developed: a news website with banners hosted in OpenX. It will also cover the tools a Plone developer must have before starting a project.

Chapter 2, *Using Development Tools,* will show you how to install and use special tools that we often need to find problems (debug), modify code on the fly, or get help on tasks during the development phase of a project.

Chapter 3, *Creating Content Types with ArchGenXML,* will introduce the ArchGenXML technology by creating a new content type (based on an existing one), and will wrap the final product into a Python egg. It is a great tool to help with the development of Archetypes-based content types.

Chapter 4, *Prevent Bugs through Testing,* will show how automatic testing helps preventing the malfunctioning of features due to lack of communication or ignorance of some parts of code when projects evolve or the development team changes.

Chapter 5, Creating a Custom Content Type with Paster will cover the creation of Archetypes content types from scratch by hand... kind of. We will actually use paster to automatically create most of it.

Chapter 6, Creating Lightweight Content Types, will introduce other technologies to create lighter content types. (Archetypes is a great, though very large, framework developing content types.)

Chapter 7, Improving Product Performance, will teach you how to reap the benefits of Plone by dealing with the problem of creating content types in which the objects' final HTML rendering performs badly, and how to benchmark these improvements.

Chapter 8, Internationalization, will cover the different tools used to offer a properly internationalized product.

Chapter 9, Adding Security to our Products will go through the steps to secure tasks and content types: permissions, roles, groups, workflows, and configuration options.

Chapter 10, Improving User Interface with KSS, will introduce the use of KSS — an AJAX framework that allows UI development without writing any JavaScript, in Plone by creating from simple client-side visual changes to server-side objects manipulation.

Chapter 11, Creating Portlets, will give you step-by-step instructions for adding portlets. Portlets are used to provide contextual information about the main contents of a page.

Chapter 12, Extending Third Party Products, will deal with what to display in the final web page and how, and will show how to add new features to existing components.

Chapter 13, Interacting with Other Systems: XML-RPC will go through some essential Python modules which are used in the advertisement service to communicate with an external non-Python-based system.

Chapter 14, Setting our Products Ready for Production, will help you create your own products repository and be ready for the website launch. After finishing the development of the products, we must make them available for future use or evolution.

Appendix, Creating a Policy Product, will introduce a special kind of product to deal with site installation, configuration, and customization with code, instead of using manual actions that are likely to be forgotten.

Our Plone development project

Although this is a cookbook, we won't give isolated recipes for each individual task, we'll follow a common theme throughout the book to make it easy to understand.

A short note about the course of the book

Some of the topics that we cover may not be all together in one chapter because:

- They don't require a whole chapter or section but are better explained in different stages of the development project.
- They need an introduction and will be complemented with tips later in the book.

Examples of these subjects are buildout recipe configuration and code testing.

In addition, we'd like to mention that, for ease of explanation and understanding, we approached the writing of the book as if this were a website project commissioned to us by a customer.

Customer requirements

The project we are tackling is the design of a digital newspaper website with a particular requirement: the customer needs, with equal importance, to publish pieces of news *and* to insert advertisements all over the place.

Below is a summarized list of the functionalities the customer requested and we will cover in this book. We will include details related to specific things that Plone doesn't provide out of the box.

1. News items will be published in several sections and must include fields like country and lead paragraph or intro.
2. Multimedia content will illustrate and complement written information.
3. Multimedia content should be played online but may also be downloaded.
4. Advertisement banners will be located in several areas of every page.
5. Advertisement banners may vary according to the section of the website.
6. Commercial (and non-technical) staff should be able to modify the location of the banners.
7. All sections will have a front page with a special layout including the last published content.

In addition, the customer is planning to release a Spanish version of the website in the near future. So they also require that:

8. Everything in the website must be translated or, at least, be translatable into other languages.

There are also two additional requirements that are not particular to this project but to everyone, and are related to the quality of the final product:

9. Accessing the website must be fast, especially for readers.
10. All of the code must be properly commented and tested so that future changes can be made, without too much effort, by a different development team.

Of course, the customer has his own branding, so they need the website to have a distinctive look and feel. This part of the project will be developed by another company (that will not be covered in this book). The process of creation and applying visual design to a Plone site is called *skinning*. The result of this process is called the *skin* or *theme*, which is usually contained in a single Plone product.

 Take a look at the list of ready-to-use themes at: `http://plone.org/products/by-category/themes`.

What you need for this book

To follow all the recipes of this book you merely need a Linux or Windows system that can run Python 2.4 or above. There are only two recipes, however, that are intended for Linux only.

Who this book is for

This book is for programmers who have some knowledge of Python, Plone, and Zope. If you want to develop feature-rich add-on products in Plone, this book is for you. It is aimed at the development of backend features, so you need not have other web-related skills such as HTML, CSS, or JavaScript.

Conventions

In this book, you will find a number of styles of text that distinguish between different kinds of information. Here are some examples of these styles, and an explanation of their meaning.

Code words in text are shown as follows: "Uses a `plone.recipe.zope2instance` recipe to install a Zope instance."

A block of code is set as follows:

```
find-links =
            http://dist.plone.org/release/3.3.3
            http://dist.plone.org/thirdparty
```

When we wish to draw your attention to a particular part of a code block, the relevant lines or items are set in bold:

```
[buildout]
parts =
      python
      virtualenv
      make-virtualenv
# Add additional egg download sources here.
# dist.plone.org contains archives
# of Plone packages.
```

Any command-line input or output is written as follows:

```
# aptitude install gcc g++ libbz2-dev zlib1g-dev libreadline5-dev libssl-dev
```

New terms and **important words** are shown in bold. Words that you see on the screen, in menus or dialog boxes for example, appear in the text like this: "In Plone literature, they are called **products**, though".

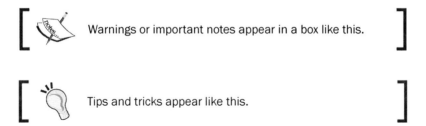

Warnings or important notes appear in a box like this.

Tips and tricks appear like this.

Reader feedback

Feedback from our readers is always welcome. Let us know what you think about this book—what you liked or may have disliked. Reader feedback is important for us to develop titles that you really get the most out of.

To send us general feedback, simply send an e-mail to feedback@packtpub.com, and mention the book title via the subject of your message.

If there is a book that you need and would like to see us publish, please send us a note in the **SUGGEST A TITLE** form on www.packtpub.com or e-mail suggest@packtpub.com.

If there is a topic that you have expertise in and you are interested in either writing or contributing to a book on, see our author guide on www.packtpub.com/authors.

Customer support

Now that you are the proud owner of a Packt book, we have a number of things to help you to get the most from your purchase.

> **Downloading the example code for the book**
>
> Visit `https://www.packtpub.com//sites/default/files/downloads/6729_Code.zip` to directly download the example code.
>
> The downloadable files contain instructions on how to use them.

Errata

Although we have taken every care to ensure the accuracy of our content, mistakes do happen. If you find a mistake in one of our books—maybe a mistake in the text or the code—we would be grateful if you would report this to us. By doing so, you can save other readers from frustration and help us improve subsequent versions of this book. If you find any errata, please report them by visiting `http://www.packtpub.com/support`, selecting your book, clicking on the **let us know** link, and entering the details of your errata. Once your errata are verified, your submission will be accepted and the errata will be uploaded on our website, or added to any list of existing errata, under the Errata section of that title. Any existing errata can be viewed by selecting your title from `http://www.packtpub.com/support`.

Piracy

Piracy of copyright material on the Internet is an ongoing problem across all media. At Packt, we take the protection of our copyright and licenses very seriously. If you come across any illegal copies of our works, in any form, on the Internet, please provide us with the location address or website name immediately so that we can pursue a remedy.

Please contact us at `copyright@packtpub.com` with a link to the suspected pirated material.

We appreciate your help in protecting our authors and our ability to bring you valuable content.

Questions

You can contact us at `questions@packtpub.com` if you are having a problem with any aspect of the book, and we will do our best to address it.

1
Getting Started

In this chapter, we will cover the following recipes:

- ► Installing Python on Linux
- ► Installing Plone on Linux
- ► Installing Plone on Windows
- ► Checking out code from a Version Control System
- ► Creating a Plone site

Introduction

Plone is probably the best Python **CMS (Content Management System)**. This means that it's a piece of software that provides all the necessary tools for people to publish content.

Why do we say that Plone is *the* CMS? For several reasons:

- ► It's easy to use
- ► It's available in more than 40 languages
- ► It has granular security
- ► It's regularly updated
- ► It's Open Source
- ► It has almost everything we need and, if it doesn't, we can add that specific need

These two last are, no doubt, its most important features: Plone is extendible, because it's also a framework, and that is what we'll mostly cover in this book—the components that are part of the framework and how to use them to build our extensions.

Find out more about Plone features at: `http://plone.org/about`.

In Plone, the extension facility is provided via the installation of *products*. Think of them as plugins, add-ons, extensions, or whatever name you want. In Plone literature, they are called **products**, though.

 While most Plone add-ons are technically Python packages, we will use the term *products* throughout this book because it is still very commonly used in Zope and Plone sphere.

As a matter of fact, Plone itself is a whole set of products, and some of its current basic features were born initially as additional characteristics, like Archetypes (more of this in the Chapter 3). With a little luck and a lot of work, one of your products may be included in a future release.

 You can find a variety of available Open Source community-developed products at `http://plone.org/products`.

In this chapter, we are going to install Plone (in both Linux and Windows). Plone is not an isolated software application, it needs Zope and other associated products to be installed as well. To understand this process and all these components, let's define a not-too-comprehensive, but sufficient glossary:

Term	Definition
Python module	A file containing Python definitions and statements.
Python **package**	A set of Python modules.
Python **egg**	A way of distributing Python packages. It is very interesting because it provides not only the programming code but also metadata like the version number, dependencies, and license terms.
Buildout	An environment or system created with a configuration file that is used by a special Python package, named **zc.buildout**, to execute a set or **parts** in a repeatable way so that it can be run on different computers or operating systems.
Buildout Recipe	A Python package, used by `zc.buildout`, that performs a particular action, like compiling the source code of an application, downloading and extracting a `tar.gz` file, executing some shell commands, and so on.
Zope installation	The set of Python packages, templates, and other files needed to execute a Zope server.
Zope **instance**	A particular Zope server installation, each of which might have its own configuration set of add-on Python packages and database.

In the following sections, we'll mainly look at a method named **buildout** for a proper Zope instance set up. However, we won't cover all of its possibilities. Throughout the whole book, after adding products to the project we are developing, we will add recipes or parameters to the `buildout` file, which we will create in this chapter.

Installing Python on Linux

Plone 3 runs only on the old Python 2.4 version. Unfortunately, almost no modern Linux distribution (or distro) ships with or supports that version. To fill this gap, we can use a special buildout to install an isolated Python environment called **virtualenv**.

Even for the most modern Plone 4, which runs on Python 2.6, this method can also be applied, as we did find problems with Python 2.6, shipped with Fedora 11 and 12.

> The idea of using virtualenv is to have a Python installation independent from the operating system's: no matter which version of Python is native in the OS, your Plone site will still work, as it will be never modified again unless you do it explicitly.

This first **buildout**, not the one that we'll use to install Plone, is a good place to start to understand its parts and the way it works.

Getting ready

To set up virtualenv, we need any version of Python installed first. So just run your own distro package manager to get it, if it is not installed yet.

> The following example installs Python 2.4.6 (the latest 2.4.x available at the time of writing) as a virtualenv. By changing the version number, you can apply the same method to create a Python 2.6 virtualenv. You can also get a copy of these two procedures in the source code that accompanies this book.

In the following procedure, we will `compile` and `make` Python, so we will need various packages installed in our system first. For Debian or Ubuntu, run this as root to get all the required dependencies:

```
# aptitude install gcc g++ libbz2-dev zlib1g-dev libreadline5-dev libssl-dev
```

In Fedora, run this command instead:

```
# yum install python-devel gcc gcc-c++ bzip2-devel gzip-devel zlib-devel readline-devel openssl-devel
```

Create a base folder for your Python 2.4 installation. We prefer ~/libexec/python2.4.

```
$ mkdir -p ~/libexec/python2.4
$ cd ~/libexec/python2.4
```

Then get the **bootstrap** Python script. This script installs the zc.buildout package inside the same buildout environment so that we won't need any other external command.

```
$ wget http://svn.zope.org/*checkout*/zc.buildout/trunk/bootstrap/
bootstrap.py
```

 Note that the *checkout* piece in the URL above is correct. It has no special meaning.

Enter the following buildout.cfg file to create virtualenv:

```
[buildout]
parts =
    python
    virtualenv
    make-virtualenv

# Add additional egg download sources here.
# dist.plone.org contains archives
# of Plone packages.
find-links =
    http://dist.plone.org
    http://download.zope.org/ppix/
    http://download.zope.org/distribution/
    http://effbot.org/downloads

[python]
recipe = zc.recipe.cmmi
url = http://www.python.org/ftp/python/2.4.6/Python-2.4.6.tgz
executable = ${buildout:directory}/parts/python/bin/python2.4
extra_options=
    --enable-unicode=ucs4
    --with-threads
    --with-readline
    --enable-ipv6

[virtualenv]
recipe = zc.recipe.egg
```

```
eggs =
    virtualenv

[make-virtualenv]
recipe = iw.recipe.cmd
on_install=true
cmds = ${python:location}/bin/python
${buildout:directory}/bin/virtualenv --clear .
```

The above buildout configuration file has three `parts`, which have their own `recipe` parameter. Let's go through each of them:

- The [python] part uses the `zc.recipe.cmmi` recipe, which downloads Python source code and compiles it. The `cmmi` suffix stands for Compile Make and Make Install.

- The [virtualenv] part uses the `zc.recipe.egg` recipe, which installs the virtualenv Python egg and creates the executable `bin/virtualenv` file.

- The [make-virtualenv] part uses the `iw.recipe.cmd` recipe, which can execute arbitrary shell commands. In this case, it runs the installation of a virtualenv to create an isolated Python 2.4 environment in your system.

As you must have noticed, there are other lines of code besides the `part` definitions and their `recipes`. These lines are **parameters** required by every recipe, like `url` for the `zc.recipe.cmmi` recipe or `cmds` for `iw.recipe.cmd`.

 Note that you can reference to variables defined in the buildout by writing ${part:parameter} as used in the last line: ${buildout:directory}.

You can correctly guess that there are many different recipes, each with their special parameter configuration and variables. For instance, there are recipes to install Varnish (a proxy cache server) and MySQL.

 For a list of available recipes, you can visit http://pypi.python.org/pypi?:action=browse&show=all&c=512.

How to do it...

So far we have just created a configuration file to create a Python 2.4 environment, but we haven't got it yet. So let's move on.

1. Run the bootstrap process:

   ```
   $ python bootstrap.py
   ```

You should get an output like this:

2. Start the `buildout` process with this command:

    ```
    $ ./bin/buildout
    ```

    Congratulations! You have successfully installed a clean Python 2.4 environment on your computer.

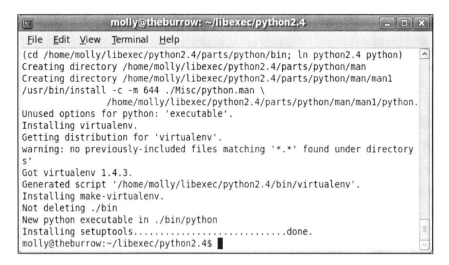

3. Now you have two different choices in how to use it:

Specifying its path:

`~/libexec/python2.4/bin/python <script>`

or by activating it to include it in your PATH environment variable:

`source ~/libexec/python2.4/bin/activate`

You'll notice that this will change your prompt, as shown in the following screenshot:

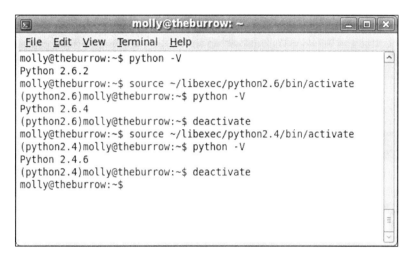

```
molly@theburrow:~$ python -V
Python 2.6.2
molly@theburrow:~$ source ~/libexec/python2.6/bin/activate
(python2.6)molly@theburrow:~$ python -V
Python 2.6.4
(python2.6)molly@theburrow:~$ deactivate
molly@theburrow:~$ source ~/libexec/python2.4/bin/activate
(python2.4)molly@theburrow:~$ python -V
Python 2.4.6
(python2.4)molly@theburrow:~$ deactivate
molly@theburrow:~$
```

4. Once activated, you can return to your original Python version by running:

`(python2.4) $ deactivate`

 In the screenshot above, you can see that there are actually three different Python versions installed. The system default version is 2.6.2, and there is also a 2.6.4 and a 2.4.6 available in separate virtual environments.

How it works...

By running the bootstrap process in Step 1, we download the `zc.buildout` package. This creates the required directory structure and generates an executable `buildout` file, which will read and process `buildout.cfg`.

In Step 2, the `buildout` process downloads the Python 2.4 source code, compiles it, and then it creates the virtualenv.

See also

▸ *Installing Plone on Linux*

Installing Plone on Linux

Now that we have a valid Python version, we can install Plone.

 There is an alternate and very handy method to install Plone on Linux (and Mac and Windows) called **Unified Installer**. It is a bundle that installs not only Zope and Plone, but also Python and other necessary packages. If you want to try it, go to http://plone.org/download and download the version of your choice.

Getting ready

ZopeSkel is a Python package that provides development templates for Zope and Plone. It will help us at several different stages of our projects. We will use it here to create a buildout environment. First, we must be sure we have it properly installed:

1. Activate your just installed Python 2.4 (or whatever version you have installed) virtualenv:

    ```
    $ source ~/libexec/python2.4/bin/activate
    ```

2. Install ZopeSkel:

    ```
    (python2.4)$ easy_install-2.4 ZopeSkel
    ```

3. If you already have it, check for the latest version by running:

    ```
    (python2.4)$ easy_install-2.4 -U ZopeSkel
    ```

How to do it...

1. Create a **buildout** with paster: Once you have the correct ZopeSkel version installed for your Python environment, run the following command to create a Zope/Plone buildout:

    ```
    (python2.4)$ paster create -t plone3_buildout
    ```

Starting with `ZopeSkel 2.15`, when creating buildout environments with `paster`, you will see a warning message informing you that **Unified Installer** is the best option for installations and `paster` is just for experts. Although Unified Installer is great and incredibly useful, we think Plone developers should know how to create a Plone environment from scratch and this is the way to do it.

2. Run the `bootstrap` process:

   (python2.4) $ cd pox

   (python2.4) $ python bootstrap.py

3. Edit the `buildout.cfg` file and locate the `eggs` parameter in the main `[buildout]` section and add `PIL` (Python Imaging Library) as a package to be downloaded and installed during buildout.

   ```
   [buildout]
   ...
   eggs =
        PIL
   ....
   ```

4. Buildout your Zope instance: This last step is to run the buildout process.

   (python2.4) $ ./bin/buildout

How it works...

Executing Step 1 will start a wizard to help with the creation of the `buildout.cfg`, we need. For each of the following options, provide these values:

Option	Value
Enter project name	pox, after Plone and OpenX, the fictitious project we are tackling in this book. Here you can choose whatever name you want and `paster` will create a directory with that name.
Expert Mode?	With the `plone3_buildout` template, no matter which mode you choose (`easy/expert/all`), you'll be prompted for the following options.
Plone Version	A valid released version of Plone. Although we have run `paster` with the `plone3_buildout` template, we can enter Plone 4 version numbers. Don't forget to choose 3.x versions for Python 2.4 and 4.x versions for Python 2.6.
Zope2 Install Path	If you want to share this instance Zope installation with another existing one, enter its path. If not, just leave it blank.
Plone Products Directory	Again, if you already have a previous installation with the list of Plone products you want to use, enter its path. If you want a fresh installation, leave it blank.
Initial Zope Username	The desired Zope administrator user.
Initial User Password	Choose one. Don't leave it blank, as you won't be able to log in.
HTTP Port	Pick a free port in your development machine.
Debug Mode	off
Verbose Security	off

A new folder named pox (the project name we used in the first option) with a basic directory structure and two very important files—`bootstrap.py` and `buildout.cfg`— will have been created.

In Step 2, we run the `bootstrap` process to complete the directory structure and generate the executable `buildout` file.

Let's see what `buildout.cfg` looks like after Step 3, where we added `PIL` in the `eggs` parameter:

```
[buildout]
parts =
    zope2
    productdistros
    instance
    zopepy
```

This is a four-part buildout. Each part will be run consecutively.

```
extends = http://dist.plone.org/release/3.3.4/versions.cfg
versions = versions
```

Egg version numbers will be fixed (or *pinned*) to the ones listed in the URL above. Note that the URL is set according to the release number you have chosen when you ran the `paster` command before.

```
find-links =
    http://dist.plone.org/release/3.3.4
    http://dist.plone.org/thirdparty
```

Downloaded and installed **eggs** should be fetched from these package **index servers**.

```
# Add additional eggs here
eggs =
    PIL


# Reference any eggs you are developing here, one per line
# e.g.: develop = src/my.package
develop =
```

We will start using the `eggs` and `develop` parameters in the next chapter as we begin adding packages to our Zope instance. Meanwhile, we will need Python Imaging Library (PIL).

```
[zope2]
# For more information on this step and configuration options:
# http://pypi.python.org/pypi/plone.recipe.zope2install
recipe = plone.recipe.zope2install
fake-zope-eggs = true
url = ${versions:zope2-url}
```

A recipe for Zope 2 installation:

```
[productdistros]
recipe = plone.recipe.distros
urls =
nested-packages =
version-suffix-packages =
```

A special recipe to download and install old-style Zope products (not released as eggs):

```
[instance]
recipe = plone.recipe.zope2instance
zope2-location = ${zope2:location}
user = admin:admin
http-address = 8080
```

```
#debug-mode = on
#verbose-security = on
eggs =
    Plone
    ${buildout:eggs}

# If you want to register ZCML slugs for any packages,
# list them here.
# e.g. zcml = my.package my.other.package
zcml =

products =
    ${buildout:directory}/products
    ${productdistros:location}
```

These are several configuration settings for the Zope instance that will be created during the `buildout` process.

```
[zopepy]
recipe = zc.recipe.egg
eggs = ${instance:eggs}
interpreter = zopepy
extra-paths = ${zope2:location}/lib/python
scripts = zopepy
```

`zopepy` is a Python interpreter with a `sys.path` variable full of the downloaded eggs and packages available at the instance's `/lib/python` folder. This is particularly useful to check if every package is available as expected.

The last step will take longer to execute than the previous steps, as it will download all the eggs listed in the `buildout.cfg` file above and all their dependencies (at the time of writing, Plone 3.3.4 has 74 direct dependencies).

This buildout executes the four parts explicitly mentioned in the `parts` definition at the top of the file:

- `[zope2]`: Its `plone.recipe.zope2install` recipe downloads and installs the Zope 2 version mentioned in `${versions:zope2-url}`. You can find this parameter at `http://dist.plone.org/release/3.3.4/versions.cfg`, the URL of the `extends` parameter.

- `[productdistros]`: It executes with its `plone.recipe.distros` recipe. In our example, we don't have any `urls` listed, so it won't process anything here.

Note that there are very few old-style Zope products that are really worth installing in a modern instance. Being old-style means being unmaintained, so use them carefully.

- ▸ [instance]: It uses a `plone.recipe.zope2instance` recipe to install a Zope instance. We can see here most of the options we set when we ran the `paster` command before.

- ▸ [zopepy]: Using `zc.recipe.egg` will create a Python `interpreter` named `zopepy` with all the `eggs` found in the `instance` section (check `${instance: eggs}`) in the `sys.path` variable.

See also

- ▸ *Installing Python on Linux*
- ▸ *Installing and configuring an egg repository*
- ▸ *Writing a production buildout*

Installing Plone on Windows

As with Linux and Mac, there is also a Windows **unified installer** (based on the buildout method described above) available, which provides the easiest way to install Plone in a Windows environment.

Download the latest Plone release from `http://plone.org/download` (3.3.4 at the time of writing) and run it.

This installation process is an easy four-step wizard that will guide you through:

1. A welcome screen, as shown in the screenshot.

2. The choice for the destination path for Plone (`c:\Program Files\Plone`, by default).

3. The configuration of the Zope instance administrator account (read: username and password).

4. A confirmation screen.

As a way of learning the buildout approach, which we introduced in the last two recipes, you are encouraged to go through the `buildout.cfg` file created in the chosen destination folder.

Although this method is really straightforward, if you plan to use several `buildouts`, Windows installer is unlikely to be the best solution, as it will reinstall the whole bundle, including the Python interpreter, every single time you create a new buildout.

As we have covered for Linux, we will see here the manual installation method to create a Zope instance on a Windows system.

How to do it...

1. Install the required Python version: If you are planning to create a Plone 4.x site, you will need Python 2.6. If not, Python 2.4 is required. Download the Windows Python installer from `http://www.python.org/download/windows` and run the installer.

2. By adding Python directory to the `PATH` environment variable, we can reuse the Python installation for other development buildouts. We are assuming here that you have installed Python 2.4 in the `c:\Python24` folder; change the paths according to your directory choices.

   - Go to the Windows Control Panel
   - Open **System options**. You can get here by pressing the *Windows logo* key + *Pause*.
   - Click on the **Advanced** tab in Windows XP or **Advanced system settings** in Windows Vista.
   - Then click on the **Environment variables** button.
   - Find the `PATH` variable and add `c:\Python24;c:\Python24\Scripts`.

3. Install the PyWin32 extension: We also need Python Win32 extensions. Download the correct file for your Python version at `http://sourceforge.net/projects/pywin32/files` and run the downloaded installer.

4. Install Python Imaging Library (PIL): download it from `http://effbot.org/downloads`. Again, pick the relevant installer for your Python version. At the time of writing, `PIL-1.1.7.win32-py2.4.exe` is the choice for Python 2.4.

5. Install a C compiler to build Zope: The easiest solution is to install MinGW, obtainable from `http://sourceforge.net/projects/mingw/files/Automated%20MinGW%20Installer`, and run the installer.

 We chose `c:\MinGW` as the installation folder. If you choose a different one, please adjust the next steps.

After the installation is finished, copy `cc1.exe` and `collect2.exe` from the `c:\MinGW\libexec\gcc\mingw32\3.4.5` folder to `c:\MinGW\bin`.

Now add `c:\MinGW\bin` to the system `PATH` environment variable the same way we did with the Python `PATH`.

6. Fix the Python compiler problem: Given that the Python-installed version has been compiled on a different machine (we installed the binaries and they are usually compiled with Visual Studio), in order to prevent problems during other packages' compilation, we must tell our environment to use the just-configured MinGW compiler.

   To do this, create or update the `distutils.cfg` file in `c:\Python24\Lib\distutils` (adjust the path to your Python installation directory) with this content:

```
[build]
compiler=mingw32
```

7. Create a buildout with paster: As with Linux, we can use `ZopeSkel` templates to create new buildouts. If you have any doubt about the following commands, refer to the instructions in the *Installing Plone on Linux* section.

   First download the **EasySetup** installation file from `http://peak.telecommunity.com/dist/ez_setup.py` and run

```
python ez_setup.py
```

   Now you can use `easy_install` to install `ZopeSkel`, and then create the buildout:

```
easy_install ZopeSkel
paster create -t plone3_buildout
cd pox
python bootstrap.py
bin\buildout.exe
```

See also

- ▸ *Installing Plone on Linux*
- ▸ *Installing and configuring an egg repository*
- ▸ *Writing a production buildout*

Checking out code from a version control system

Developing without a Version Control System (VCS) is strongly discouraged: you may not want to use VCS while simply following the recipes in this book. However, any project, large or small, should use a VCS wherever possible. In the next chapter, we will start developing a package, so we'll adjust our buildout with a handy extension to support the development of products: **mr.developer**.

How to do it...

Edit buildout.cfg and add the following lines:

```
[buildout]
...
extensions = mr.developer
sources = sources

[sources]
# repository information here
# format <name> = <kind> <url>
# my.package = svn http://example.com/svn/my.package/trunk
```

How it works...

By adding the mr.developer extension, we can define a new [sources] section with settings to automatically checkout our projects—at buildout time—from whatever version control system we use. This will facilitate the repetitive task of updating every package we develop.

Supported *kinds* of repositories are:

- ▸ svn, for subversion: http://subversion.tigris.org/
- ▸ hg, for mercurial: http://mercurial.selenic.com/wiki/
- ▸ git, at http://git-scm.com/./

More information about `mr.developer` is available at `http://pypi.python.org/pypi/mr.developer`.

There's more...

If you are interested in any of the above VCS, read more about them at:

- `http://svnbook.red-bean.com`
- `http://hgbook.red-bean.com`
- `http://book.git-scm.com`

Creating a Plone site

We have no Plone site to play with yet (if you used the unified installer method, you should already have one though). A Plone site lives in the **Zope Object Database** (**ZODB**) and can be created by starting the instance and going through the **Zope Management Interface** (**ZMI**) (instructions for this a bit later). However, there is a better method to create a Plone site using the buildout automation process.

How to do it...

Edit `buildout.cfg` and add `[plonesite]` in the main `parts` parameter:

```
[buildout]
parts =
    zope2
    productdistros
    instance
    zopepy
    plonesite
...
```

And then add this new section at the bottom of the file:

```
[plonesite]
recipe = collective.recipe.plonesite
site-id = plone
instance = instance
```

The new recipe, `collective.recipe.plonesite`, can be used to create or update Plone sites. We'll learn more about it in the following chapters.

Now we're ready to rebuild and start the instance.

```
./bin/buildout
./bin/instance fg
```

Finally, on browsing to `http://localhost:8080/plone`, you'll see a Plone site.

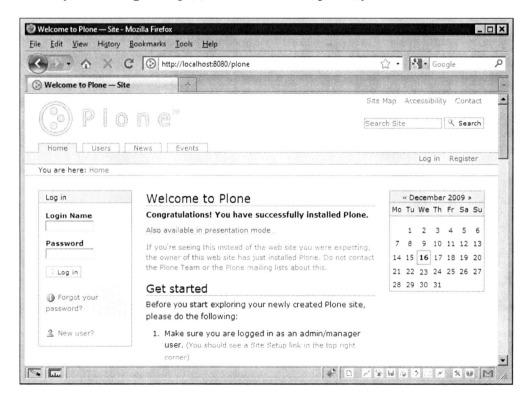

How it works...

The new `[plonesite]` part makes the buildout process run the `collective.recipe.plonesite` recipe. With the correct parameters (`site-id`, `instance`, and some other ones that you might need), it will create or update a Plone site inside the Zope instance.

A particularly useful parameter is `products`, which automatically installs a list of products when `buildout` is run. We will use it in *Opening an online Python shell on Plone using Clouseau*.

For more information about this recipe and its options visit `http://pypi.python.org/`
`pypi/collective.recipe.plonesite`.

There's more...

As we said earlier, you can also create as many Plone sites as you need through the Web, that
is to say, from the **ZMI** at the Zope root. This could be especially handy during development.

By going to `http://localhost:8080/manage`, you will be asked to authenticate yourself.
Use the `admin` user you defined in the `buildout.cfg` file.

Depending on your Plone version, you will use different methods to create a Plone site:

Up to version 3.x of Plone, pick the **Plone Site** option from the combo-box at the top-right
corner, and then click on the **Add** button (or just leave the combo-box). Then fill the short form
and submit your changes. A new Plone site will be created with the ID you have specified.

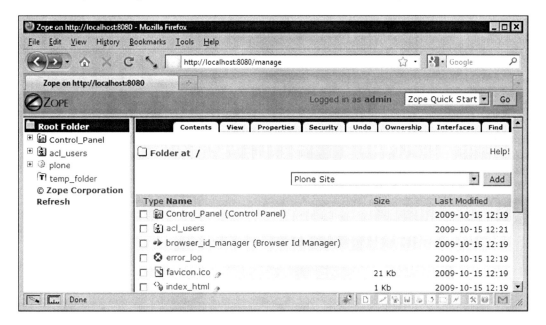

With Plone 4.x, there is a new **Add Plone Site** button at the top-right corner, above the combo-box we have just mentioned.

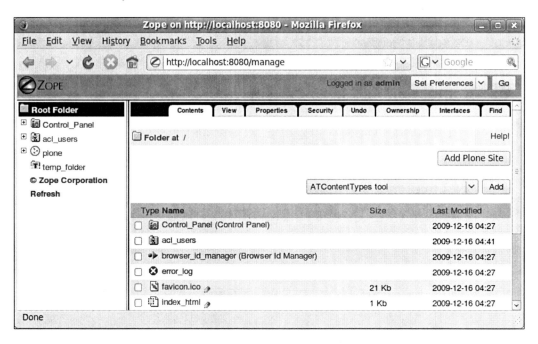

As mentioned at the beginning of this chapter, we'll incorporate more configuration options to our `buildout.cfg` as we create products in the project. So keep an eye open or just go to the *Index* of the book and look for "buildout" to go straight to them.

See also

▸ *Opening an online Python shell on Plone using Clouseau*

▸ *Testing server load and benchmarking our code*

▸ *Installing and configuring an egg repository*

2
Using Development Tools

In this chapter, we will cover:

- ▶ `IPython`: An interactive Python shell
- ▶ `ipdb`: A replacement for regular Python debugger and usage from URL
- ▶ `DocFinderTab`: Online Plone products documentation
- ▶ `Clouseau`: Online Python shell
- ▶ `PDBDebugMode`: Post-mortem debugger
- ▶ `plone.reload`: Application of code changes without restarting Zope

 You can find more tools at `http://plone.org/products?getCa tegories=dev`. Especially, you should consider adding `Products. PrintingMailHost` in any development environment you are working on to help you with tasks involving sending e-mails.

Introduction

This chapter has a twofold purpose:

- ▶ The first and main one is to introduce several Python packages and Plone products that will help us during the development of any Plone project.
- ▶ The second is to deepen our knowledge and skill in dealing with the buildout configuration files.

Although the latter is the core of the previous chapter, there will be lots of examples in the book (and especially in the following pages) that will help us get used to this technique.

Some of these developer-essential tools will be available only when running the Zope instance in debug-mode. To set this mode, we have two choices:

- ▸ Changing debug mode parameter in configuration file
- ▸ Running Zope instance in foreground mode

Changing debug mode parameter in configuration file

To change debug-mode parameter in the configuration file of our instance, do the following:

1. Change `debug-mode` parameter under `[instance]` part of the `buildout.cfg` file:

   ```
   [buildout]

   ...

   [instance]
   ...
   debug-mode=on

   ...
   ```

2. Build your instance again:

   ```
   ./bin/buildout
   ```

Alternatively, if you need a quick change, you can also modify `debug-mode` value in `parts/instance/etc/zope.conf`. However, bear in mind that its value will be overwritten the next time you build your instance.

Running Zope instance in foreground mode

The second and more direct option is to run the Zope instance in **foreground** mode. This will automatically launch Zope in `debug-mode`, no matter what your configuration files are. It will also keep open the Zope console to let us debug it with any of the **pdb** alternatives we are going to see.

In Linux run:

```
$ ./bin/instance fg
```

In Windows use:

```
> .\bin\instance fg
```

From now on, we'll use the Linux command, but you'll need to use the appropriate one for your system.

We want to clarify, before going on, that all the tools we will use and install in our Zope instance will be included via buildout. Nevertheless, this doesn't mean that we are going to spoil or get our `buildout.cfg` dirty. As we will see in *Writing a production buildout* (in the last chapter), there are means to separate environment from production options in buildout files. So don't worry, relax and enjoy the show!

Accessing an IPython powered shell

IPython, a Python shell on steroids, provides an interactive environment for programmers, enriching and easing their experience during the development and debugging stages of the project. Some of its highlighted features are:

- Object introspection
- Code introspection
- Documentation introspection (`%pdoc` magic command)
- Input history, persistent across sessions
- *Tab* auto-completion

 To learn more about IPython visit the project website at: `http://ipython.scipy.org/moin.`

These and more of its features will be quite useful to get used to Plone's code and to get to know better its API and documentation. IPython's particular mode to write **doctests** will also be a great help when working with them (refer to *Creating doctests with IPython* in Chapter 4 for more details about this).

How to do it...

To take full advantage of IPython inside Zope, we will create a new executable file in the `bin` directory: `ipzope`. To do so, we will add some lines in the `buildout.cfg` file:

1. Include a new `[ipzope]` part at the bottom of the file:

```
[ipzope]
# an IPython Shell for interactive use with zope running.
# you also need to put
# https://svn.plone.org/svn/collective/dotipython/trunk/
# ipy_profile_zope.py
```

```
# to your $HOME/.ipython directory for the following to work.
recipe = zc.recipe.egg
eggs =
    ipython
    ${instance:eggs}
initialization =
    import sys, os
    os.environ["SOFTWARE_HOME"] = "${zope2:location}/lib/python"
    os.environ["INSTANCE_HOME"] = "${instance:location}"
    sys.argv[1:1] = "-p zope".split()
extra-paths = ${zope2:location}/lib/python
scripts = ipython=ipzope
```

2. Add the just created `ipzope` to the `parts` definition at the top of the file:

```
parts =
    zope2
    productdistros
    instance
    zopepy
    plonesite
    ipzope
```

3. Install Python required modules (just for Windows): On Windows, you will need the PyReadline and ctypes packages. The easiest way to install PyReadline is to use the binary installer available at `https://launchpad.net/pyreadline/+download`. Download `ctypes` from `http://python.net/crew/theller/ctypes` and install it.

4. Build your instance. Finally, build again the Zope instance to let it know that IPython is available:

```
./bin/buildout
```

How it works...

Once built the new improved instance, we can run it in a special mode (when run in this mode, Zope won't listen to any port but to the direct console input) to get access to an IPython-powered shell:

```
./bin/ipzope
```

The first time you run `ipzope`, a new IPython profile directory will be created in your home folder. You'll be notified of this as shown in the following screenshot:

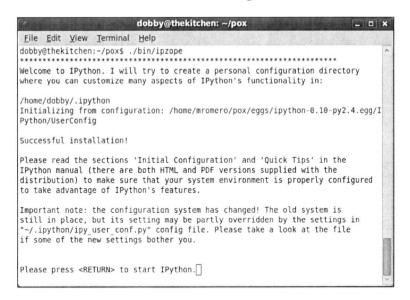

In Linux, you can find this new folder at `$HOME/.ipython`. In Windows, it will be created in `%userprofile%\_ipython` (notice the underscore instead of a dot).

There's more...

To get used to `ipzope` and IPython facilities, we will launch `ipzope` and play around with our Plone site by setting some properties in its `error_log` tool:

1. Open an IPython shell by running `./bin/ipzope`.

2. Write `portal.error_log.get` and then press the *Tab* key to get the list of `error_log`'s available methods beginning with `get`.

3. Check the results of `getProperties` by running `portal.error_log.getProperties()`.

4. After this, you should see that `setProperties` method is the one to use. But what is the syntax? Try `%pdoc` to get its docstring: `%pdoc portal.error_log.setProperties`.

5. Was this helpful? Not really, so let's try with a different one. Try `%psource` to get the source code: `%psource portal.error_log.setProperties`.

6. Great! So we now know how to pass the parameters to the previously mentioned `setProperties` method. Go ahead and clean the `ignored_exceptions` property by running `portal.error_log.setProperties(20, True, ())`.

7. Done. Sure? Let's check: `portal.error_log.getProperties()`.

8. Don't forget to save the changes (that is, commit): `utils.commit()`.

9. Although we are working in a standalone Zope instance (`ipzope` doesn't listen to any port), it is always worthwhile to synchronize our session with changes other people might have made while we were working by using `utils.sync()`.

Now, if you close the IPython session (by pressing *Ctrl + D*) and launch your Zope instance to open the Plone site in a browser, you'll see your changes at `http://localhost:8080/plone/prefs_error_log_form`.

 More information about IPython can be found at: `http://ipython.scipy.org/moin/`.

See also

▸ *Creating doctests with IPython*

Taking advantage of an enhanced interactive Python debugger with ipdb

As a Python developer, you should already be familiar with pdb. So think of ipdb as a Python debugger with many of the advantages IPython provides. ipdb, for example, is much easier to use thanks to the IPython autocomplete feature.

 You can find the official documentation for pdb for Python 2.4 at
http://www.python.org/doc/2.4.4/lib/module-pdb.html.

ipdb has another very useful and important feature which is the ability to get an IPython shell in our instance console whenever we want by means of adding the /ipdb suffix to any URL.

 ipdb is only available when Zope is running in the **foreground mode**.

How to do it...

1. Add the iw.debug line in eggs parameter of [buildout] part:

```
[buildout]

...

# Add additional eggs here
eggs =
    iw.debug
```

2. Insert an iw.debug line in the zcml parameter of [instance] part:

```
[instance]

...

# If you want to register ZCML slugs for any packages,
# list them here.
# e.g. zcml = my.package my.other.package
zcml =
    iw.debug
```

3. Rebuild your instance. We need to build our Zope instance again to let it know that there were some changes:

    `./bin/buildout`

4. Run your instance. Then run the instance in **foreground** mode to get a handle of its console:

    `./bin/instance fg`

How it works...

Given that we haven't written any line of code yet, we won't call ipdb from inside the (non-existing) code. What we need to know is that by adding these lines anywhere in the code, we will get the prompt from the improved debugger:

```
import ipdb; ipdb.set_trace()
```

 If you leave any ipdb (or pdb) call in your code when running Zope in any but foreground mode, then you'll get a BdbQuit exception.

But we do have a Plone site running, so let's try to get an IPython shell on demand. Access http://localhost:8080/plone/ipdb and go to your foreground console.

There will be an ipdb prompt waiting for you. Use the ll command (double "L" in lowercase) to get a list of local variables. Then test some other things: context, is the object we called ipdb from, in our example, the Plone site. In this particular case, it also happens to be the portal variable.

 Don't forget to use *Tab* key to let ipdb auto-complete.

```
                                          dobby@thekitchen: ~/pox              _  □  ✕
 File   Edit   View   Terminal   Help
       91              else:
 ---> 92                  set_trace()
       93

 ipdb> ll
 Out[0]:
 {'context': <PloneSite at /plone>,
  'meth': None,
  'portal': <PloneSite at /plone>,
  'request': <HTTPRequest, URL=http://localhost:8080/plone/ipdb/pdb>,
  'view': None}
 ipdb> context
 Out[0]: <PloneSite at /plone>
 ipdb> context == portal
 Out[0]: True
 ipdb> portal.Title()
 Out[0]: 'Plone site'
 ipdb> portal.portal_quickinstaller.listInstallableProducts()
 Out[0]:
 [{'status': 'new', 'hasError': False, 'id': 'Marshall', 'title': 'Marshall'},
  {'status': 'new', 'hasError': False, 'id': 'NuPlone', 'title': u'NuPlone'},
  {'hasError': False,
   'id': 'plone.app.openid',
   'status': 'new',
   'title': u'OpenID Authentication Support'},
  {'hasError': False,
   'id': 'CMFPlacefulWorkflow',
   'status': 'new',
   'title': u'Workflow Policy Support (CMFPlacefulWorkflow)'},
  {'hasError': False,
   'id': 'plone.app.iterate',
   'status': 'new',
   'title': u'Working Copy Support (Iterate)'}]
 ipdb> c
```

More information about `ipdb` can be found at:
http://pypi.python.org/pypi/iw.debug.

Discovering Zope/Plone APIs and docstrings with DocFinderTab

Although Zope and Plone documentation is really good, sometimes it's so comprehensive that we must read and browse lots of code before we get what we are looking for. `DocFinderTab` provides a great way of finding it.

How to do it...

1. Add the `Products.DocFinderTab` line in the `eggs` parameter of `[buildout]` part:

    ```
    [buildout]


    ...


    # Add additional eggs here
    eggs =
        iw.debug
        Products.DocFinderTab
    ```

2. Build your instance again and launch it:

    ```
    ./bin/buildout
    ./bin/instance fg
    ```

Now you can navigate to your **ZMI (Zope Management Interface)** instance to see a new **Doc** tab. For instance, browse to the URL `http://localhost:8080/plone/showDocumentation` to get the documentation tab as shown in the following screenshot:

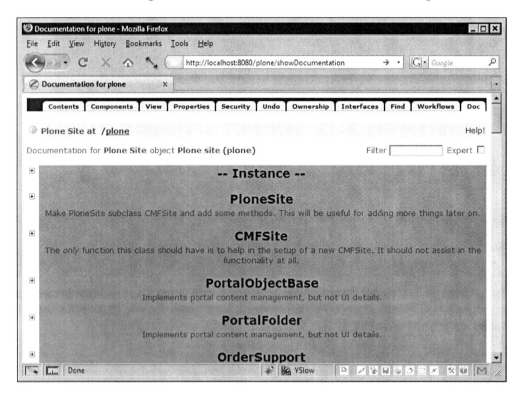

You can also do this with a particular document, folder, or tool of your site:

- `http://localhost:8080/plone/front-page/showDocumentation`.
- `http://localhost:8080/plone/events/showDocumentation`.
- `http://localhost:8080/plone/portal_catalog/showDocumentation`.

How it works...

`DocFinderTab` is an introspection tool to expose Zope and Plone documentation from inside the **ZMI**.

The following paragraph explains how `DocFinderTab` works:

It analyses any Zope object inside a running Zope, determines which classes have been used in the object's makeup and provides information about their class level attributes: name, allowed roles, arguments, documentation strings. It provides (read only) access to source code of Python implemented classes and methods.

The excerpt was taken from Dieter Maurer's website (`http://www.dieter.handshake.de`). He's the creator of `DocFinder`, the Zope product used by `DocFinderTab`.

There's more...

More information on `DocFinderTab` is available at:
`http://plone.org/products/docfindertab`.

To learn about how `DocFinder` works visit
`http://www.dieter.handshake.de/pyprojects/zope/DocFinder.html`.

If you are interested in more Python introspection, then visit
`http://diveintopython.org/power_of_introspection/index.html`.

Opening an online Python shell on Plone using Clouseau

If IPython already offers a great add-on for development, **Clouseau** takes us a step further with an AJAX-based Python shell interface integrated within our Plone site.

 Please be advised that Clouseau hasn't been updated since December 2008 and it has not been officially tested in Plone 3. However, it still works like a charm.

How to do it...

1. Add the `Products.Clouseau` line in the `eggs` parameter of `[buildout]` part:

    ```
    [buildout]

    ...

    # Add additional eggs here
    eggs =
        iw.debug
        Products.DocFinderTab
        Products.Clouseau
    ```

2. Auto-install Clouseau during buildout: Add it to the `products` parameter in `[plonesite]` part if you want Clouseau to be automatically installed during the buildout process:

    ```
    [plonesite]
    recipe = collective.recipe.plonesite
    site-id = plone
    instance = instance
    products =
        Clouseau
    ```

3. Rebuild and re-start:

    ```
    ./bin/buildout
    ./bin/instance fg
    ```

4   Open a new Clouseau session and once logged in you'll see at the bottom of any content on your Plone site a new link called **python prompt**. Click on it to open an online Python shell:

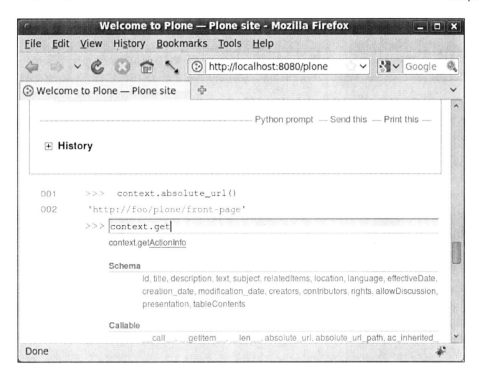

As you see you can play with local variables bound to context, portal, Zope root, and so on. You can also use the *Tab* key to let Clouseau autocomplete your code.

 Clouseau is available only when running Zope in debug mode.

There's more...

In the site setup of your Plone portal, you can also find a new Clouseau configlet, where you can store or load sessions. Most importantly, however, is the recommendation you'll see to read online help. We want to share with you just a few tips:

> ▶ Regarding security, users with "Manager" role can have access to a Clouseau shell only if the instance is in debug mode (read security is not an issue). Just in case, do not leave a public instance running in debug-mode.

> ▶ Thanks to the already installed `DocFinderTab` product, Clouseau can show a comprehensive list of available properties and methods when typing commands in its shell.

- ▸ To see other people's changes and to avoid conflict errors, you must run `utils.sync()`.
- ▸ If you plan to make permanent changes in your instance database from inside Clouseau, you must call the `utils.commit()` method.

For more information, visit the Clouseau help page at:
`http://localhost:8080/plone/clouseau_help`.

 More information about Clouseau can be found at at: `http://plone.org/products/clouseau`.

Debugging Zope exceptions with PDBDebug Mode

Whenever an exception is fired by some situation not foreseen during development, we can trace the exception in Zope logs or in the console itself. Many times during development, it's more useful to get direct access to the exception's context to better understand the problem. **PDBDebugMode**, a postmortem debugger, allows us to do that. It opens a `pdb` prompt to let us get our hands dirty.

How to do it...

1. Add a `Products.PDBDebugMode` line in the `eggs` parameter of the `[buildout]` part.

   ```
   [buildout]
   ...

   # Add additional eggs here
   eggs =
       iw.debug
       Products.DocFinderTab
       Products.Clouseau
       Products.PDBDebugMode
   ```

2. Rebuild the Zope instance:

   ```
   ./bin/buildout
   ```

3. Test `PDBDebugMode`. As we said earlier, from now on every time Zope fires an exception (if running in debug mode), a `pdb` (not an `ipdb` though) will prompt us to inspect the context.

   ❑ For an easy test, we must first tell Zope to pay attention to (that is, not ignore) the kind of exceptions we are going to produce. Open your browser and go to `http://localhost:8080/plone/prefs_error_log_form` and delete the `NotFound` line in **Ignored exception types** field (or you can also follow the `ipzope` example we included in *Accessing an IPython powered shell* earlier).

   ❑ Then type any URL that you know doesn't exist, like `http://localhost:8080/plone/doesnt-exist`.

Now check your console. You will see a `pdb` prompt waiting for you. Unluckily, this example is not a very good one because the exception was fired by the `ZPublisher` (try writing `self` in the console), so we can't see familiar code.

You can suffer problems with `PDBDebugMode` such as triggering on at unexpected times, causing apparent slowness, or freezes. Thus, if your instance doesn't seem to be responding, check its console.

More information about `PDBDebugMode` is available at: `http://plone.org/products/pdbdebugmode`.

See also

▸ *Accessing an IPython powered shell*

Applying code changes on-the-fly using plone.reload

When a Zope instance is running in debug mode, most of the changes made in the underlying code (except for templates, Python scripts, and some other resources like CSS) won't be refreshed in the server until it is restarted. This means that if we want to test a new method or if we had detected a problem and solved it, we must restart our Zope server to see the results. At first glance, it doesn't seem to be a big deal. However, in the rush of development or when making lots of little changes in the code, this could really be a pain in the neck. This is especially true if we are working with a production database because they normally take a long time during server launch.

Fortunately, `plone.reload` can come to our rescue. In a fraction of a second it detects and refreshes all the changes made to the code. Moreover, if we had modified configuration options (not `.py` files but `.zcml`, as we'll see in future chapters), we can apply them on-the-fly also.

How to do it...

1. Add a `plone.reload` line in the `eggs` parameter of the `[buildout]` part.

```
[buildout]

...


# Add additional eggs here
eggs =
    plone.reload
```

How it works...

You just need to point your browser URL to `http://localhost:8080/@@reload` (notice that `@@reload` is called on Zope instance root and not on Plone site) and click on the corresponding button to:

- Reload code (`.py` files).
- Reload code and configuration options (`.py` and `.zcml`).

After doing this, you'll get a short log about the files that were detected during reload.

 `plone.reload` is available only when Zope is running in debug mode.

Unfortunately, `plone.reload` does not always work. If you find unexpected error messages (typically `ComponentLookupError` or `could not adapt`) in your console, it is most likely that `plone.reload` couldn't do the whole job properly. In these situations, just restart your instance to continue working.

There's more...

You may want to remember (or save a bookmark in your browser) the URL of the resulting action to speed up your code changes:

- `http://localhost:8080/@@reload?action=code`, for code changes
- `http://localhost:8080/@@reload?action=zcml`, for code and configuration changes

 More information about `plone.reload` is available at: `http://pypi.python.org/pypi/plone.reload`.

3
Creating Content Types with ArchGenXML

In this chapter, we will cover:

- ▸ Installing **ArchGenXML**
- ▸ Configuring **ArgoUML**
- ▸ Creating a model
- ▸ Generating code
- ▸ Customizing generated code
- ▸ Installing the product

Introduction

ArchGenXML is a great tool to ease the development of archetypes-based content types. It provides a graphic and bug-proof alternative to code products for Plone. It also allows the generation of workflow code or even portal tools.

 Content type is the name of the different kinds of objects we can create in a Plone site such as News Items, Events, Pages, and so on.

We don't aim to review comprehensively the whole set of ArchGenXML features but to introduce it as a trigger for learning it more deeply and as an introduction to the **Archetypes** framework.

In this chapter, we'll tackle the first item in the Customer requirements list we have exposed in the preface.

 News items will be published in several sections and must include some fields like country and lead.

Installing ArchGenXML

Although ArchGenXML documentation provides several installation options, we have chosen the recommended one, that will help us in strengthening an already introduced concept: **buildout**. In addition, this method will let you share the buildout configuration file with your team and help them by easing their ArchGenXML installation as well.

Getting ready

On Linux as on Windows, we must have already installed Python 2.4. Check *Installing Python on Linux* and *Installing Plone on Windows* for details on this.

We'll proceed with the ArchGenXML installation.

How to do it...

1. Create a directory for the target ArchGenXML installation and choose the installation directory of your preference. We have chosen `libexec` at the home folder (denoted by ~ on Linux):

   ```
   mkdir -p ~/libexec/archgenxml
   cd ~/libexec/archgenxml
   ```

2. Download (or copy from an existing location) the `bootstrap.py` file.

   ```
   wget http://svn.zope.org/*checkout*/zc.buildout/trunk/bootstrap/bootstrap.py
   ```

3. Create a `buildout.cfg` file for ArchGenXML like the following one:

   ```
   [buildout]
   parts =
       archgenxml

   [archgenxml]
   recipe = zc.recipe.egg:scripts
   eggs = archgenxml
   ```

4. Bootstrap and build ArchGenXML. Before proceeding make sure you use a Python 2.4 interpreter. If you are using **virtualenv** on Linux, you can activate it first as explained in *Installing Python on Linux*. You can also invoke the Python interpreter directly on its installation directory.

    ```
    /location_of_python_2.4/python bootstrap.py
    ```

    ```
    ./bin/buildout
    ```

How it works...

We now have a correct installation of ArchGenXML. Now we just need to use it. To do so, we need an application to create **UML (Unified Modeling Language)** models that can export them into XMI format like ArgoUML, Poseidon, or ObjectDomain.

The following examples will be done on ArgoUML. You can get it from `http://argouml.tigris.org/`.

See also

- ▸ *Installing Python on Linux*
- ▸ *Installing Plone on Windows*

Configuring ArgoUML

ArgoUML runs on any Java platform. If you don't have it yet, install JRE version 5 or higher.

 Installation details can be found at `http://argouml-stats.tigris.org/documentation/quick-guide-0.28/ch02.html`.

The first step in using ArchGenXML from a UML model is to associate a proper **profile** (with widgets, fields, and stereotypes information) to the UML application.

Getting ready

To get an ArchGenXML profile with all the information we'll use during Plone models generation, we can:

1. Download it from `http://svn.plone.org/svn/archetypes/ArchGenXML/trunk/umltools/argouml/archgenxml_profile.xmi`

2. Generate it with our just installed ArchGenXML application. The following command will create an `archgenxml_profile.xmi` file in the `./bin` folder:

   `~/libexec/argchgenxml/bin/agx_argouml_profile`

   Whatever method you choose, move the profile file to a new `profiles` folder inside `archgenxml`.

   Another better choice is to generate the profile file automatically during ArchGenXML buildout. If you want to, just modify your ArchGenXML `buildout.cfg` file:

3. Add a new `agx-profile` line to the `parts` definition at the top of the file:

   ```
   [buildout]
   parts =


       . . .
       agx-profile
   ```

4. And then include the new `[agx-profile]` part definition at the bottom of the file:

   ```
   [agx-profile]
   recipe = iw.recipe.cmd
   on_install=true
   on_update=false
   cmds =
       mkdir ${buildout:directory}/profiles
       cd ${buildout:directory}/profiles
       ${buildout:directory}/bin/agx_argouml_profile
   ```

 In Windows, surround all paths with quotation marks to prevent errors when using long directory names including white spaces.

The `iw.recipe.cmd` recipe runs arbitrary shell commands—the ones listed after the `cmds` parameter.

The `on_install` and `on_update` parameters tell the recipe when it must be executed.

How to do it...

To associate the just generated profile to ArgoUML, we have to add it as a default profile for all upcoming projects, and then change a property in every new project.

Let's edit ArgoUML general settings:

1. Launch ArgoUML.

2. Go to the **Edit | Settings** menu option, and then to the **Profiles** section.

3. In the **Default XMI Directories** list, click on the **Add** button, then browse to the `profiles` folder and select it.

4. Click on the **OK** button and restart ArgoUML.

5. Again go to the **Edit | Settings** menu option, and then to the **Profiles** section.

6. You'll now see a new **AGXProfile** option in the **Available Profiles** list; select it and click on the **>>** button to include it in the **Default Profiles** list.

7. Remove any other profile in the **Default Profiles** list, except **UML 1.4** (you can't remove it from **Profile Settings**).

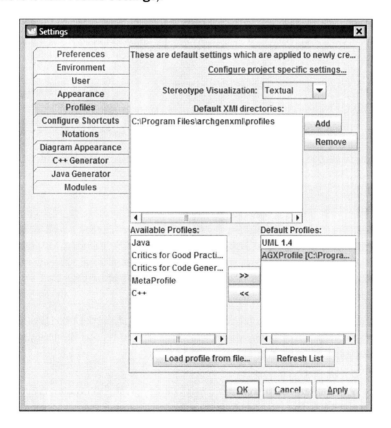

Every time you create a new project, you have to modify the per-project properties as follows:

1. Go to the **File | Project Properties** menu option, and then to the **Profiles** section.

2. Select the **UML 1.4** option in the **Active Profiles** list on the right; then click on the **<<** button to make it inactive.

3. Make sure there is no other profile set as active except **AGXProfile**.

4. Click on **OK** to save these settings.

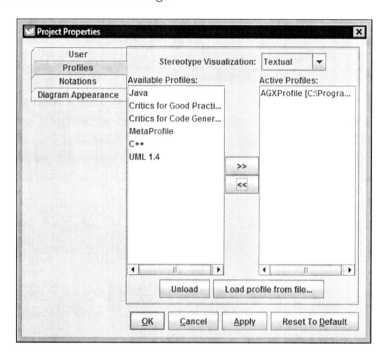

How it works...

By leaving just `AGXProfile` in the **Active Profiles** list, we make sure no other stereotypes, data types or tags will be available in ArgoUML except the ones we need for ArchGenXML. This will save us from mistakes like typos, or using data types that are not really useful for a Plone project. Moreover, this will give us the chance of learning by seeing tags that we didn't know existed.

Due to a restriction in ArgoUML, we can't remove the **UML 1.4** profile from the **Active Profiles** list in the **Settings** window. That's why we leave it in Step 1 and then we finally remove it in Step 2, in the project-specific properties.

Once we have applied all these changes, we should see the left-hand navigator as in the screenshot below:

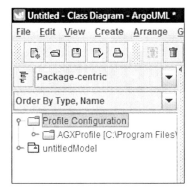

There's more...

For more about ArgoUML configuration, see Plone's Developer Manual at:
`http://plone.org/documentation/manual/archgenxml2`.

Creating a model

We are now ready to start with the creation of a new UML model. Once finished, we will use ArchGenXML to turn our model into the expected content type.

Getting ready

Before going on, let's create a new `models` folder inside our ArchGenXML installation folder to store the following example code:

```
cd ~/libexec/archgenxml
mkdir ./models
```

 Yes, we could have also created this folder during buildout. If you want, help yourself.

And don't forget to set project properties as explained in *Configuring ArgoUML*.

How to do it...

After having created a new project and set its properties as above, and before starting to draw, we must define the product name:

1. Click on the **untitledModel** branch on the left navigator to select it. You'll now be able to set its properties on the bottom-right panel.

2. In the **Name** field, write the model's name; it will be the product name in the installation area of Plone. In our case, type `poxContentTypes` (after PloneOpenX ContentTypes).

>
> All products created with ArchGenXML will have a name beginning with `Products` followed by the model name. In this example, it is `Products.poxContentTypes`.

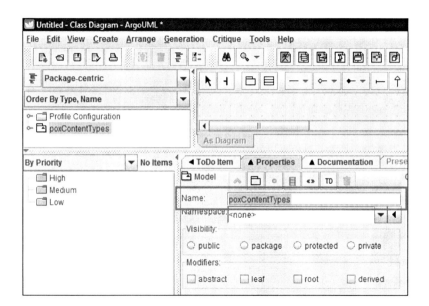

The top-right panel is where we're going to draw the model. Add a new package to our model:

1. Click on the third icon (**New Package**) in the toolbar.

2. Click on the top-right "drawing" panel to create the package.

3. You can drag and drop its corners to make it bigger.

4. Double-click its header and change its title into `content` to set its name. Using `content` as the package name for content type definitions is common practice in Plone products.

Inside this package we'll create the class (or classes) we need.

1. Click on the fourth icon (**New Class**) in the toolbar.

2. Click inside the `content` package to create the class inside it. If you are not sure whether it is inside the package, check on the left-hand navigator and expand the branches.

3. Double-click the class header (first rectangle) and change its title to `XNewsItem` (after eXtended News Item).

Many times during products development we will already have a base class to **inherit** from. In this particular case, we want the `XNewsItem` content type to inherit all the functionalities, which the native Plone `News Item` content type has.

To **inherit from existing classes**, we have several options; the most straightforward one is applying **stereotypes**.

1. Click on the **XNewsItem** class just drawn and go to the **Stereotype** tab in the bottom-right panel.

2. Click on the **atnewsitem [Class]** option in the **Available Stereotypes** list on the left and press the **>>** button to apply that stereotype. This will add a **<<atnewsitem>>** line on the class header.

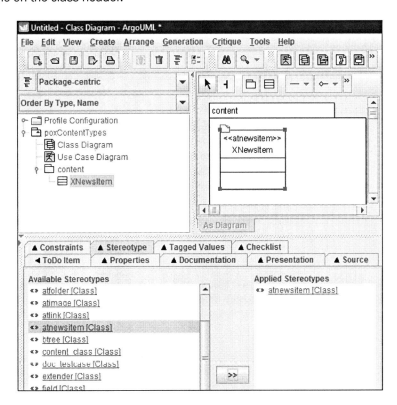

After having turned our class into a News Item, let's add new fields to get it closer to the requirements.

1. Double-click on the class attributes panel (middle rectangle) to add a new attribute. Add a name, a colon, and a type. The new attribute **Properties** tab will automatically open. You can change the name, type, and other properties here.

 There's a corresponding Archetypes data type for every type we choose for our attributes.

2. If not specified during creation, add the name of the new attribute: `lead`.

3. If not specified on creation, add the type of the new attribute: `string`.

4. Go to the **Tagged Values** tab to set some other advanced properties:

Tag	Value	Comments
`widget:label`	Lead	If not specified, ArchGenXML will automatically create the label with the name of the field.
`widget:description`	Whatever descriptive text you want to add.	When possible, try to use English text for static text like labels or field description. This will help when dealing with **internationalization**.

 Almost all the **Tagged Values** will be treated by ArchGenXML as `string` values. There are a few exceptions like `required`, which expects a `bool` value. If you want to make sure ArchGenXML will get the correct data type, add a `python:` prefix; for instance: `python:True` or `python:['high', 'medium', 'low']`.

For a complete list of available Archetypes fields and their properties, go to `http://plone.org/documentation/manual/archetypes-developer-manual/fields/fields-reference`.

5. Let's add another field with some more options. Double-click on the class attributes panel and add a new attribute with these characteristics:

   ▶ **Name:** `country`
   ▶ **Type:** `string`

6. Then go to the **Tagged Values** tab and add the following tags:

Tag	Value	Comments
widget:label	Country	
widget:type	SelectionWidget	A widget to display an options list: radio button or combo box.
vocabulary	python:"countryVocabulary"	The source for the options list. In this case, we're specifying a method called countryVocabulary. We'll define the method later.
enforceVocabulary	python:True	This will assure us that no other option can be used in this field except for the one provided by the countryVocabulary method. Although the SelectionWidget above won't allow this to happen, it means an extra validation.

For a complete list of available Archetypes widgets and their configuration options go to http://plone.org/documentation/manual/ archetypes-developer-manual/fields/widgets-reference.

Sometimes we learn that there are already some fields in the base class we're working with (ATNewsItem, in our example) that might need various minor changes to meet our requirements. Instead of creating new fields and hiding or removing them, we can **reuse** the existing fields.

Plone's News Item content type has a special **relatedItems** field in the **Categorization** tab to select already created content that will be displayed as links when reading the document.

1. Double-click on the class attributes panel (second rectangle) to add a new attribute. Add relatedItems as its name, a colon, and copy as its type. The new attribute **Properties** tab will open automatically. Ensure that copy is the selected type: copy is a special data type that tells ArchGenXML that it must reuse an existing field and override some of its properties.

2. Go to the **Tagged Values** tab to make the relatedItems field the one we want: add a **schemata** tag and set its value to default. This is the way to change the tab where this field will appear in edition mode.

We now have an `XNewsItem` content type that looks a lot like how we expected. However, there's a `countryVocabulary` method required by `country` field that we must define in order to prevent errors on instance start-up. Let's see how to add methods to the content type class:

1. Double-click on the class operations panel (third rectangle) to add a new method. Add its name. The new method **Properties** tab will automatically open. You can change its name there if you have misspelled it.

2. If not specified on creation, add the name of the new method: `countryVocabulary`.

3. Go to the **Tagged Values** tab to add some other changes: if your method is a one-liner, go ahead and add a **code** tag and set its value:

```
return (('AQ', 'Antartiqa'), ('BS', 'Bahamas'),
('CM', 'Cameroon'), ).
```

How it works...

After having defined the product name (Steps 1 and 2) and added a new package (Steps 3 to 6), we finally created a new class (Steps 7 to 9), which will be, at the end of the day, our content type's class.

At that stage `XNewsItem` is just a copy of `BaseContent` class, which is the core of almost every content type in Plone. It has an id, a `title`, `description`, and all the metadata fields and methods to support the **Dublin Core** convention.

By applying `atnewsitem` stereotype (Steps 10 to 11), we change the base class of `XNewsItem` from `BaseContent` to `ATNewsItem`. But again, there already is a News Item content type in Plone; we must keep making changes in our model for it to be of use. In Steps 12 to 17, we added new fields and reused some other existing ones.

Finally, in Steps 20 to 22, we added a short method that will be used to provide the options in the just created `country` field.

There's more...

We have specified the `countryVocabulary` method as the list of options for the `country` field. This isn't a really good example. It's more likely that we will want to use a configurable list of countries; even better, a list of countries with their ISO 3166 two-digit codes. To achieve this, we can use **ATVocabularyManager** and take advantage of its integration on ArchGenXML. Nevertheless, take our choice as a simple example.

The ATVocabularyManager project page is `http://plone.org/ products/atvocabularymanager`.

More about ATVocabularyManager-ArchGenXML integration can be found at `http://plone.org/documentation/manual/archgenxml2/ 3rdparty/atvocabularymanager`.

We can also use a Zope 3 **vocabulary**—it is actually a **named utility**—together with the `vocabulary_factory` attribute for an options field. Although there's no `vocabulary_factory` tagged value in AGXProfile, you can manually add it in ArgoUML. For instructions on creating a Zope 3 vocabulary, check *Adding configuration options in Plone control panel*.

See also

- ▸ *Adding configuration options in Plone control panel*
- ▸ *Configuring ArgoUML*

Generating code

At this stage, we have drawn the definitions for a new content type based on Plone's default `News Item` but with some differences: there's a `lead` field, a `country` field, and a modified `relatedItems` field. There's also a new `countryVocabulary` method that will provide the country options list for that field.

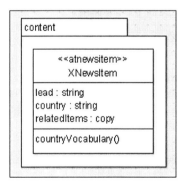

To turn all these drawings into a Plone usable content type, we must finally use ArchGenXML.

How to do it...

1. Save the model as `poxContentTypes.zargo` inside the `models` folder we created before.

2. Go to your ArchGenXML `models` folder and run:

```
cd ~/libexec/archgenxml/models
../bin/archgenxml ./poxContentTypes.zargo
```

3. If everything is okay, you'll get an output similar to this:

INFO ArchGenXML Version 2.4.1

(c) 2003-2009 BlueDynamics Alliance, Austria, GPL 2.0 or later

INFO Directories to search for profiles: ['~/archgenxml/profiles']

INFO Parsing...

INFO Profile files: '{u'archgenxml_profile.xmi': u'~/archgenxml/profiles/archgenxml_profile.xmi'}'

INFO Directory in which we're generating the files: ".

INFO Generating...

INFO Starting new Product: 'poxContentTypes'.

INFO   Generating package 'content'.

INFO   Generating class 'XNewsItem'.

INFO generator run took 1.00 sec.

 You might get this message while generating the code: **WARNING Can't build i18n message catalog. Module 'i18ndude' not found.** If that is the case, read *Adding i18ndude support to ArchGenXML* to add internationalization support.

4. After this, you'll see a new `poxContentTypes` folder inside `models` with a main structure like:

poxContentTypes

+ content

+ locales

+ profiles

+ skins

- __init__.py

- config.py

- configure.zcml

- profiles.zcml

- refresh.txt

- setuphandlers.py

 The + preceded lines are folders and the - preceded ones are files.

There's more...

We suggest you to:

▶ Browse and see the generated code to start getting used to it, especially `XNewsItem.py` file.

▶ Continue with the great ArchGenXML documentation to explore even more of its features:

  ❑ `http://plone.org/documentation/manual/archgenxml2`.

  ❑ `http://plone.org/products/archgenxml/documentation`.

See also

▶ *Adding i18ndude support to ArchGenXML*

Customizing generated code

Although ArchGenXML builds all the necessary boilerplate to create Plone Archetypes-based content types, there are some pieces of code that we can't specify anywhere in a UML model. Fortunately, we can modify the automatically generated code in different places so that ArchGenXML won't overwrite it in future builds.

Typical examples of code customization are setting the order of the widgets in the edition form and defining the body of complicated methods.

Getting ready

Every time we customize ArchGenXML-generated code, we must do it inside the special comment blocks placed everywhere in the source files like the following:

```
##code-section class-header #fill in your manual code here
##/code-section class-header

##code-section module-footer #fill in your manual code here
##/code-section module-footer
```

 Notice the `#fill in your manual code here` legend.

How to do it...

We will first define the order for the widgets when displayed in standard edit form and view page.

1. Go to the `models/poxContentTypes/content` folder inside your ArchGenXML installation directory and open `XNewsItem.py` file in your favorite code editor.

2. Find the following comment block placed just after the definition of `XNewsItem` schema:

   ```
   ##code-section after-schema #fill in your manual code here
   ##/code-section after-schema
   ```

3. Add the following lines to alter the order of the widgets in the resulting schema:

   ```
   ##code-section after-schema #fill in your manual code here
   XNewsItem_schema.moveField('lead', after='title')
   XNewsItem_schema.moveField('country', before='text')
   XNewsItem_schema.moveField('relatedItems', pos='bottom')
   ##/code-section after-schema
   ```

Look at the highlighted lines:

- ▸ We get `lead` field and put it next to the `title`.
- ▸ Then we get `country` field and place it before the body `text` field.
- ▸ Finally, we get `relatedItems` field and send it to the bottom of the schema.

We have only one method in our `XNewsItem` class: `countryVocabulary`. For teaching purposes, we have defined its body as a line of code returning just three countries (check _Creating a model_). However, we are now going to add more options. We could actually get and return a list of countries from somewhere, like a special tool in Plone or even a Web service. Instead, we are just going to increase the list with a static one. This is the way ArchGenXML lets us define the body of complicated methods.

We must first remove the body of the method in the UML model:

1. Select the `countryVocabulary` method in the operations panel (the third one in the `XNewsItem` class).

2. Open the **Tagged Values** tab in the bottom-right panel.

3. Remove the `code` tagged value and its associated value. Place the cursor in the corresponding row and press the trash icon. Be sure to remove not the contents but the whole row to prevent ArchGenXML parsing errors.

4. Open `XNewsItem.py` file again (inside `models/poxContentTypes/content` folder) and locate the `countryVocabulary` definition line.

5. You'll see the old three-country list. Remove it and modify the code as follows:

```
security.declarePublic('countryVocabulary')
def countryVocabulary(self):
    """

    Returns a list of country codes and their names for the
    "country" field
    """

    return (\
            ('AQ', 'Antartiqa'),\
            ('AR', 'Argentina'),\
            ('BS', 'Bahamas'),\
            ('BR', 'Brazil'),\
            ('CM', 'Cameroon'),\
            ('CL', 'Chile')\
            )
```

How it works...

ArchGenXML is so great that if there's no way to turn UML into code, it lets us insert our own code in places that won't be modified in subsequent builds.

In the procedure above, we covered two typical examples of code customization.

In Steps 1 to 3, we moved the fields we used in *Creating a model* to be placed exactly where we wanted.

Although we can set widgets order via tagged values, we wanted to show how to do this for other Archetypes content types that might be created without ArchGenXML.

 To learn how to use `move:after`, `move:before`, `move:bottom`, `move:top`, and `move:pos` tagged values, check the documentation at `http://plone.org/documentation/manual/archgenxml2/reference/tagged-values`.

As you may have guessed, `moveField` is a schema method aimed to place the fields in the order we want. If we don't use this method, fields' widgets will be placed in the order of declaration in the source file. In our case, due to the way that ArchGenXML generates the final schema, the `News Items` inherited fields are placed first followed by the fields we added manually in the UML model.

In Steps 4 to 8, we modified the body of a method with a more complicated functionality. If ArchGenXML finds a piece of code for a method, it won't try to write its body even if there's a `code` tagged value defined in the UML model. However, it's a good practice to keep things clean and clear.

Because we have placed these two changes in special parts of the source files (Step 3 above), ArchGenXML won't touch them in next runs.

See also

▸ *Creating a model*

Installing the product

Congratulations! You have created your first Archetypes-based content type.

Let's add it in our already configured Zope instance to see what it looks like.

Instead of using the ArchGenXML product as it is, we will wrap it in an **egg** structure and install it in the `src` folder of our **buildout**.

How to do it...

First of all, we must **create the egg structure** that will hold the ArchGenXML generated code:

1. Go to your `buildout` folder and create — if not created yet — a `src` folder.

   ```
   mkdir ./src
   ```

2. Then call `paster` to create the egg folder structure:

   ```
   paster create -t plone
   ```

It will start a very short wizard to select some options for our product. Most important is the first one:

Option	Value
Enter project name	`Products.poxContentTypes`: Although the project name might not necessarily match the full name of the package, they usually do.
Expert mode	`easy`: The `expert mode` option is new with ZopeSkel 2.15. If you choose other than `easy`, you will be prompted for the `namespace` and `package` names, which we don't need here because they will be automatically taken from the project's name.

Add whatever you want to the remaining options or just hit *Enter* to each one.

Once finished, `paster` should have created a folder structure like:

Products.poxContentTypes

+ docs

+ Products

  + poxContentTypes

  ...

  - __init__.py

+ Products.poxContentTypes.egg-info

  - dependency_links.txt

  ...

- README.txt

- setup.cfg

- setup.py

The new egg product is empty, but we already have some code that ArchGenXML has generated. So let's use it to make things work.

1. Copy all the contents of `./models/poxContentTypes` inside your ArchGenXML folder, (not the `poxContentTypes` folder itself, but its contents) into the `src/Products.poxContentTypes/Products/poxContentTypes` folder inside your `buildout` folder. Some of the existing files will be overwritten, don't worry about them.

   We are done! We have a working content type. Now we should tell our Zope instance to be aware of it. To do that, modify the buildout and build the instance again.

2. In the main `[buildout]` part, modify the `eggs` parameter by adding a new line:

   ```
   [buildout]

   . . .

   eggs =

   . . .

           Products.poxContentTypes
   ```

3. Given that our product is in development stage (that is, it's inside the `src` folder of our instance), we must also change the `develop` parameter to tell our instance where to fetch its code from:

   ```
   [buildout]

   . . .

   develop =
           src/Products.poxContentTypes
   ```

4. Build your instance again and re-launch it:

   ```
   ./bin/buildout
   ./bin/instance fg
   ```

How it works...

Unfortunately, ArchGenXML doesn't create the **egg** structure together with the product. Neither does it allow us to use arbitrary namespaces. This is why we have chosen a simple word for the package name: poxContentTypes that will be preceded by the *Zope-ish* Products to create the final **namespace**: Products.poxContentTypes.

 If you choose a dotted package name, ArchGenXML will automatically replace the dots by underscores in the final product namespace.

Nevertheless we can still use ArchGenXML's power to generate the necessary code and insert it into an egg structure we create ad-hoc with **paster**.

Automatically installing products in your Zope instance

When working on a project like ours, you will find it very useful to automatically install some products in your Zope instance at buildout time.

How to do it...

1. If not done yet, add a new line in the parts definition at the top of buildout.cfg to tell buildout to create a Plone site automatically:

   ```
   [buildout]

   ...

   parts =

   ...

       plonesite
   ```

2. And then add a new [plonesite] part at the bottom of the file:

   ```
   [plonesite]
   recipe = collective.recipe.plonesite
   site-id = plone
   instance = instance
   products =
       Products.poxContentTypes
   ```

3. Don't forget to build your instance and launch it once more.

```
./bin/buildout
./bin/instance fg
```

How it works...

The recipe used in [plonesite] part here — collective.recipe.plonesite — will create or update a new Plone site when the buildout is run. In addition, if any product is specified in the products parameter, it will be automatically installed.

Once your Zope instance is up, you can open your Plone home page and click on the **Add new** drop-down menu. By clicking on the **XNewsItem** option, a new form should open as shown in the following screenshot:

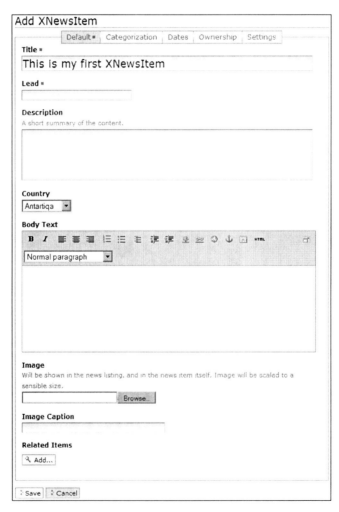

There's more...

You also have the option to install products manually:

1. Log into your Plone site as admin user.

2. Click on the **Site Setup** link on the top-right corner and then click on the **Add-on Products** link, or just go to `http://localhost:8080/Plone/prefs_install_products_form`.

3. In the **Add/Remove Products** page, select **poxContentTypes** in the **Products available for install** list and press the **Install** button below.

See also

▸ *Creating a Plone site*

▸ *Opening an online Python shell on Plone using Clouseau*

▸ *Creating a policy product*

▸ *Installing and configuring an egg repository*

4
Prevent Bugs through Testing

In this chapter, we will cover:

- ▸ Working with paster-generated test suites
- ▸ Creating a test suite with ArchGenXML
- ▸ Creating doctests with iPython
- ▸ Zope functional testing
- ▸ Using Selenium functional tests

Introduction

After working with the same development environment (Plone in our case) for a while, we tend to get more confident in our code. It's natural to believe that the more I know about something, the more I can do something similar correctly the first time I try it. Paradoxically, this is a mistake in programming, as it will lead to more mistakes.

During development, automated testing is the key practice we should keep as a continuous process of evolution to prevent these errors. It allows us to write testing code that can be run automatically after every code change in order to verify the consistency and correctness of those changes.

 Testing is a means of assuring programming quality.

In the following sections, we'll introduce some core concepts of testing and create some rather straightforward examples to demonstrate all the tests we'll add to our products in further chapters:

- ▶ Unit tests
- ▶ Integration tests
- ▶ Functional tests.

The following glossary contains a short explanation of basic testing notions.

Glossary

Term	Explanation
Unit test	A test for small (the smallest possible) units of code. For example, the setting and retrieving of a particular attribute in a class.
Integration test	A test for code as a component related with other components. Most of the tests we'll write for Plone products will be integration tests, as we'll need the whole Plone framework and some of its products to get the expected results. For example, the possibility of creating objects of a new content type after a product has been installed.
Functional test	A test from the end user standpoint. It usually refers to a use case or user story. For example, assuring a descriptive message is shown if a form is submitted without required data.
Test case	A set of tests commonly grouped because they all check a single component like a class or a short module.
Test suite	A set of test cases that will be run all together.
PyUnit	The standard unit testing framework for Python.
doctest	A special syntax for writing tests. The main benefit of doctests is that it is not only a test but the documentation of the code itself. Anybody can read it and understand it better because it provides real examples.

 All along the book we will mainly write doctest, our choice over PyUnit.

Working with paster-generated test suites

Products created with **paster** already come with four different types of test suites ready to be used:

- Unit test in doctest syntax
- Unit test inside the method's docstring
- Integration test in doctest syntax
- Functional test in doctest syntax

The automatically generated `tests` module provides the necessary code to run the test cases.

Getting ready

We are going to use the same egg-structured product we created with `paster` in the *Installation of the product* recipe. If you didn't read that one, you can use the example code available for download on the Packt Publishing website.

How to do it...

Open the `tests` module in `Products.poxContentTypes/Products/poxContentTypes` to see four commented test suites:

```
...
def test_suite():
    return unittest.TestSuite([

        # Unit tests
        #doctestunit.DocFileSuite(
        #    'README.txt', package='Products.poxContentTypes',
        #    setUp=testing.setUp, tearDown=testing.tearDown),

        #doctestunit.DocTestSuite(
        #    module='Products.poxContentTypes.mymodule',
        #    setUp=testing.setUp, tearDown=testing.tearDown),

        # Integration tests that use PloneTestCase
        #ztc.ZopeDocFileSuite(
        #    'README.txt', package='Products.poxContentTypes',
        #    test_class=TestCase),

        #ztc.FunctionalDocFileSuite(
        #    'browser.txt', package='Products.poxContentTypes',
        #    test_class=TestCase),

        ])
...
```

How it works...

By uncommenting the testing code above and writing some test code, we will learn each of the above testing variations.

Unit test DocFileSuite

The first testing technique available in `test_suite` method is a **unit test** that should be defined in a `README.txt` file inside the package we are developing.

 Writing tests in separate files (separate from source modules) is preferable when tests are long or they have so many cases that it would damage the readability of the code itself.

Uncomment the lines:

```
doctestunit.DocFileSuite(
    'README.txt', package='Products.poxContentTypes',
    setUp=testing.setUp, tearDown=testing.tearDown),
```

Create a `README.txt` file inside the package. If you are using the code from the previous chapter, the file should be created in `./src/Products.poxContentTypes/Products/poxContentTypes/` in your buildout directory.

Then add the following lines:

```
>>> from Products.poxContentTypes import config
>>> from Products.poxContentTypes.content.XNewsItem import XNewsItem

>>> xni=XNewsItem('dummy')

>>> xni
<XNewsItem at dummy>

>>> xni.countryVocabulary()
(('AQ', 'Antartiqa'), ('AR', 'Argentina'), ('BS', 'Bahamas'), ('BR',
'Brazil'), ('CM', 'Cameroon'), ('CL', 'Chile'))
```

 Look at the way this doctest is written. It's exactly the same way the Python interpreter should have behaved if we were testing our code. Every >>> preceded line is an input command and the other lines are the corresponding output.

After the initial imports, we create an instance of our `XNewsItem` class. Bear in mind that this is not the way objects are created in a Plone site. But because we don't want to test our class interacting in a Plone site but the `countryVocabulary` method (this is a unit test, not an **integration** one), we just need a proper class' instance. On creation, we add the `dummy` argument because all **Archetypes** objects need an `id` as an initialization parameter.

After that, we just call the method in question to check if its returned values are the expected ones.

Running tests

Now we have to run all the tests (just one for the time being) in the package.

Inside your instance folder run this command:

```
./bin/instance test -s Products.poxContentTypes
```

We use the `-s` option to specify the package we want to test. By default Zope seeks a `tests` module or package inside the packages to be tested.

> You can get more available options to use when testing by running this command:
> ```
> ./bin/instance test --help
> ```

When done, we'll get an output similar to the following screenshot:

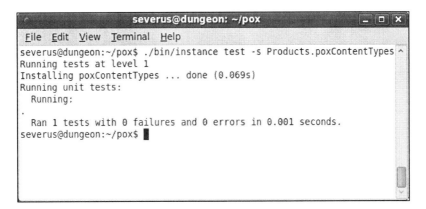

We could have written this unit test even if we hadn't known anything about Plone but plain Python: we have instantiated the class and executed a method.

Unit test DocTestSuite

The second testing technique available in `test_suite` method is, again, a **unit test**. But we won't create any external file this time; tests will be written in **docstring**s.

 Tests written as docstrings (that is, inside source modules) are preferable when testing simple pieces of code with few cases.

Uncomment the following code and replace `mymodule` with the module we are testing:

```
doctestunit.DocTestSuite(
    module='Products.poxContentTypes.content.XNewsItem',
    setUp=testing.setUp, tearDown=testing.tearDown),
```

Now modify the `countryVocabulary` method's docstring by adding the same test as in the previous section. The file to be modified is `XNewsItem.py` in `src/Products. poxContentTypes/Products/poxContentTypes/content`.

```
security.declarePublic('countryVocabulary')
def countryVocabulary(self):
    """
    Returns a list of country codes and their names for the
    "country" field

    >>> from Products.poxContentTypes import config
    >>> from Products.poxContentTypes.content.XNewsItem import
    XNewsItem

    >>> xni=XNewsItem('dummy')

    >>> xni
    <XNewsItem at dummy>

    >>> xni.countryVocabulary()
    (('AQ', 'Antartiqa'), ('AR', 'Argentina'), ('BS', 'Bahamas'),
    ('BR', 'Brazil'), ('CM', 'Cameroon'), ('CL', 'Chile'))
    """
    return (
            ('AQ', 'Antartiqa'),
            ('AR', 'Argentina'),
            ('BS', 'Bahamas'),
            ('BR', 'Brazil'),
            ('CM', 'Cameroon'),
            ('CL', 'Chile')
        )
```

As you can see, comments can be inserted together with testing code. This is the way doctests meet the "doc" part of their name.

Now, again test the package by running:

```
./bin/instance test -s Products.poxContentTypes
```

You should get an output as shown in the following screenshot:

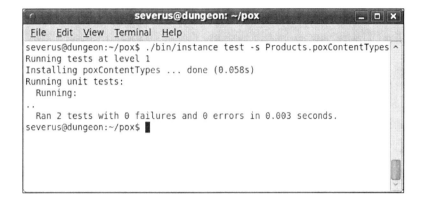

You might have noticed that the only difference between this output and the one when we had one unit test (except for the obvious summary information at the end) is the number of dots between **Running** and **Ran 2 tests...**

There's one dot for every passing test.

Integration test ZopeDocFileSuite using PloneTestCase

The third testing technique available in `test_suite` method is an **integration test**. This means that we are going to test our class as a component of a bigger environment: a Plone site.

Uncomment the next group of lines and replace README.txt with INTEGRATION.txt: we'll create a new file instead of overwriting our first unit test.

```
        ztc.ZopeDocFileSuite(
            'INTEGRATION.txt', package='Products.poxContentTypes',
            test_class=TestCase),
```

Integration tests based on the `PloneTestCase` class set a whole Plone site on the fly. For this particular one, we'll need our product to be installed, so open the `tests.py` file and change the `setupPloneSite` call after initial imports and replace it with the following lines of code:

```
# ptc.setupPloneSite()
ztc.installProduct('poxContentTypes')
ptc.setupPloneSite(products=['poxContentTypes',])
```

Then create a new `INTEGRATION.txt` file inside your package folder, which is `./src/Products.poxContentTypes/Products/poxContentTypes/` in your buildout folder.

```
>>> self.loginAsPortalOwner()
>>> portal.invokeFactory('XNewsItem', 'dummy')
'dummy'
>>> portal.dummy
<XNewsItem at /plone/dummy>

>>> portal.dummy.countryVocabulary()
(('AQ', 'Antartiqa'), ('AR', 'Argentina'), ('BS', 'Bahamas'), ('BR',
'Brazil'), ('CM', 'Cameroon'), ('CL', 'Chile'))
```

Spot the big difference with the previous unit tests regarding initialization of our objects. We are now using the `invokeFactory` method in the `portal` object to create an instance of our `XNewsItem` class. Furthermore, we need special permissions to create content in a Plone `portal`, that's why we first `loginAsPortalOwner()`.

We could have added a line like:

```
xni=XNewsItem('dummy')
```

This would use `xni` as in the previous examples. However, we wanted to emphasize the integration nature of this test by using the `portal` object repeatedly.

 If you have any iPython-related egg (`ipython`, `ipdb`, or `iw.debug`) installed in your instance, you would probably want to uninstall them by commenting their lines in the `buildout.cfg` file. iPython changes the way of printing into the standard output, so the expected output won't match the actual one.

Test the package again by running:

./bin/instance test -s Products.poxContentTypes

You should get an output like the following (we have removed several Zope warnings during instance start up):

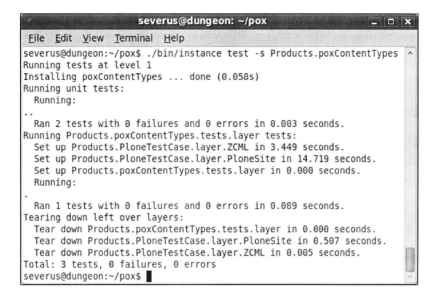

Execution time now is much longer than in previous test runs. This is due to the recently added integration test because a new full Plone site is being automatically created.

Functional test

We'll cover how to create **functional tests** later on in this chapter. Yet, we can also run them with the **paster**-created **test suite**. Uncomment the following lines if you want to run a functional test defined in the `browser.txt` file:

```
ztc.FunctionalDocFileSuite(
    'browser.txt', package='Products.poxContentTypes',
    test_class=TestCase),
```

See also

▸ *Installation of the product*

Creating a test suite with ArchGenXML

Up till now we have created and run different kinds of test suites based on **paster**-generated products. Nevertheless **ArchGenXML** can also create all the necessary boilerplate we need for testing.

We are going to use the same UML model and product that we developed in the *Creating a model* and *Generating code* tasks in the previous chapter. If you didn't read that one, you can use the example code available for download. We'll also use ArgoUML in the next examples.

Getting ready

In the previous chapter, we created two products (one with ArchGenXML in the *Generating code* recipe and the other one with paster in *Installation of the product*) and merged them in an egg directory structure. If we plan to model tests suites with a UML application, we need to remove the `tests` module from the paster-created package.

In your instance folder, run the following command to remove `tests.py`:

```
rm src/Products.poxContentTypes/Products/poxContentTypes/tests.py
```

In Windows, run:

```
del src\Products.poxContentTypes\Products\poxContentTypes\tests.py
```

How to do it...

Launch ArgoUML or your favourite UML program, and then open the model you have been working with (`poxContentTypes.zargo` in our case, available also for download).

1. Create a new package (third icon in the toolbar) and name it `tests`.

2. Add a new class to it (fourth icon in the toolbar) and name it `poxContentTypesTestCase`. Make sure the class is inside the package.

3. Apply the **<<plone_testcase>>** stereotype to `poxContentTypesTestCase` class. You can do this in the **Stereotype** tab in the bottom right pane.

4. Create a new class inside the `tests` package, name it `testXNewsItem`, and then apply the **<<doc_testcase>>** stereotype to it. We could have used **<<testcase>>** stereotype, but we prefer using doctests. Make this class derive from `poxContentTypesTestCase` with a generalization arrow (ninth icon in the toolbar).

5. Optionally, you can add a `testSetup` class with a **<<setup_testcase>>** stereotype. Make it also derive from `poxContentTypesTestCase` with a generalization arrow. This will make ArchGenXML create a new `testSetup` module with some general checks (the correct installation of a tool, a content type, skins, workflows, among others) that you can take as examples of how to perform your own tests.

After these steps, you should have arrived at a model like the one shown below:

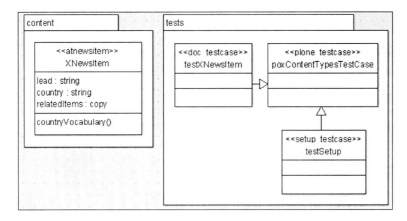

Don't forget to save your work before running ArchGenXML to generate the code.

Go to your ArchGenXML `models` folder (or where you placed the model) and run:

`../bin/archgenxml ./poxContentTypes.zargo`

If everything goes well, you'll see these lines as ArchGenXML output:

```
kreacher@headquarters: ~/libexec/archgenxml/models
 File  Edit  View  Terminal  Help
kreacher@headquarters:~/libexec/archgenxml/models$ ../bin/archgenxml
poxContentTypes.zargo
INFO  ArchGenXML Version 2.4.1
(c) 2003-2009 BlueDynamics Alliance, Austria, GPL 2.0 or later
INFO  Directories to search for profiles: ['/home/kreacher/libexec/ar
chgenxml/profiles/']
INFO  Parsing...
INFO  Profile files: '{u'archgenxml_profile.xmi': u'/home/kreacher/li
bexec/archgenxml/profiles/archgenxml_profile.xmi'}'
INFO  Directory in which we're generating the files: ''.
INFO  Generating...
INFO  Starting new Product: 'poxContentTypes'.
INFO      Generating package 'content'.
INFO          Generating class 'XNewsItem'.
INFO      Generating package 'tests'.
INFO          Generating testcase 'poxContentTypesTestCase'.
INFO          Generating testcase 'testXNewsItem'.
INFO          Generating testcase 'testSetup'.
INFO  generator run took 1.40 sec.
kreacher@headquarters:~/libexec/archgenxml/models$ 
```

How it works...

You'll now have two new packages inside the poxContentTypes product folder: doc and tests. The first one will have the doctest file textNewsItem.txt and the second one will have all the test machinery, including a testSetup module. Let's go through some of the files there.

The poxContentTypesTestCase module contains the base test case class which we'll use for all the tests we are going to write:

```
. . .
testcase = PloneTestCase.PloneTestCase
. . .

PloneTestCase.setupPloneSite(products=PRODUCTS)

class poxContentTypesTestCase(testcase):

    """Base TestCase for poxContentTypes."""
. . .

def test_suite():
    from unittest import TestSuite, makeSuite
    suite = TestSuite()
    suite.addTest(makeSuite(poxContentTypesTestCase))
    return suite
. . .
```

ArchGenXML test cases are based on (that is, inherited from) the PloneTestCase class. This automatically turns them into **integration tests**, not **unit tests**. We can use them as a unit test, though. However, they will take longer to run.

testXNewsItem.py file is the test file:

```
. . .

from Testing import ZopeTestCase
from Products.poxContentTypes.tests.poxContentTypesTestCase import
poxContentTypesTestCase

# Import the tested classes

class testXNewsItem(poxContentTypesTestCase):
    """Test-cases for class(es) ."""
```

```
##code-section class-header_testXNewsItem #fill in your manual
code here
##/code-section class-header_testXNewsItem

def afterSetUp(self):
    pass

# Manually created methods


def test_suite():
    from unittest import TestSuite
    from Testing.ZopeTestCase.zopedoctest import ZopeDocFileSuite
    from Testing.ZopeTestCase import ZopeDocFileSuite
    ##code-section test-suite-in-between #fill in your manual code
    here
    ##/code-section test-suite-in-between


    s = ZopeDocFileSuite('testXNewsItem.txt',
                         package='Products.poxContentTypes.doc',
                         test_class=testXNewsItem)
    ...
```

This test case, created by ArchGenXML, inherits from the base poxContentTypesTestCase class as defined in the previous module. In turn it will call a doctest (ZopedocFileSuite) inside our product documentation folder: doc/testXNewsItem.txt. If you open this file, you'll see a less useful test. However, you can replace it with the unit or integration tests, which we have already seen in *Working with paster-generated test suites*.

See also

▶ *Creating a model*

▶ *Generating code*

▶ *Installation of the product*

▶ *Working with paster generated test suites*

Creating doctests with iPython

doctests are a great means of testing because they can better describe the code they are testing, with examples and comments in a very natural way for programmers.

However, Python editors are short of support for the crucial task of writing them; that is to say we lack auto-complete, Python syntax help, access to methods' docstrings, and so on. As a sad result, writing doctests is a pain in the neck.

Fortunately, **iPython** comes to the rescue with a special (and very nice, indeed) doctest compatibility mode: `%doctest_mode`.

```
In [1]: %doctest_mode
*** Pasting of code with ">>>" or "..." has been enabled.
Exception reporting mode: Plain
Doctest mode is: ON
>>>
```

When entering in **doctest_mode**, the regular iPython prompts changes into the usual Python `>>>` sign.

```
>>> i = 1
>>> i
1
>>> i += 1
>>> i
2
>>> a = (1,2,3,)
>>> a
(1, 2, 3)
```

After finishing the test, we can go back to the iPython shell via the `%doctest_mode` command again:

```
>>> %doctest_mode
Exception reporting mode: Context
Doctest mode is: OFF

In [10]:
```

iPython magic commands begin with % and provide special functionalities not available in a regular Python shell. For more information about them, type `%magic` in your iPython interpreter.

Now that we know how to write doctests with iPython, let's create one.

 Please note that we are about to hack a regular test suite to let us work more comfortably while writing doctests. By no means is this something you should leave in a final package but should be used just for debugging or development purposes.

Getting ready

First of all, we need an embedded iPython inside the test suite. This will let us use it, enter in **doctest_mode**, and then copy and paste all we need.

 From now on we will continue working with **paster**-generated test suites. You should slightly adjust these steps if you prefer to work with the **ArchGenXML**-created test suite.

Edit `tests.py` in the `Products.poxContentTypes` package and add the following block of code:

```
import sys
from IPython.Shell import IPShellEmbed
def ipython(locals=None):
    """Provides an interactive shell aka console inside your testcase.

    It looks exactly like in a doctestcase and you can copy and paste
    code from the shell into your doctest. The locals in the testcase
    are available, because you are in the testcase.

    In your testcase or doctest you can invoke the shell at any point
    by calling::

        >>> from Products.poxContentTypes.tests import ipython
        >>> ipython( locals() )

    locals -- passed to InteractiveInterpreter.__init__()
    """

    savestdout = sys.stdout
    sys.stdout = sys.stderr
    sys.stderr.write('='*70)
    embedshell = IPShellEmbed(argv=[],
                              banner="""
IPython Interactive Console
```

```
Note: You have the same locals available as in your test-case.
""",
                              exit_msg="""end of ZopeTestCase
Interactive Console session""",
                              user_ns=locals)
    embedshell()
    sys.stdout.write('='*70+'\n')
    sys.stdout = savestdout
```

This `ipython` method is inspired by the `interact` method created by **ArchGenXML**.

How to do it...

Once the `ipython` method is available, we'll call it from any of the test cases we want to work with (unit or integration test):

1. Open the `INTEGRATION.txt` file in the `Products.poxContentTypes` package and add these lines at the beginning:

    ```
    >>> from Products.poxContentTypes.tests import ipython
    >>> ipython(locals())
    ```

    The first import line must point to the module where we have added the `ipython` method.

2. Make sure the following lines are uncommented in `tests` module:

    ```
    ztc.ZopeDocFileSuite(
        'INTEGRATION.txt', package='Products.poxContentTypes',
        test_class=TestCase),
    ```

3. Run the new test with this command:

    ```
    ./bin/instance test -s Products.poxContentTypes
    ```

4. You'll get an iPython interpreter session in the console. Enter in `doctest_mode` by running:

    ```
    In [1]: %doctest_mode
    *** Pasting of code with ">>>" or "..." has been enabled.
    Exception reporting mode: Plain
    Doctest mode is: ON
    >>>
    ```

    This will leave you in a fresh Plone site with new ZODB just as if you were running a test (we are indeed).

5. After we have finished writing tests, we can exit `doctest_mode` (or not), copy the iPython session into the test file, and finally exit the iPython shell with `%exit` command.

```
...
>>> %doctest_mode
Exception reporting mode: Context
Doctest mode is: OFF
In [4]: %exit
```

The test suite we were running (and paused to write the actual testing routine) will finish with a success status.

In the following screenshot, you can see how to use iPython's `%doctest_mode` to write an integration test:

 You can also use iPython to write unit tests in which case you won't be able to work with a Plone site but just with your (or others') Python packages.

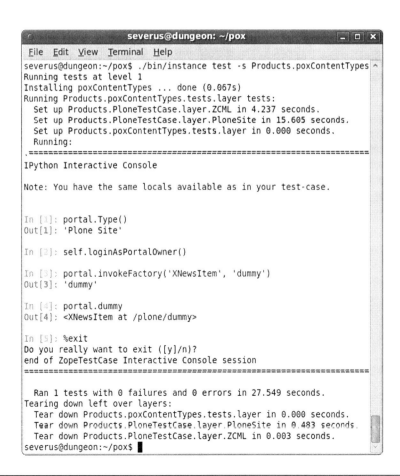

Zope functional testing

So far we have tested our class and its methods from the developer's point of view. However, Zope (and thus Plone) allows us to test our code in a **black-box** fashion from the end user standpoint.

As far as Plone is concerned, end users will use, in most cases, a web browser to interact with the final application. Zope provides a web browser simulator in its `zope.testbrowser` package, which behaves almost in the same way every modern and real browser does, except for the lack of JavaScript support.

> In *Using Selenium functional tests* section, we'll cover testing with the Selenium framework, which does support JavaScript.

By using this library, we can easily create automated **functional tests**.

Getting ready

Just like iPython turns to be the easiest way of writing `doctests`, there's a great tool to help us during functional test creation: `zope.testrecorder`, a browser session recorder.

> `zope.testrecorder` is a good starting point for developers with little experience on Zope functional testing. However, as you will see in this section, several changes must be applied to its output to get a working test. As you get more used to functional tests in Zope, you'll probably leave `zope.testrecorder` behind to write your test cases from scratch.
>
> Please refer to the `zope.testbrowser README.txt` file for full details on its API.

In order to use it, we must include it beforehand in our `buildout` configuration file.

Add the `zope.testrecorder` line in the `eggs` parameter of `[buildout]` part:

```
[buildout]

. . .

# Add additional eggs here
eggs =
    . . .
    zope.testrecorder
```

And then a `zope.testrecorder` line in `zcml` parameter of `[instance]` part:

```
[instance]
...
zcml =
...
    zope.testrecorder
```

 For recently created or updated eggs (`zope.testrecorder` is not one of them), you'll rarely need their inclusion in the `zcml` parameter. This is due to a package named `z3c.autoinclude` that automatically includes eggs' **ZCML slugs**. More information on it can be found at: `http://pypi.python.org/pypi/z3c.autoinclude`.

Finally, rebuild your instance by running:

```
./bin/buildout
```

How to do it...

We are going to create a test to verify all the functionalities we have developed so far. We will see whether there's an available XNewsItem content type and whether it has all the regular News Item fields, and also a required lead field and a combo box for country selection.

1. Start your instance:

    ```
    ./bin/instance fg
    ```

     Make sure you are not logged in; despite just having launched the instance, you might have a previous open session.

2. Point your browser to,
    `http://localhost:8080/++resource++recorder/index.html`
3. In the URL field box, enter your Plone site URL, in this case
    `http://localhost:8080/plone/`
4. Click on the **Go** button. This will load your Plone site in the lower frame.

    Once you hit the **Go** button, `zope.testrecorder` will begin recording everything you type, press or click on your browser.

It's highly advisable to have a testing plan beforehand in order not to get lost during the session and not to obtain a resultant useless functional test.

Perform several tasks until the test is finished:

1. First of all, we must be logged in with proper access rights in order to create some content. Thus, click on the **Log in** link.
2. Log in with your administrator username and password: **admin** for both fields in our case. Then click on the **Log in** button.
3. Click on the **Add new...** drop-down menu.
4. Select **XNewsItem** from the list.
5. Fill the **Title** field with **This is an XNewsItem title**.
6. The **Lead** field is also required, so fill it with **Lead field is required**
7. Select the **Argentina** option in the **Country** combo box.
8. Click on the **Save** button to submit the changes.

   Once the changes are submitted, you'll be automatically redirected to the recently saved XNewsItem document.
9. Select **Changes saved.** text appearing above the document title.
10. Right-click on it and select the **Check Text Appears On Page** option in the context menu.

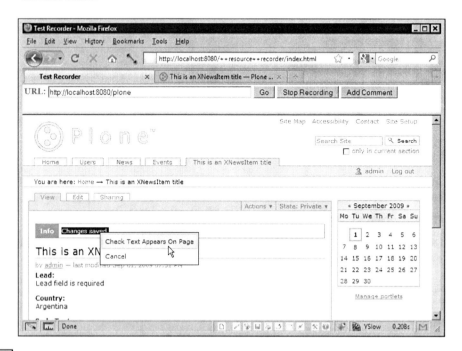

That's it, the test has been completed.

1. Click on the **Stop recording** button in the upper frame and then render the test as **Python Doctest**.

   The test recorder will output the doctest we need for the just finished functional test.

2. Copy the output and paste it in a new `browser.txt` file inside the `Products/poxContentTypes` folder.

   Create the browser object we'll be using:

```
>>> from zope.testbrowser import Browser
>>> browser = Browser()
>>> browser.open('http://localhost/plone')
>>> browser.getLink('Log in').click()
>>> browser.getControl('Login Name').value = 'admin'
>>> browser.getControl('Password').value = 'admin'
>>> browser.getControl('Log in').click()
>>> browser.open('http://localhost/plone/portal_factory/XNewsItem/
xnewsitem.2009-08-31.7524887510/edit')
>>> browser.getControl('Title').value = 'This is an XNewsItem
title'
>>> browser.getControl('Lead').value = 'Lead field is required'
>>> browser.getControl('Country').value = 'AR'
>>> browser.getControl('Save').click()
>>> 'Changes saved.' in browser.contents
    True
```

 We have highlighted the lines we must modify.

3. After this, some changes must be applied to the just created test file. We will explain them in the *How it works...* section. The final `browser.txt` file should look like this:

   Create the browser object we'll be using:

```
>>> from Products.Five.testbrowser import Browser
>>> from Products.PloneTestCase.setup import portal_owner,
default_password
>>> browser = Browser()
>>> portal_url = self.portal.absolute_url()
>>> browser.open(portal_url)
>>> browser.getLink('Log in').click()
>>> browser.getControl('Login Name').value = portal_owner
```

```
>>> browser.getControl('Password').value = default_password
>>> browser.getControl('Log in').click()
>>> browser.open(portal_url + '/createObject?type_name=XNewsItem')
>>> browser.getControl('Title').value = 'This is an XNewsItem
title'
>>> browser.getControl('Lead').value = 'Lead field is required'
>>> browser.getControl('Country').value = ('AR',)
>>> browser.getControl('Save').click()
>>> 'Changes saved.' in browser.contents
True
```

 We have highlighted the lines we just modified.

4. Open the `tests` module and uncomment the last available test suite we were working with at the beginning of this chapter:

```
ztc.FunctionalDocFileSuite(
    'browser.txt', package='Products.poxContentTypes',
    test_class=TestCase),
```

5. In the same `tests` module, make sure you have your product properly installed in Zope and Plone, so change `setupPloneSite` call like this:

```
# ptc.setupPloneSite()
ztc.installProduct('poxContentTypes')
ptc.setupPloneSite(products=['poxContentTypes',])
```

6. Test the package by running:

```
./bin/instance test -s Products.poxContentTypes
```

You should get an output like this:

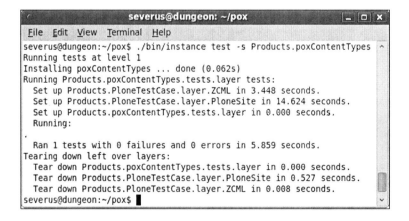

As we stated in *Integration test ZopeDocFileSuite using PloneTestCase* previously, make sure that no iPython-related package is interfering with the standard output or you will get failing tests when you shouldn't.

How it works...

For the above functional test to work properly in our Zope instance, we must make some manual changes.

First of all, instead of using the `zope.testbrowser` module, we'll use the `Products.Five.testbrowser` variation with Zope 2 support.

```
>>> from Products.Five.testbrowser import Browser
```

Second, when running functional tests, the Zope host name is not configured for the real instance. It is actually `http://nohost/` (no port number). So we should adjust it wherever it is used in the test. Nevertheless, there's an alternative that may help us elsewhere in the test. We can use the `self.portal` variable to get a handle on the Plone site (`self` refers to the test case being executed). Then we'll alter every appearance of `http://localhost/plone` or `http://localhost:8080/plone` to `self.portal.absolute_url()`.

```
>>> portal_url = self.portal.absolute_url()
>>> browser.open(portal_url)
```

After directing the browser to the portal home page, we clicked the **Log in** link in order to authenticate ourselves. During a test run, no existing user is available; actually no data at all is there because the ZODB is a new one. So we must use a generic manager user:

```
>>> from Products.PloneTestCase.setup import portal_owner,
default_password
>>> browser.getLink('Log in').click()
>>> browser.getControl('Login Name').value = portal_owner
>>> browser.getControl('Password').value = default_password
>>> browser.getControl('Log in').click()
```

As we mentioned earlier, `zope.testbrowser` is not JavaScript aware, so it won't record any JavaScript interaction. When we want to add a new `XNewsItem` in our site, `zope.testrecorder` learns that we opened the final URL, which won't work during the test run. We can change it with the one used to create objects:

```
>>> browser.open(portal_url + '/createObject?type_name=XNewsItem')
```

The last change we should make is regarding the setting of a combo box value. Unfortunately, `zope.testrecorder` doesn't realize that a combo box is a special kind of control. When setting their values, lists or tuples must be used instead of plain strings.

```
>>> browser.getControl('Country').value = ('AR',)
```

Finally, you should get a doctest like the one shown in the last step of the *How to do it...* section above.

Using Selenium functional tests

Selenium functional tests may be rarely used, but they are very useful if we are to test user interactions using JavaScript, like AJAX-based components in our user interface.

Plone supports Selenium tests in two different ways:

- ▶ `collective.ploneseltest` package provides a `PloneTestCase`-like class to run Selenium tests. With this approach, tests behave like regular Zope functional tests. A Zope instance is started with an empty ZODB and a new Plone site. Selenium RC must be installed separately.
- ▶ `rcom.recipe.selenium` recipe installs **Selenium RC** and creates a test runner. All tests must be run in a living and existing Plone site.

We'll look at the second alternative because it shows a new mode to run tests in existing Plone sites, which might have already created content and it will be available in further test runs.

Getting ready

To record and run a Selenium test we must install both Selenium IDE and Selenium RC. Find installation instructions in the *There's more...* section.

So far, most of our test cases were all included together in a `tests` module inside our product package (`src/Products.poxContentTypes/Products/poxContentTypes/tests.py`). However, we must change this if we want to use the `rcom.recipe.seleniumenv` recipe and all its goodness. (Refer to the *There's more...* section for a detailed explanation.)

How to do it...

1. We are now going to record a Selenium test, so start your instance:

   `./bin/instance fg`

2. Open your Firefox browser and go to your Plone site home page, `http://localhost:8080/plone` in our case, and then go to **Tools | Selenium IDE** to open and start the **Selenium IDE** test recorder. Make sure the red recording button is pressed and that the top **Base URL** top shows `http://localhost:8080/plone`; if not, set it.

The next procedure is the same as the one we followed in followed in Zope functional testing to record a functional test using `zope.testrecorder`.

3. First of all, we must be logged in with proper access rights in order to create some content. Click on the **Log in** link for that.

4. Log in with your administrator username and password: **admin** for both fields in our case. Then click on the **Log in** button.

5. Click on the **Add new...** drop-down menu.

6. Select **XNewsItem** from the list.

7. Fill the **Title** field with **This is another XNewsItem title**.

8. The **Lead** field is also required, so fill it with **Lead field is still required**.

9. Select **Argentina** option in the **Country** combo box.

10. Click on **Save** button to submit the changes.

When the changes are submitted, you'll automatically be redirected to the recently saved XNewsItem document.

11. Select **Changes saved.** text appearing above the document title.

12. Right-click on it and select the **verifyTextPresent Changes saved.** option in the Firefox context menu.

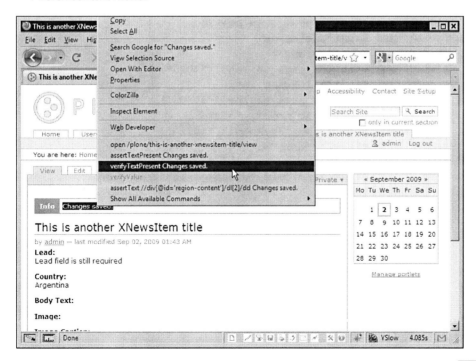

13. That's it! The test has finished, so click on the red button icon in Selenium IDE to stop the recorder.

14. In the Selenium IDE window, go to the **File | Export Test Case As... | Python— Selenium RC** menu option. Save the test case as `testXNewsItem.py` inside a new seleniumtests sub-package (more of this in Organizing packages, in *There's more...* section).

15. Go back to the `__init__.py` file inside `seleniumtests` sub-package and edit it to import the just created test case:

```
echo import testXNewsItem >> __init__.py
```

16. Now open the `testXNewsItem.py` file and modify the port number, browser, and URL according to the following (commented lines are replaced from the original by the next one):

```
from selenium import selenium
import unittest, time, re

class testXNewsItem(unittest.TestCase):
    def setUp(self):
        self.verificationErrors = []
        # self.selenium = selenium("localhost", 4444, "*chrome",
        "http://localhost:8080/plone")
        self.selenium = selenium("localhost", port, browser, url)
        self.selenium.start()

    def test_test_x_news_item(self):
        sel = self.selenium
        sel.open("/plone")
        sel.wait_for_page_to_load("30000")
        sel.click("link=Log in")
        sel.wait_for_page_to_load("30000")
        sel.type("__ac_name", "admin")
        sel.type("__ac_password", "admin")
        sel.click("submit")
        sel.wait_for_page_to_load("30000")
        sel.click("//dl[@id='plone-contentmenu-factories']/dt/a/
        span[1]")
        sel.click("//a[@id='xnewsitem']/span")
        sel.wait_for_page_to_load("30000")
        sel.type("title", "This is another XNewsItem title")
        sel.type("lead", "Lead field is still required")
        sel.select("country", "label=Argentina")
        sel.click("form.button.save")
        sel.wait_for_page_to_load("30000")
        try: self.failUnless(sel.is_text_present("Changes
        saved."))
```

```
except AssertionError, e: self.verificationErrors.
append(str(e))

def tearDown(self):
    self.selenium.stop()
    self.assertEqual([], self.verificationErrors)

if __name__ == "__main__":
    unittest.main()
```

We have also added a `wait_for_page_to_load` call after the first `open` action to let the test runner wait until the home page is available.

17. Given that Selenium tests run on existing Plone sites, as opposed to previous test suites, we must start our Zope instance before running them.

    `./bin/instance fg`

    You can also start it regularly with the start option instead of fg.

18. Then run the tests with the following command.

    `./bin/seleniumRunner -s Products.poxContentTypes -i plone`

    In Windows:

    `python .\bin\seleniumRunner -s Products.poxContentTypes -i plone`

    The `-s` option specifies the product to be tested so that `seleniumRunner` will retrieve all tests inside a `tests.seleniumtests` sub-package. The `-i` option tells what Plone site all tests must be run on.

For other available options, open and see `seleniumRunner` file inside your instance `bin` folder.

19. If everything goes well, you'll get an output like this:

    ```
    test_test_x_news_item (seleniumtests.testXNewsItem.testXNewsItem)
    ... ok


    ----------------------------------------------------------------
    Ran 1 test in 43.012s

    OK
    ```

More information about the **seleniumenv** project can be found at: http://pypi.python.org/pypi/rcom.recipe.seleniumenv

There's more...

As we said at the beginning of this recipe, we must set our environment properly in order for Selenium tests to be recorded and run.

Further reading

To speed up test runs, you can install `roadrunner`, which preloads Python code and sets up a default Plone site to be used during testing. More about it at: `http://pypi.python.org/pypi/roadrunner`.

Martin Aspeli's testing tutorial is a must for learning testing: `http://plone.org/documentation/tutorial/testing`.

He has also written the Plone bedside book, *Professional Plone Development*, which has an extensive treatment of this subject: `http://www.packtpub.com/Professional-Plone-web-applications-CMS/book`.

Philipp von Weitershausen has contributed on the testing tutorial above. He has also written a terrific book, *Web Component Development with Zope 3*, with a broad introduction on testing and further examples throughout the book: `http://www.springer.com/computer/programming/book/978-3-540-76447-2`.

Installing Selenium RC and IDE

Include a new `[seleniumenv]` part at the bottom of the `buildout.cfg` file:

```
[seleniumenv]
recipe = rcom.recipe.seleniumenv
seleniumversion = 1.0.1
eggs = ${instance:eggs}
```

This `rcom.recipe.seleniumenv` recipe will set a Selenium RC environment to test products in our instance. The `seleniumversion` parameter is to select the version that must be fetched. The `eggs` parameter tells which eggs will be available during test runs.

Then add the just created `seleniumenv` to the `parts` definition at the top of the file:

```
[buildout]

...

parts =
    ...
    seleniumenv
```

To prevent version conflicts when building the upgraded instance, add this line in the [versions] section to stick zc.buildout egg version:

```
[versions]
...
zc.buildout = 1.4.1
```

Finally, rebuild your instance by running:

./bin/buildout

You must also install the **Selenium IDE** add-on for Firefox available at http://seleniumhq.org/projects/ide. This Firefox plugin is the test recorder.

Organizing packages

When running Selenium tests based on the rcom.recipe.seleniumenv recipe, (as we have covered here) we must make sure that our package has a special organization.

Go to your buildout directory and then to the product package folder:

cd ./src/Products.poxContentTypes/Products/poxContentTypes/

Create a tests sub-package inside your product package and move the tests.py existing file there:

mkdir ./tests

mv ./tests.py ./tests

cd ./tests

touch __init__.py

This last __init__.py file turns a folder into a valid Python package.

Create a new seleniumtests sub-package inside tests:

mkdir ./seleniumtests

cd ./seleniumtests

touch __init__.py

Debugging tests

Do not forget that tests are Python code, so you can do whatever you want and need inside them. For example, you can invoke your good friend pdb.

```
>>> import pdb; pdb.set_trace()
```

See also

> ▸ *Writing a production buildout*

> ▸ *Testing server load and benchmarking our code*

5
Creating a Custom Content Type with Paster

In this chapter, we will cover:

- ▸ Creating an Archetypes product with paster
- ▸ Adding a content type into a product
- ▸ Changing a base class in paster content types
- ▸ Adding fields to a content type
- ▸ Adding a custom validator to a content type
- ▸ Modifying the view of a content type with jQuery

Introduction

In this chapter, we'll address the second and third points of the customer requirement list, which we included in preface:

- ▸ Multimedia contents will illustrate and complement written information
- ▸ Multimedia contents should be played online but may also be downloaded

Previously in the book, we have used a graphic application (**ArgoUML**) to draw a **UML** model that was automatically transformed by **ArchGenXML** into an **Archetypes**-based content type for Plone.

In this chapter, we'll create a content type product with another tool, **paster**. It's not a graphic application, but it's as easy to use as writing a few characters.

We used paster earlier to create a **buildout**-based Zope instance and an **egg**-structured Plone product. Here we'll use it to create a full Archetype product, its **schema** fields, and even the required **tests** to make sure everything is working as intended.

Creating an Archetypes product with paster

There are several steps to take with paster to produce a full and useful content type. The first one should be the creation of the structure, meaning the product directory organization.

Getting ready

The final destination of this product, at least at development stage, is the `src` folder of our buildout directory. There is where we place our packages source code while we are working on them, until they become **eggs** (to see how to turn them into eggs read *Submitting products to an egg repository*). Thus go to your buildout directory and then get inside the `src` folder:

```
cd ./src
```

Make sure you have the latest `ZopeSkel` installed. `ZopeSkel` is the name of a Python package with a collection of skeletons and templates to create commonly used Zope and Plone projects via a `paster` command.

```
easy_install -U ZopeSkel
```

How to do it...

1. Create a package for the new add-on product:

    We are going to create a new package called `pox.video`. The *pox* prefix is taken from PloneOpenX (the website we are working on) and will be the namespace of our product.

    ```
    paster create -t archetype
    ```

In the **ArchGenXML** chapter, we didn't have the choice of a namespace other than `Products`, which is a limitation of ArchGenXML. Choosing a proper and project-specific namespace is more common in Python sphere.

2. Fix the main `configure.zcml` file to prevent errors:

   Open the just created `configure.zcml` file in the `pox/video` folder and comment the **internationalization** registration like this:

   ```
   <!--  <i18n:registerTranslations directory="locales" /> -->
   ```

3. Update the Zope instance with the new product:

   To let Zope know that there's new code to be used, let's update our instance `buildout.cfg` file.

   In the main `[buildout]` section, modify the `eggs` and `develop` parameters like this:

   ```
   [buildout]
   ...
   eggs =
   ...
        pox.video
   ...
   develop =
        src/pox.video
   ```

4. Automatically add the product in a Plone site:

   We can install our brand new product automatically during buildout. So add a `pox.video` line inside the `[plonesite]` part's `products` parameter:

   ```
   [plonesite]
   recipe = collective.recipe.plonesite
   ...
   products =
   ...
        pox.video
   ```

5. Rebuild and relaunch the Zope instance:

   Build your instance and, if you want to, launch it to check that the `pox.video` product is installed (not strictly necessary though).

   ```
   ./bin/buildout
   ./bin/instance fg
   ```

How it works...

So far we have a skeleton product, which is composed basically of boilerplate (we will build on it further). However, it has all the necessary code to be installed, which is important.

The `paster` command of Step 1 in *How to do it...* creates a package using the `archetype` available template. When run, it will output some informative text and then a short wizard will be started to select some options. The most important are the first five ones:

Option	Value
Enter project name	`pox.video`
Expert mode?	Choose whatever option you like.
Project Title	Video
Version	1.0
Description	Video content type for PloneOpenX website

Add whatever you want to the remaining options (if you chose other than `easy` mode), or just hit *Enter* to each one. After selecting the last option, you'll get an output like this (a little longer actually):

```
Creating template basic_namespace
Creating directory .\pox.video
Creating template archetype
  Recursing into +namespace_package+
    Recursing into +package+
      Recursing into content
      Recursing into interfaces
      Recursing into portlets
      Recursing into profiles
      Recursing into tests
...
The project you just created has local commands. These can be used
from within the product.

usage: paster COMMAND

Commands:
  addcontent  Adds plone content types to your project

For more information: paster help COMMAND
```

The first group of lines tells us something about the created directory structure. We have a pox.video (project name) folder, containing a pox (namespace) folder, which contains a video (package) folder, which in turn contains several sub-packages: content, interfaces, portlets, profiles, and tests. In the following sections, we are going to deal with all of them except portlets, which will be tackled in *Creating a portlet package*, *Customizing a new portlet according to our requirements*, and *Testing portlets*.

The second group of lines (after the ellipsis) gives us very important information: we can use particular **local commands** inside our fresh product. More of this in the next section.

Step 2 in the preceding procedure is to tell Zope about the new available package. By adding pox.video in the eggs parameter, we add it in Zope's PYTHONPATH. We also have to add the package's location in the develop parameter. If not, the buildout process would try to fetch it from some of the URLs listed in the find-links parameter.

During start up, Zope 2 loads (Five does the job actually) configuration files, usually configure.zcml, for all the products and packages inside the folders that are listed in the [instance] section's products parameter. For other Python packages outside those folders, a **ZCML slug** is required for the product to be loaded.

Fortunately, from Plone 3.3 onwards, the ZCML slug is not needed if packages to be installed use z3c.autoinclude, which automatically detects and includes ZCML files.

Although we were not aware of that, when we created the pox.video package with paster, z3c.autoinclude was added as an entry point in the setup.py file. Open it in the main pox.video folder to check it:

```
. . .
setup(name='pox.video',
      version=version,
      description="Video content type for PloneOpenX website",
      . . .
      entry_points="""
      # -*- entry_points -*-
      [z3c.autoinclude.plugin]
      target = plone
      """,
      . . .
      )
```

For those packages that don't have this feature, we must explicitly insert a reference to the package in the `zcml` parameter of the `[instance]` section like we did in *Taking advantage of an enhanced interactive Python debugger with ipdb*:

```
[instance]

...

# If you want to register ZCML slugs for any packages,
# list them here.
# e.g. zcml = my.package my.other.package
zcml =
    iw.debug
```

There's more...

Do not forget to test your changes (`paster` changes in fact)!

Fortunately, `paster` creates automatically a `tests` sub-package and a package-level `README.txt` file with the first part of a test (logging into our website). Feel free to take a look at it, as it is a very good example of **doctest**. Nevertheless, it really doesn't test too much for the time being. It will be more productive after adding some features to the product.

 You may find it really useful to read the content types section from the online Plone Developer Manual at `http://plone.org/documentation/manual/developer-manual/archetypes`.

See also

- *Submitting products to an egg repository*
- *Taking advantage of an enhanced interactive Python debugger with ipdb*
- *Adding a content type into a product*
- *Adding fields to a content type*
- *Adding a custom validator to a content type*
- *Creating a portlet egg with paster*
- *Customizing a new portlet according to our requirements*
- *Testing portlets*

Adding a content type into a product

In *Creating an Archetypes product with paster,* we were able to create a package shell with all the necessary code to install a product, although it was unproductive.

We are now going to add some useful functionality by means of, again, our dear `paster`.

Getting ready

When we ran `paster` in *Creating an Archetypes product with paster*, we highlighted some of its output, copied below:

```
The project you just created has local commands. These can be used
from within the product.
```

Paster **local commands** are available inside the project folder. So let's move inside it:

```
cd ./src/pox.video
```

How to do it...

To add a new content type inside the product, run the following command:

```
paster addcontent contenttype
```

How it works...

This will run the `addcontent paster` command with its `contenttype` template. After a short wizard asking for some options, it will produce all the code we need.

Option	Value
Enter `contenttype_name`	Video
Enter `contenttype_description`	FLV video file
Enter `folderish`	False
Enter `global_allow`	True
Enter `allow_discussion`	True/False, whatever.

You'll get an output like this:

```
...
   Inserting from README.txt_insert into /pox.video/pox/video/README.
txt
   Recursing into content
   Recursing into interfaces
   Recursing into profiles
     Recursing into default
       Recursing into types
```

If you need more than just one content type in your product, you can run the `paster addcontent contenttype` command as many times as you want.

There's no need to modify, `buildout.cfg` file, as we have already made all the required changes. If you didn't make these modifications, please refer to *Creating an Archetypes product with paster*.

Open the interface file in `./src/pox.video/pox/video/interface/video.py`:

```python
from zope import schema
from zope.interface import Interface

from pox.video import videoMessageFactory as _


class IVideo(Interface):
    """Description of the Example Type"""

    # -*- schema definition goes here -*-
```

Empty interfaces, like this one, are called **marker interfaces**. Although they provide some information (they can be used to associate a class with some functionality as we will see in *Using the ZCA to extend a third party product: Collage*), they lack attributes and methods information (that is, their promised functionalities), and consequently and worse, they don't document.

Interfaces don't exist in Python. However, **Zope 3** has incorporated this concept to let components interact easier. All attributes and methods declarations in interfaces are a contract (not a binding one, though) with the external world. For more information about `zope.interface`, visit `http://wiki.zope.org/Interfaces/FrontPage`.

The new content type class is in the `video.py` file located in the `./src/pox.vieo/pox/video/content` package. Let's go through it and explain its pieces.

```python
"""Definition of the Video content type
"""

from zope.interface import implements, directlyProvides

from Products.Archetypes import atapi
from Products.ATContentTypes.content import base
from Products.ATContentTypes.content import schemata

from pox.video import videoMessageFactory as _
from pox.video.interfaces import IVideo
from pox.video.config import PROJECTNAME
```

All `paster`-generated content types inherit from basic `ATContentTypes`, which is good given the large number of products available for them.

> Check the `Products.ATContentTypes` package for plenty of good working examples.

```python
VideoSchema = schemata.ATContentTypeSchema.copy() + atapi.Schema((
    # -*- Your Archetypes field definitions here ... -*-

))
```

Schemas specify the fields available in content types. In our case, the `Video` content type is a plain copy of `ATContentTypeSchema`, which already includes all fields necessary to support **Dublin Core** convention.

> Dublin Core is supported thanks to the `BaseObject` and `ExtensibleMetadata` modules in the `Products.Archetypes` package.

`VideoSchema` here is the result of the addition (yes, we can actually *add* schemas) of two other schemas: the aforementioned `ATContentTypeSchema` and the new empty one created with the `atapi.Schema(())` method, which expects a `tuple` argument (check the double brackets).

>
>
> Up to ZopeSkel 2.16 (paster's package) the `storage` of `title` and `description` fields are changed to `AnnotationStorage`. This reduces performance and therefore it would be better to change it by removing these lines letting **Archetypes** deal with regular `AttributeStorage`:
>
> ```
> # Set storage on fields copied from
> ATContentTypeSchema,
>
> # making sure
> # they work well with the python bridge properties.
> VideoSchema['title'].storage = atapi.
> AnnotationStorage()
>
> VideoSchema['description'].storage = atapi.
> AnnotationStorage()
> ```
>
> There are plans to remove this from `ZopeSkel`, but there's no release date yet for it.

After schema definition, we call `finalizeATCTSchema` to re-order and move some fields inside our schema according to Plone standard. It's advisable to get familiar with its code in the `Products.ATContentTypes.content.schema` module:

```
schemata.finalizeATCTSchema(VideoSchema, moveDiscussion=False)
```

Once defined its schema the real class is created. As we said earlier, it inherits from `base.ATCTContent`; this will be changed for our Video content type.

```
class Video(base.ATCTContent):
    """FLV video file"""
    implements(IVideo)

    meta_type = "Video"
    schema = VideoSchema

    title = atapi.ATFieldProperty('title')
    description = atapi.ATFieldProperty('description')

    # -*- Your ATSchema to Python Property Bridges Here ... -*-


atapi.registerType(Video, PROJECTNAME)
```

The first line in our class body specifies that it implements `IVideo` interface (`interfaces/video.py` file).

Then `VideoSchema` is associated with the class.

ATFieldProperty is required to create ATSchema to Python Property **bridges**. These are recommended for fields of a schema using AnnotationStorage. If you still have title and description fields storage as AnnotationStorage, you should keep these lines. Otherwise you can safely remove them.

And finally, the atapi.registerType() call adds all **getters** and **setters** to the Video class. This is **Archetypes**' magic. You define just a schema and Archetypes will automatically create all methods needed to interact with the class.

There's more...

We do have some more interesting code now, that's why we should be more careful with it and test it. Again, paster has appended several **functional tests** in the README.txt file, including the creation (as Manager and Contributor users), modification, and deletion of a Video object.

Test the product with the following command:

```
./bin/instance test -s pox.video
```

We'd like to highlight the block of statements regarding the creation of content as a contributor member:

```
Let's logout and then login as 'contributor', a portal member that has
the
contributor role assigned.

    >>> browser.getLink('Log out').click()
    >>> browser.open(portal_url)
    >>> browser.getControl(name='__ac_name').value = 'contributor'
    >>> browser.getControl(name='__ac_password').value =
    default_password
    >>> browser.getControl(name='submit').click()
```

This contributor member isn't mentioned anywhere inside the test. Nevertheless the login action doesn't fail. How can that be possible if there's no contributor member included by default in the PloneTestCase base class, like default_user or portal_owner?

If we check the base.py file inside the tests sub-package of our product, we'll see that the FunctionalTestCase class has a special afterSetUp method, which is called just before the real test begins and registers the contributor member above.

Could we have created the user inside the test? Definitely, because test code is a set of Python statements and we can do whatever we want with them.

Is it sensible to perform this kind of set up actions inside the test code? Absolutely not. As we said in *Zope Functional testing*, in Chapter 4, **functional tests** should be conceived as **black-box** tests, from the sheer end-user point of view. This means that code inside a functional test shouldn't assume anything about the underlying environment, but behave as if a regular user were acting through the user interface. Anything we need during testing that shouldn't be done by the user must be placed outside the test code, as in this example.

See also

▸ *Creating an Archetypes product with paster*

▸ *Working with paster generated test suites*

▸ *Zope Functional testing*

▸ *Using the ZCA to extend a third party product: Collage*

Changing the base class in paster content types

All `paster`-created (non-folderish) content types inherit from the basic `ATCTContent` class, which comes with `ATContentTypeSchema`. However, this is a very basic content type: `title`, `description`, and some more metadata fields. On top of this, we intend to upload videos to our website, not just text.

ATContentTypes are native to Plone and many community developers had released extensions or plugins for them, such as LinguaPlone. That's why it is prudent to stay close to them. We are now going to change the `ATCTContent` parent class for `ATFile` to automatically inherit all the benefits, including the file upload field.

How to do it...

Open the `video.py` file inside the `content` sub-package of your product and make these changes. Be aware of commented lines — they can be just removed, but we wanted to keep them here to remark what's going on.

1. Import the base class and interface to be used:

   ```
   from Products.Archetypes import atapi
   # from Products.ATContentTypes.content import base
   from Products.ATContentTypes.content import file
   from Products.ATContentTypes.interface.file import IATFile
   from Products.ATContentTypes.content import schemata
   ```

   This way we are importing interface and class of the out-of-the-box `File` content type.

2. Change original `schema`:

```
# VideoSchema = schemata.ATContentTypeSchema.copy() + \
#   atapi.Schema((
VideoSchema = file.ATFileSchema.copy() + atapi.Schema((

    # -*- Your Archetypes field definitions here ... -*-

))
```

Now, our `VideoSchema` includes `File` fields.

3. Change the base class and implemented interface:

```
# class Video(base.ATCTContent):
class Video(file.ATFile):
    """
    pox Video
    """
#   implements(IVideo)
    implements(IATFile, IVideo)
```

The last step is to change the parent class of `Video` so that now it inherits from `ATFile` instead of just `ATCTContent`. And then we adjust the interfaces this class now implements.

4. Change the view action URL: Open `profiles/default/types/Video.xml` file and amend the `url_expr` attribute in `View` action by adding `/view`.

```
<?xml version="1.0"?>
<object name="Video"
    meta_type="Factory-based Type Information with dynamic views"
    i18n:domain="pox.video" xmlns:i18n=
                        "http://xml.zope.org/namespaces/i18n">
    ...
    <action title="View" action_id="view" category=
                                        "object" condition_expr=""
    url_expr="string:${object_url}/view" visible="True">
    <permission value="View" />
    </action>
    ...
</object>
```

5. Tell Plone to use the new action URL in listings: Add a `propertiestool.xml` file inside the `profiles/default` folder with this code:

```xml
<?xml version="1.0"?>
<object name="portal_properties" meta_type=
                                        "Plone Properties Tool">
 <object name="site_properties" meta_type="Plone Property Sheet">
  <property name="typesUseViewActionInListings" type=
                                        "lines" purge="False">
   <element value="Video"/>
  </property>
 </object>
</object>
```

6. Relaunch your instance and reinstall the product. By restarting the Zope instance all of the latest changes will be applied:

   `./bin/instance fg`

   Go to `http://localhost:8080/plone/prefs_install_products_form` and reinstall the product.

7. Create a new Video object:

   Inside your Plone site, click on the **Add new...** drop-down menu and select the **Video** option. It should look like this.

How it works...

Since the first creation of the almost empty product (full of boilerplate, though), in *Creating an Archetypes product with paster*, we haven't tried to use it, except for the tests we have run. We can now say that it has grown up and it's ready to be seen in action.

In Steps 1 to 3 above, we changed some of the basics in paster's original `class` and its `schema` to inherit all the benefits of another existing content type: `ATFile`.

If you had tried to create a `Video` content type before Step 4, after saving, you would have been automatically prompted to download the file you just uploaded. Why's that? The reason is we inherited our class from `ATFile`, which has a special behavior (like `ATImage`) regarding its URLs.

Files and images uploaded to a Plone site (using regular content types) are downloadable via their *natural* URL. For example, if you browse to `http://yoursite.com/document.pdf`, you will be asked to download the file. Alternatively, if you want to open the web page with a download link and metadata, you should use `http://yoursite.com/document.pdf/view`.

That's why we had to change the view URL for our content type in `Video.xml` (Step 4) for users to be able to open an inline video player (as we plan to).

All files included in the **profiles** folder are used by **GenericSetup** during installation of the product and are to give some information that Python code doesn't provide, such as whether we'll let users post comments inside the content types (`allow_discussion`).

Plone object listings (including search results) tend to create links to contents without the `/view` suffix. We must explicitly tell Plone that when listing videos, the suffix should be appended to prevent a download attempt. Fortunately, Plone has foreseen this could have happened. Thus there's no need to modify or override every single list. If the content type name is listed in the special `typesUseViewActionInListings` property, it will work as expected.

Changes in Step 5 will make the `site_properties` update its `typesUseViewActionInListings` property. By including `purge="False"` in `<property />` tag, we prevent other existing values (typically `File` and `Image`) in the property from being removed.

There's more...

We have definitely made some changes in the code. And this time it wasn't `paster`, it was us! Wouldn't it be advisable to test the package?

```
$ ./bin/instance test -s pox.video
```

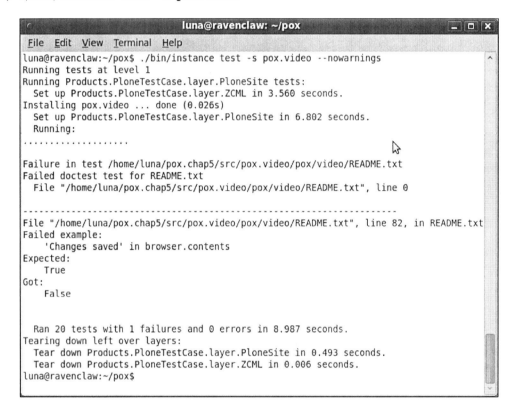

```
luna@ravenclaw: ~/pox                                    _ □ ✕
File  Edit  View  Terminal  Help
luna@ravenclaw:~/pox$ ./bin/instance test -s pox.video --nowarnings
Running tests at level 1
Running Products.PloneTestCase.layer.PloneSite tests:
  Set up Products.PloneTestCase.layer.ZCML in 3.560 seconds.
Installing pox.video ... done (0.026s)
  Set up Products.PloneTestCase.layer.PloneSite in 6.802 seconds.
  Running:
..................

Failure in test /home/luna/pox.chap5/src/pox.video/pox/video/README.txt
Failed doctest test for README.txt
  File "/home/luna/pox.chap5/src/pox.video/pox/video/README.txt", line 0

----------------------------------------------------------------
File "/home/luna/pox.chap5/src/pox.video/pox/video/README.txt", line 82, in README.txt
Failed example:
    'Changes saved' in browser.contents
Expected:
    True
Got:
    False


  Ran 20 tests with 1 failures and 0 errors in 8.987 seconds.
Tearing down left over layers:
  Tear down Products.PloneTestCase.layer.PloneSite in 0.493 seconds.
  Tear down Products.PloneTestCase.layer.ZCML in 0.006 seconds.
luna@ravenclaw:~/pox$
```

Wow! What happened? Did we get a failure?

Normally, you would add a `pdb` line before the reported as failing comment:

```
>>> import pdb; pdb.set_trace()
```

Or you might consider dumping `browser.contents` into a file to check what is wrong.

```
>>> open('/tmp/contents.html', 'w').write(browser.contents)
```

We'll skip that and jump straight into the problem. The new `file` field in our upgraded `Video` content type is required. We should adjust our **functional test** to upload a file.

Open the `README.txt` file in the `pox.video` package and search for the following lines to make the changes below (you must change it twice in `README.txt`):

```
>>> browser.getControl(name='title').value = 'Video Sample'
>>> browser.getControl('Save').click()
>>> 'Please correct the indicated errors.' in browser.contents
True
>>> 'File is required, please correct.' in browser.contents
True
>>> import cStringIO
>>> browser.getControl(name='file_file').\
... add_file(cStringIO.StringIO('File contents'), \
... 'text/plain', 'test.txt')
>>> browser.getControl('Save').click()
>>> 'Changes saved' in browser.contents
True
```

We first try to save the video with no uploaded file and get a validation error message. Then we create and upload an on-the-fly text file and everything works fine.

See also

- ▸ *Creating an Archetypes product with paster*
- ▸ *Adding a custom validator to a content type*

Adding fields to a content type

According to "Video metadata model" available in **Microformats.org** (`http://microformats.org/wiki/video-metadata-model`) the `Video` content type, as a mere copy of `ATFile`, has just one metadata field left: creation date. We are now going to add this missing field with a different name—Original date—to avoid mistaking it with the creation date of the object.

Getting started

As we are going to run `paster` **local commands,** we must move inside the product folder.

```
cd ./src/pox.video
```

How to do it...

To add new fields in the `Video` class schema run the following command:

```
paster addcontent atschema
```

How it works...

The above `paster addcontent` command with the `atschema` template will start a short wizard asking for some options, to give us with all the code we need:

Option	Value
Enter `content_class_filename`	video
Enter `field_name`	originalDate
Enter `field_type`	datetime
Enter `widget_type`	default, or hit *Enter*
Enter `field_label`	Original date
Enter `field_desc`	Date this video was recorded

Hit *Enter* to accept the next default values.

You may get a warning message but almost no output. However, your `video.py` file will be upgraded.

The `VideoSchema` definition now has this new field including a specific **validator**:

```
atapi.DateTimeField(
    'originalDate',
    storage=atapi.AnnotationStorage(),
    widget=atapi.CalendarWidget(
        label=_(u"Original date"),
        description=_(u"Date this video was recorded"),
    ),
    validators=('isValidDate'),
),
```

There's also a new ATSchema to Python Property **bridge** within the class body:

```
originalDate = atapi.ATFieldProperty('originalDate')
```

As we said in *Adding a content type into a product*, AnnotationStorage is not recommended for schema fields, so you can safely remove the `storage=atapi.AnnotationStorage()` line and then remove the Python bridge.

And last, but not least, the `interfaces/video.py` file has also changed:

```
class IVideo(Interface):
    """FLV video file"""

    # -*- schema definition goes here -*-
    originalDate = schema.Date(
        title=_(u"Original date"),
        required=False,
        description=_(u"Date this video was recorded"),
    )
```

Again, if you are keeping `AttributeStorage`, the default one, instead of `AnnotationStorage`, remove this schema definition.

There's more...

We should update the test to verify everything is still working and, of course, any update works as expected.

Search for the first saving action and change the test according to the following:

```
>>> browser.getControl(name='title').value = 'Video Sample'
>>> browser.getControl(name='originalDate_year').value = \
... ('2009',)
>>> browser.getControl(name='originalDate_month').value = \
... ('12',)
>>> browser.getControl(name='originalDate_day').value = \
... ('31',)
>>> browser.getControl('Save').click()
```

To set a `datetime` field, we must fill all of its date combo-boxes; time is not required though.

Now run the test; you should see no failures:

```
./bin/instance test -s pox.video
```

See also

▶ *Adding a content type into a product*
▶ *Adding a custom validator to a content type*

Adding a custom validator to a content type

Given that we plan to show an embedded video player when opening a Video page in our website, we must ensure that users won't be able to upload any kind of file other than FLV videos.

Archetypes can validate field inputs in different ways; the most common one is the use of a `validators` property inside the schema *field* definition, as it's used in the previous section for the `originalDate` field.

We prefer using a more modern way to call a validator, a **subscription adapter**, which is basically a special class that declares to *adapt* another one and, in the case of Archetypes **validators**, it implements a specific event interface.

How to do it...

1. Create this `validators.py` file inside the `contents` sub-package of your product:

```
from zope.interface import implements
from zope.component import adapts
from Products.Archetypes.interfaces import IObjectPostValidation
from pox.video import videoMessageFactory as _
from pox.video.interfaces import IVideo
from flvlib.tags import FLV

# class name could be any one
class ValidateFLVFile(object):
    """
    Checks if file field has a real FLV file
    """
    implements(IObjectPostValidation)
    adapts(IVideo)
    field_name = 'file'

    def __init__(self, context):
        self.context = context

    def __call__(self, request):
        value = request.form.get(self.field_name + '_file',
        request.get(self.field_name + '_file', None))
        if value is not None:
            flv_file=FLV(value)
            try:
                flv_file.parse_header()
            except:
```

```
        return {self.field_name :
                    _(u"Uploaded file is not FLV")}
    if not flv_file.has_video:
        return {self.field_name :
                    _(u"Uploaded file is not FLV")}
# Returning None means no error
return None
```

2. Configure the validator as a subscription adapter. Open the `configure.zcml` file inside the `contents` sub-package and add these lines at the bottom of the file (before the `</configure>` close tag):

```
<subscriber
    provides= "Products.Archetypes.interfaces.
IObjectPostValidation"
    factory=".validators.ValidateFLVFile"
/>
```

3. Add dependent packages in our egg: Open the `setup.py` file in the root `pox.video` folder of your product and modify the `install_requires` variable of the `setup` call:

```
setup(name='pox.video',
    ...
    install_requires=['setuptools',
                    # -*- Extra requirements: -*-
                    'flvlib',
                    ],
    ....
```

4. Rebuild, relaunch your instance, and reinstall the product:

```
./bin/buildout
```

```
./bin/instance fg
```

How it works...

When Archetypes-based content types are being saved, after schema-defined validation has taken place, all factory classes providing or implementing `IObjectPostValidation` interface (an *event* interface actually) will be called as event handlers. According to their return values, the content type will be saved or returned to the user to fix the presented errors.

The `adapts(IVideo)` line in the code of Step 1 is vital and introduces a key concept of Zope 3 component architecture, **adapters**. We can alter the original behavior of a class object by means of another class (that is, we don't need to modify the source code of the first one).

The rest of the code is the validation itself. When calling the validation routine, there's a `request` argument available from which we can get all submitted fields (including the file we want to check). The expected return value can be:

- A dictionary with an error message for every non-passing field
- None, in which case validation succeeds

 There's also an `IObjectPreValidation` interface whose subscription adapters will be called *before* schema-specific validation takes place.

The difference between this subscription adapter and other adapters is that it implements an *event* interface, that's why it must be configured as `<subscriber />` instead of a regular `<adapter />`.

Finally, as we have used a special Python package (`flvlib`), we can include it as an **egg dependency** in the product in order to tell the **buildout** process to download and install it automatically.

There's more...

At this stage, you already know that our **doctest** in the `README.txt` file will fail. Until now we were uploading a plain text file. But the new validator will make things stop working or at least, it should.

 You might want to download the source files accompanying this book from its web page to get the `video.flv` file mentioned below. You could also use any other `FLV` video, and update paths and filenames accordingly.

To check that validation is working as expected, add these lines in the `README.txt` file:

```
>>> browser.getControl('Save').click()
>>> 'Please correct the indicated errors.' in browser.contents
True
>>> 'File is required, please correct.' in browser.contents
True
>>> import cStringIO
>>> browser.getControl(name='file_file').\
... add_file(cStringIO.StringIO('File contents'), \
... 'text/plain', 'test.txt')
>>> browser.getControl('Save').click()
>>> 'Uploaded file is not FLV' in browser.contents
True
```

We make sure that uploading anything but an FLV file is not allowed.

```
>>> import os
>>> pkg_home = os.path.dirname(pox.video.tests.__file__)
>>> samplesdir = os.path.join(pkg_home, 'samples')
```

Then get the location of a `samples` folder inside the `tests` sub-package. In that folder, there's a `video.flv` file that we will upload:

```
>>> browser.getControl(name='file_file').add_file( \
... file(os.path.join(samplesdir, 'video.flv')).read(), \
... 'application/x-flash-video', 'video.flv')
>>> browser.getControl('Save').click()
>>> 'Changes saved' in browser.contents
True
```

There's another upload attempt at the end of the test. Modify it as well:

```
>>> browser.getControl(name='title').value = 'Video Sample'
>>> browser.getControl(name='file_file').add_file( \
... file(os.path.join(samplesdir, 'video.flv')).read(), \
... 'application/x-flash-video', 'video.flv')
>>> browser.getControl('Save').click()
>>> 'Changes saved' in browser.contents
True
```

That's it. Test your instance to see if everything is okay.

See also

▸ *Changing the base class in paster content types*

▸ *Subscribing to others' events*

Modifying the view of a content type with jQuery

Normally, after creating a content type, you'd like to make some visual adjustments for users to view it according to the website specifications. Given that this is directly related to the **theming** phase, which is not covered in this book, we won't dive into those details. However, we will make some minor changes in the basic view template and supply an inline video player.

Getting ready

We will use Flowplayer (a GPL-licensed video player) to watch videos online. Version 3.1.5 is included in the code associated with this book, but any newer version should work as well.

 There is a Plone add-on product named `collective.flowplayer` that works perfectly well for these requirements and it has even more options than we are developing here. The following is just for demonstration purposes. More information about this package is at: `http://pypi.python.org/pypi/collective.flowplayer`.

As suggested by the online documentation at `http://flowplayer.org/documentation`, we will use `<a />`-tagged HTML elements pointing to `FLV` files and turn them into video players via **JavaScript** code.

 More information about Flowplayer is available at their website: `http://flowplayer.org/`.

How to do it...

1. Install Flowplayer. Create a new `flowplayer` folder inside the `browser` sub-package of your product. Download Flowplayer and add the following files inside it (filenames may change according to the latest release):

   - `flowplayer-3.1.5.swf`: the base player.

   - `flowplayer.controls-3.1.5.swf`: a plugin with play button, stop button, and other controls. It's called automatically by the base FlowPlayer SWF file.

   - `flowplayer.min-3.1.5.js`: a minified JavaScript file containing all the necessary code to use Flowplayer.

 Since the `flowplayer` folder won't store any Python files, we don't need to turn it into a package with a `__init__.py` file.

2. Create this `video.js` **JavaScript** file in the same `browser` folder:

```
/* When DOM element is ready
 * call the following function
 */
jQuery(document).ready(function() {
```

```
/* Get all links, inside the automatically generated view
 * template, pointing to the download link of a FLV file
 */

    jQuery.each(jQuery('#archetypes-fieldname-file span
a[href$=".flv/at_download/file"]'), function() {

/* Get the jQueried link and
 * a copy of it to be inserted later
 */

        var jq = jQuery(this);
        var clone = jq.clone()

/* Change some style options, like display (required)
 * width and height, depending of the video dimensions
 */
        jq.attr('style', 'display: block; width: 425px; height:
300px;');

/* Create a flash object based on given SWF file and passing
 * a config object to the *flashvars* parameter
 * Notice the use of encodeURIComponent to prevent flowplayer
 * from throwing an error while trying to load its controls
 * plugin
 */
    jq.flashembed(encodeURIComponent('++resource++pox.video.
flowplayer/flowplayer-3.1.5.swf'), {
            config: {
                clip:  {
                    autoPlay: false,
                    autoBuffering: true,
                    url: this.href
                }
            }
        });
/* Copy the link below the flash video player
 * to provide the user a download link
 */
        jq.after(clone);
    });
});
```

3. Register the new `flowplayer` directory available in the website. In the `configure.zcml` file in the `browser` package, add the following block:

```
<browser:resourceDirectory
    name="pox.video.flowplayer"
    directory="flowplayer"
/>
```

4. Add a new `jsregistry.xml` file inside the `profiles/default` folder of your product:

```
<?xml version="1.0"?>
<object name="portal_javascripts" meta_type="JavaScripts Registry"
    autogroup="False">
 <javascript cacheable="True" compression="safe" cookable="True"
    enabled="True" expression=""
    id="++resource++pox.video.flowplayer/flowplayer.min-3.1.5.js"
    inline="False"/>
 <javascript cacheable="True" compression="none" cookable="True"
    enabled="True" expression=""
    id="++resource++pox.video.flowplayer/video.js"
inline="False"/>
</object>
```

5. Launch the Zope instance and re-install the product.

How it works...

The `video.js` file is a **jQuery** based **JavaScript** that adds a Flowplayer whenever it finds particular HTML elements in the web page. Refer to the inline comments to understand how it works.

 jQuery JavaScript library is by default included with Plone.

That file and the previous three ones mentioned in the preceding Step 1 should be available on our website to be used from the `Video` view template. To achieve this, we must define **browser resources** as in Step 3.

 If we had a single or particular files to publish as browser resources, we could have used the `<browser:resource />` directive for each of them instead of `<browser:resourceDirectory />`.

This change will let all files in the `browser/flowplayer` folder be available via a URL like `http://localhost:8080/plone/++resource++pox.video.flowplayer/file.txt`. This is what we have used in the `video.js` JavaScript above to create the embedded flash object.

Step 4 is to register the two new JavaScript files in **portal_javascripts**. This tool merges several JavaScript source files into a single one so that fewer requests are made by the browser.

The **GenericSetup** handlers, called during product installation, make it easy to add, remove, or modify configuration options in almost every tool available in Plone. These handlers can read XML files with particular syntax and translate them into the proper settings.

 If you go to `portal_javascripts` tool, you'll be able to automatically make an association between every `<javascript />` directive and every JavaScript resource in **ZMI**.

Once reinstalled, when opening a `Video`, you should see something like this:

There's more...

How could we test these little changes we have made? We could just try to access every resource's URL and check if they are available as intended. But would that be a real functional test from the user standpoint? Certainly not.

What the final user would like to test is whether uploaded videos are really playable online. Given that `zope.testbrowser` doesn't support JavaScript, we must create a **Selenium** test.

As we did in *Using Selenium functional tests* in Chapter 4, we must create a `seleniumtests` sub-package within `tests`:

```
cd ./src/pox.video/pox/video/tests/
mkdir seleniumtests
cd seleniumtests
```

The `__init__.py` file inside `seleniumtests` must import the tests modules we are going to run:

```
echo import testFlowPlayer >> __init__.py
```

Then we place the `testFlowPlayer.py` file inside the same folder. The source Selenium testing code of this file is not fully copied here due to its length, you can find it in the downloadable code associated with this book. However, we want to highlight the following line in the test:

```
self.failUnless(sel.is_element_present("//*[@id=\"archetypes-
fieldname-file\"]/span/a/object"))
```

This is the way Selenium can verify if there's a specific HTML element inside a web page. The XPath expression here is almost the same as the one in the jQuery we used for fetching links to be converted in `video.js` of the previous section.

Feel free to check the whole `testFlowPlayer.py` for other details, like how to upload a file.

To run this test, you should have a running instance and then, in another shell, run the following command:

```
.\bin\seleniumRunner -s Products.poxContentTypes -i plone
```

In Windows, run:

```
python .\bin\seleniumRunner -s Products.poxContentTypes -i plone
```

See also

- ▸ *Creating the user interface for Zope 3 content types*
- ▸ *Using Selenium functional tests*

6
Creating Lightweight Content Types

In this chapter, we will cover:

- ▶ Creating a product package structure
- ▶ Creating a folderish content type
- ▶ Creating the user interface for Zope 3 content types
- ▶ Creating content types with Dexterity

Introduction

In the last chapter, we introduced some of the main concepts of **Zope 3** component architecture such as subscription adapters, browser views and resources, among others. In the next few pages, we will fully explore the Zope 3 world by creating **content components** (that is, **content types** in the Zope 3 way).

At the time of writing this book, Plone did not run on the Zope 3 application server, but **Zope 2**. How's it possible then to use Zope 3 modules in Plone? Fortunately, Zope 3 has been conceived, from its very beginning, as a collection of software components (read Python packages) that can be integrated within other software components. Thanks to the **Five** project, Zope 3 technology can be plugged into Zope 2 so that we can use most of the new ways of doing things when developing for Plone.

We have already covered the first three requirements of our customer (see preface of the book). We will now start the tasks to accommodate the following two:

- ▸ Advertisement banners will be located in several areas of every page
- ▸ Advertisement banners may vary according to the section of the website

To do this, we will logically organize our banners inside sections, which will be located in strategic areas of the final page. To better understand this approach, look at the following wireframe of the *Economy* front page in our news website:

In the preceding prototype, we can spot three sections of banners:

- **Economy Logo Section**
- **Economy Right Column Section**
- **Economy Headlines Section**

Each of these sections is actually a set that will help us organize banners in the layout of the web page. Banners are specific for every content area of the website. There will be special ads for Economy, Politics, Sports, and so on.

This organization naturally suggests the hierarchic structure of the next picture:

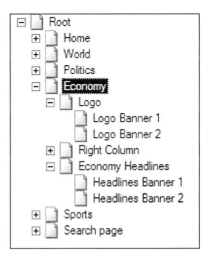

To achieve this, we could create just another archetype and organize it in folders. Unfortunately, due to its versatility, the **Archetypes** framework is quite large and therefore sometimes inefficient. And given that banners will be located all over the place, we need them to be extremely efficient.

Using components from Zope 3, we can create more lightweight and simple content types for our banners and their folders or sections. Furthermore, we can gain more control over them: we can do without **Dublin Core** support, and we can customize **add and edit forms** as we wish, instead of dealing with Archetypes' auto-generated forms.

We'd like to make a general warning to the developer beginning this chapter. At the time of writing, core content types of Plone are built with **Archetypes** (**ATContentTypes** product). We are introducing the Zope 3 substitute for a very specific requirement and application. In consequence, if you are to create custom content types for your website, it's more likely that the option is still Archetypes (and some ATContentTypes extension actually, like in *Creating an Archetypes product with paster* in *Chapter 5*).

We'll still use **Zope 3** practices in further chapters, not for **content components** but for related concepts.

There are many resources available on the Web, which tell us about the relationship between Archetypes, Zope 3, Five, and Plone. We kindly invite you to read these or just *google* "plone and zope 3":

- `http://plone.org/documentation/tutorial/borg/to-archetype-or-not-to-archetype`

- `http://plone.org/documentation/faq/zope-3-and-plone`

Creating a product package structure

As in the previous chapter, we'll create the egg structure for the banner's product with `paster`.

Getting ready

As in previous examples, during development phase, we must locate our products inside the buildout's `src` folder. Thus go to your buildout folder and run:

```
cd ./src
```

How to do it...

1. Once inside the `src` folder, create a basic Plone project by running:

```
paster create -t plone
```

This command will ask you some questions regarding the names you want to use in your product:

Option	Value
Enter project name	pox.banner
Expert mode?	`easy`. We don't need `expert` mode for this example.
Version	1.0
Description	Banners administration for PloneOpenX website

When done, we'll have a new product waiting to be used. Therefore, we should tell Zope about its existence.

2. Edit the `buildout.cfg` file and change it accordingly. In the main `[buildout]` section, modify the `eggs` and `develop` parameters:

```
[buildout]
...
eggs =
...
    pox.banner
...
develop =
    ...
    src/pox.banner
```

Optionally, if you want the product to be installed at building time, modify the `[plonesite]` section:

```
[plonesite]
recipe = collective.recipe.plonesite
...
products =
...
    pox.banner
```

3. Build your instance by running:

```
./bin/buildout
```

How it works...

The above `paster` command has created an **egg**-structured add-on product with all the required code to be installed, used, and even tested in Zope. However, since we have only created the shell of the product (that is, no functionality), we won't use it or test it now.

See also

- ▸ *Creating an Archetypes product with paster*
- ▸ *Creating a folderish content type*

Creating a folderish content type

To ease the banner administration in our website, we have decided to organize banners within folders or containers; we will call them "Sections". We could have chosen to use existing folder content types, but, as stated in this chapter's introduction, we want to maximize lightness in these products.

Getting ready

The `plone` template we used with `paster` to create this new product does not know anything about its final usage. That's why, unlike in the last chapter—when we run `paster` with the `archetype` template—we must create every sub-package we need—in this case, the `content` sub-package.

Get inside the `pox.banner` product and run:

```
mkdir src/pox.banner/pox/banner/content
touch src/pox.banner/pox/banner/content/__init__.py
```

 In Linux, we usually run `touch <name_of_file>` to create an empty file. The alternative for Windows is a command like `echo # > <name_of_file>`.

How to do it...

1. Create a new `interfaces.py` file inside the `pox/banner` folder including the following code:

```
from zope import schema
from zope.interface import Interface
class ISection(Interface):
    """A Section
    """
    title = schema.TextLine(title=u"Title",
                            description=u"Section title.",
                            required=True)
```

2. Add a new `section.py` file inside the `pox.banner.content` sub-package and add the following code (explained in How it works...):

```
from zope.interface import implements
from zope.component.factory import Factory
from plone.app.content.container import Container
from plone.app.content.interfaces import INameFromTitle
from pox.banner import interfaces
class Section(Container):
    """
    A section to contain other sections or banners
    """
    implements(interfaces.ISection, INameFromTitle)
    title = u""
    portal_type = "Section"

    sectionFactory = Factory(Section, 'Section', ' A section to
contain other sections or banners')
```

3. Modify `configure.zcml` in the `pox.banner` package to register everything we need to be accessible in Zope.

```
<configure
  xmlns="http://namespaces.zope.org/zope"
  xmlns:five="http://namespaces.zope.org/five"
  xmlns:i18n="http://namespaces.zope.org/i18n"
  xmlns:genericsetup="http://namespaces.zope.org/genericsetup"
>

  <five:registerPackage package="." initialize=".initialize" />
<!-- <i18n:registerTranslations directory="locales" /> -->

  <genericsetup:registerProfile
      name="default"
```

```
          title="pox Banners and Sections"
          description="Banners administration for PloneOpenX website"
          directory="profiles/default"
          provides="Products.GenericSetup.interfaces.EXTENSION"
   />

     <five:registerClass
          class=".content.section.Section"
          meta_type="Section"
          permission="cmf.AddPortalContent"
     />

     <utility
          provides="zope.component.interfaces.IFactory"
          component=".content.section.sectionFactory"
          name="addSection"
     />
</configure>
```

4. Include **Factory Type Information** (**FTI**) for **GenericSetup**: Add the `types.xml` file inside a new `profiles/default` folder of the package:

```
<object name="portal_types">
<object name="Section" meta_type="Factory-based Type
 Information" />
</object>
```

And then create the `Section.xml` file inside the `profiles/default/types` folder (you'd probably have to create it):

```
<?xml version="1.0"?>
<object name="Section"
     meta_type="Factory-based Type Information with dynamic views"
     xmlns:i18n="http://xml.zope.org/namespaces/i18n"
     i18n:domain="pox.banner">

 <!-- Basic information -->
 <property name="title">Section</property>
 <property name="content_icon">folder_icon.gif</property>
 <property name="product"></property>
 <property name="content_meta_type">Section</property>
 <property name="global_allow">True</property>
 <property name="allow_discussion">False</property>

 <property name="filter_content_types">False</property>
 <property name="allowed_content_types"/>
```

```
<property name="factory">addSection</property>

<alias from="(Default)" to="view"/>
<alias from="edit" to="@@edit"/>
<alias from="sharing" to="@@sharing"/>
<alias from="view" to="@@view"/>

<action title="View" action_id="view" category="object"
condition_expr=""
   url_expr="string:${object_url}" visible="True">
 <permission value="View"/>
</action>

<action title="Edit" action_id="edit" category="object"
condition_expr=""
   url_expr="string:${object_url}/edit" visible="True">
 <permission value="Modify portal content"/>
</action>

</object>
```

5. Create a README.txt file inside the pox.banner package and add these lines with the following tests:

    Get the Section factory by its named utility

    ```
    >>> from pox.banner.content.section import *
    >>> from zope.component import getUtility
    >>> from zope.component.interfaces import IFactory
    >>> addSection = getUtility(IFactory, 'addSection')
    ```

    Let's create a Section object by calling the factory

    ```
    >>> first_section = addSection('first_section')
    >>> first_section
    <Section at first_section>
    >>> first_section.id
    'first_section'
    >>> first_section.title = "A sample section"
    ```

    **We need to add it to an object manager for acquisition to do
    its magic.**

    ```
    >>> self.portal[first_section.id] = first_section
    >>> self.portal.first_section
    <Section at /plone/first_section>
    ```

    Section can contain sections

```
>>> first_subsection = addSection('first_subsection')
>>> first_subsection.title = "A sample subsection"
>>> self.portal.first_section[first_subsection.id] = \
first_subsection
>>> self.portal.first_section.first_subsection
<Section at /plone/first_section/first_subsection>
```

Sections have been cataloged.

```
>>> from Products.CMFCore.utils import getToolByName
>>> catalog = getToolByName(self.portal, 'portal_catalog')
>>> from pox.banner.interfaces import ISection
>>> [brain.getObject() for brain in catalog(object_provides =
ISection.__identifier__)]
[<Section at /plone/first_section>, <Section at
/plone/first_section/first_subsection>]
```

6. Edit the `tests.py` file and uncomment these lines:

    ```
    # Integration tests that use PloneTestCase
    ztc.ZopeDocFileSuite(
        'README.txt', package='pox.banner',
        test_class=TestCase),
    ```

7. Then test the package by running:

    `./bin/instance test -s pox.banner`

How it works...

Unlike **Archetypes**, Zope 3 content components are based on the **interfaces** they implement, which, in turn, are their schemas. Thus we have started, in Step 1, by defining what fields we must include to fulfill our needs.

> An `interfaces` module is the common means of writing down the interfaces we'll use in a package. If we had several interfaces or they were long, then we could create an `interfaces` package instead.

Once we have specified the `Section`'s schema in the `interfaces` module, we also create, in Step 2, a class to implement it—that is to say, a class that will obey the `ISection` interface.

> Quick reminder: Zope interfaces are not enforced, but they establish a *gentlemen's agreement* with classes implementing them.

The `Section` class is based on the `Container` class, which provides all the functionalities we need for these simple *folders*.

 We could have created a lighter content type by inheriting from `OFS.Folder.Folder`. However, we'd have been missing some essential features such as auto-indexing in catalog. That's why we decided to use the mixin `plone.app.content.container.Container` class.

The `implements(interfaces.ISection, INameFromTitle)` line promises that `Section` objects will satisfy `ISection` interface (that is, it will have a `title` text field, which is all the interface says about itself).

 Given that the `Section` class implements `INameFromTitle`, when saved for the first time, any of its content objects will automatically get a normalized ID based on the title field. For more information about it read `plone/app/content/namchooser.txt`.

Then we set a default value for the `title` attribute during initialization and the `portal_type` value required by catalog index and metadata.

When creating `Section` objects, we won't need to use (to be bound to) any specific implementation of them, but just call a proper **factory**. A matching utility should be registered in `configure.zcml`. Anyway, we are providing a factory in the last line of `section.py`.

 A factory is a **utility** component that implements the `IFactory` interface and creates and returns the expected object instance.

In Step 3, we highlighted lines and directive that must be added or changed in the original `paster`-created `configure.zcml` file:

- `genericsetup` namespace is used in the `<genericsetup:registerProfile />` directive, which will be used in the `portal_quickinstaller` tool and in the **Add/Remove Products** configlet in the control panel. Title and description will be used there.
- Make sure to comment the `<i18n:registerTranslations />` line in case there's no `locales` folder created in the package.
- We use `<five:registerClass />` to register `Section` class and let it be available in Zope 2.
- The new `addSection` **utility** is registered so that we can use it regardless of the implementation of the interface.

During product installation, **GenericSetup** takes several steps according to what it finds in the `profiles` folder, including information about new content types to let Plone know how to deal with them. This information is stored in the **portal_types** tool, and is taken from the `types.xml` file and one or more XML files depending on how many content types we want to register. These files are shown in Step 4 of the aforementioned procedure. By opening `http://localhost:8080/plone/portal_types/manage` you will find the list of all the types that are already available in your Plone site. It is important to notice that, unlike in **Archetypes**-based content types, Zope 3 pure `content components` need the `product` property to be undefined or empty.

Although this product is already installable in Plone, we can't do anything with it from a web browser. If we were to add it from the **Add new** drop down menu, we would create it without being able to set any of its fields. This is because we don't have any **add or edit form**, or even a view page (one big difference from **Archetypes**, which automatically creates them). We'll see how to achieve this in *Creating the user interface for Zope 3 content types*.

Regardless of whether the product is usable or not, we now have some code, so we can write a test to make sure it's working and it will still work in the future. We have highlighted the comments inside the **doctest** of Step 5 to spot which feature we want to test. These ones are the key elements we'll use later in this and future chapters.

Since the tests require an actual Plone portal, with a functional catalog, they are actually **integration tests**, we modified the `tests` module in Step 7 to tell Zope's testing machinery which kind of test to run.

See also

▶ *Adding a content type into a product*

▶ *Creating the user interface for Zope 3 content types*

▶ *Customizing a new portlet according to our requirements*

Creating the user interface for Zope 3 content types

The `Section` class developed in *Creating a folderish content type* is working as expected, nevertheless it's not yet usable from a web browser. Like most content types in Plone, we need it to have **add and edit forms** and a view page. Fortunately, **Zope 3** is on our side, so we will squeeze it.

Getting ready

 By convention, components are separated into modules or packages according to their intended target. Thus, all browser-related components will reside in a `browser` sub-package.

In your `pox/banner` folder, create the package by running:

```
mkdir src/pox.banner/pox/banner/browser
touch src/pox.banner/pox/banner/browser/__init__.py
```

 In Linux, we usually run `touch <name_of_file>` to create an empty file. The alternative for Windows is a command like `echo # > <name_of_file>`.

How to do it...

In the just created `browser` sub-package, add a new `section.py` file.

1. Create a class required by the **Add form**:

```
import zope.formlib
from zope.component import createObject
from Acquisition import aq_base
from Products.Five.formlib import formbase as fiveformbase
from plone.app.form import base as formbase
from pox.banner import interfaces

class Add(formbase.AddForm):
    form_fields = \
zope.formlib.form.FormFields(interfaces.ISection)
    def create(self, data):
        content = createObject(self.__name__)
        zope.formlib.form.applyChanges(content,
        self.form_fields, data)
    return aq_base(content)
```

2. Add a class required by the **Edit form**. In the same `section.py` file, add these lines:

```
class Edit(formbase.EditForm):
    form_fields = zope.formlib.form.FormFields(interfaces.
ISection)
```

3. Include a class required by the **View page**:

```
class View(fiveformbase.DisplayForm):
    form_fields = zope.formlib.form.FormFields(interfaces.
ISection)
```

4. Register components in `configure.zcml`. Add this `configure.zcml` file in the `browser` sub-package:

```
<configure
    xmlns="http://namespaces.zope.org/zope"
    xmlns:browser="http://namespaces.zope.org/browser"
    i18n_domain="pox.banner">

    <!-- Add form -->
    <browser:page
        for="zope.app.container.interfaces.IAdding"
        name="addSection"
        class=".section.Add"
        permission="cmf.AddPortalContent"
        />

    <!-- Edit form -->
    <browser:page
        for="..interfaces.ISection"
        name="edit"
        class=".section.Edit"
        permission="cmf.ModifyPortalContent"
        />

    <!-- View page -->
    <browser:page
        for="..interfaces.ISection"
        name="view"
        class=".section.View"
        permission="zope2.View"
        />

</configure>
```

5. Including component registration during instance start-up. Modify the `configure.zcml` file in the `pox/banner` folder by adding this line:

```
<configure
    xmlns="http://namespaces.zope.org/zope"
    xmlns:genericsetup="http://namespaces.zope.org/genericsetup"
    xmlns:five="http://namespaces.zope.org/five">
    ...
    <include package=".browser" />

</configure>
```

6. Create a doctest in a new pox/banner/browser.txt file with this **functional test**:

```
Initial steps
-------------
Create the browser object we'll be using.

    >>> from Products.Five.testbrowser import Browser
    >>> browser = Browser()
    >>> portal_url = self.portal.absolute_url()
    >>> self.portal.error_log._ignored_exceptions = ()


Necessary import for logging in as manager.

    >>> from Products.PloneTestCase.setup import portal_owner,
    default_password


Login action
    >>> browser.open(portal_url)
    >>> browser.getLink('Log in').click()
    >>> browser.getControl(name='__ac_name').value = portal_owner
    >>> browser.getControl(name='__ac_password').value = \
default_password
    >>> browser.getControl(name='submit').click()


Adding a new Section content item
---------------------------------


We use the 'Add new' menu to add a new content item.

    >>> browser.getLink('Add new').click()
```

Then we select the type of item we want to add. In this case we select 'Section' and click the 'Add' button to get to the add form.

```
>>> browser.getControl('Section').click()
>>> browser.getControl(name='form.button.Add').click()
>>> 'Section' in browser.contents
True
```

Now we fill the form and submit it.

```
>>> browser.getControl(name='form.title').value =
'Sample Section'
>>> browser.getControl(name='form.actions.add').click()
>>> browser.url
'http://nohost/plone/sample-section/view'
>>> 'Sample Section' in browser.contents
True
```

Default view

```
>>> browser.open(portal_url + '/sample-section')
>>> browser.url
'http://nohost/plone/sample-section'
>>> 'Sample Section' in browser.contents
True
```

7. Enable the functional test. To be able to run the test, we must first uncomment these lines in the `tests` module.

```
ztc.FunctionalDocFileSuite(
    'browser.txt', package='pox.banner',
    test_class=TestCase),
```

Besides, we must be sure that the `pox.banner` product is correctly installed in the Plone site for us to be able to create content objects. Modify this line at the top of the `tests.py` file:

```
#ptc.setupPloneSite()
ptc.setupPloneSite(products=['pox.banner', ])
```

8. Run this test suite with this command in your buildout directory:

```
./bin/instance test -s pox.banner
```

How it works...

The form generator `AddForm`—Step 1—needs a `form_fields` attribute with the set of *form* fields to include. The `FormFields` call turns *schema* fields defined in `ISection` into *form* fields.

The `create` method is called when the user submits the data, which is very important because, if not saved, the object won't be created, unlike with Archetypes. In detail:

- `createObject` method creates a content object with the factory named as the passed argument.
- `applyChanges` loops through all the fields and sets their values according to the submitted `data`.
- by returning `aq_base(content)` we make sure that the resulting object is devoid of any context, as it will be placed in a new one according to the container where it was created.

 More about Zope Acquisition can be found at: `http://plone.org/documentation/glossary/acquisition` and `http://docs.zope.org/zope2/zope2book/Acquisition.html`.

As above, an Edit form—Step 2—needs a `form_fields` attribute with the list of fields to include. Zope 3 will do the magic to turn it into a web browser form.

To create add and edit forms, we used the `plone.app.form.base` class, that redirects us to the view page when submitting data.

Given that the `View` class in Step 3 is based on `DisplayForm`, instead of creating a form, it will render a view page.

As in the previous examples, we must tell Zope about the existence of all these classes and functionalities. Thus we created, in Step 4, a new configuration (component registration) file inside the new `browser` sub-package:

- First we register an `addSection` browser page available for objects providing the `IAdding` interface (the one used to get all addable content types inside a container). When used, this page will call the `.section.Add` class (note the initial dot indicating the `section` module is located in the same package) and it will be displayed just for members with the `cmf.AddPortalContent` permission.
- The second block is like the previous one with some differences. The new `edit` browser page will be available for objects providing `..interfaces.ISection` interface (here two consecutive dots mean that the `interfaces` module lives in the parent package). The callable class will be `.section.Edit` and another permission is required.
- This last `<browser:page />` directive registers the display form we just created.

If you check the `Section.xml` file inside the `profiles/default/types` folder, you will see how `view` and `edit` actions match the names we have chosen for the browser pages above. You'll also spot that the `factory` property corresponds to the name we have given to the **factory** utility in *Creating a folderish content type*.

The Zope instance processes the package's main `configure.zcml` file during start-up (this is due to the `z3c.autoinclude` plugin as explained in *Creating an Archetypes product with paster* in *Chapter* 5). However, nothing tells Zope that there might be other configuration files to be treated, like the one in browser sub-package. To tell Zope of this, we modified the main package `configure.zcml` file in Step 5.

There's more...

With the above code, we have included in the source files accompanying this book an alternative to the **edit form** and **view page**. It won't be explained here, though. We think it is worth having a look at it because it uses a different approach. Instead of using the `zope.formlib` package and its Five's implementation, it uses the `z3c.form` package (Zope 3 Community form), which is newer, better documented, and better maintained. We will cover the `z3c.form` in *Creating a configuration form*, *Adding configuration options in Plone control panel*, and *Preparing a form to take full advantage of KSS*.

See also

- ▸ *Creating an Archetypes product with paster*
- ▸ *Creating a folderish content type*
- ▸ *Creating a product package structure*
- ▸ *Creating a configuration form*
- ▸ *Adding configuration options in Plone control panel*
- ▸ *Preparing a form to take full advantage of KSS*

Creating content types with Dexterity

Is Dexterity yet another content type framework? Haven't we just seen Zope 3 techniques for creating content types? Wasn't it lighter than Archetypes? Yes, yes, yes! Why learn another way to code content types, then? Because Dexterity is taking the shape of the future content types framework.

Dexterity combines the lightness of Zope 3 content components with Archetypes' key concept of code-it-easy:

▸ It requires significantly less code than Archetypes (it's based on Zope 3).

▸ It has better test coverage, which provides examples and documentation about use cases.

▸ It relies on a widely used forms library (`z3c.form`), which is also useful for creating standalone forms not connected to a content object.

▸ It supports **add forms** (unlike Archetypes, which uses the `portal_factory` tool to create temporary objects before saving them for the first time).

▸ It more closely follows Python and Zope 3 conventions.

▸ It lets extend content type's functionalities with reusable behaviors.

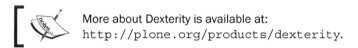

> More about Dexterity is available at:
> `http://plone.org/products/dexterity`.

Is it sensible to move to Dexterity? Probably not. Not yet, at least. At the time of writing, Dexterity is alpha software and even the examples below might stop working (to prevent this, we have included packages version numbers). However, we still think it's valuable to include a short example in order to know what probably will be coming up.

How to do it...

1. Modify the `interfaces.py` file in your `pox.banner` package like this:

```python
from plone.directives import form
class IBanner(form.Schema):
    """A Banner interface
    """
    title = schema.TextLine(
            title=u"Title",
            description=u"Section title.",
            required=True)

    body = schema.Text(
            title=u"Banner HTML",
            required=True,
            default=u"<h1>Banner code goes here</h1>")
```

2. Include portal types information for **GenericSetup**. Modify the `types.xml` file in the `profiles/default` folder to provide Banner content type information:

```
<object name="portal_types">
 <object name="Section" meta_type="Factory-based Type
 Information" />
 <object name="Banner" meta_type="Dexterity FTI" />
</object>
```

We must also supply Banner's metadata (**FTI**) in a `Banner.xml` file inside the `profiles/default/types` folder. Here are some snippets of the file (full version available in this chapter's source code):

```
<?xml version="1.0"?>
<object name="Banner" meta_type="Dexterity FTI"
    xmlns:i18n="http://xml.zope.org/namespaces/i18n"
    i18n:domain="pox.banner">

 <!-- Basic information -->
 <property name="title">Banner</property>
 <property name="global_allow">False</property>
 ...
 ...
 <property name="klass"> plone.dexterity.content.Item</property>
 ...
 <!-- Schema - here described inline for TTW editing -->
 <property name="schema">pox.banner.interfaces.IBanner</property>
 ...
<!-- enabled behaviors -->
 <property name="behaviors">
     <element value="plone.app.content.interfaces.
     INameFromTitle" />
 </property>
 ...
```

3. Update components registration in main `configure.zcml`:

```
<configure
     ...
     xmlns:grok="http://namespaces.zope.org/grok"
     ...>
     <!-- Include configuration for dependencies listed in
     setup.py  -->
     <includeDependencies package="." />
     <grok:grok package="." />
     ...
</configure>
```

4. Add required dependencies in `setup.py`. Open the `setup.py` file in the root `pox.banner` folder of your product and modify the `install_requires` variable of the `setup` call:

```
setup(name='pox.banner',
    ...
    install_requires=['setuptools',
                      # -*- Extra requirements: -*-
                      'plone.app.dexterity',
                      ],
    ....
```

5. Extend the **buildout** with a **Known Good Set** of dependencies for Dexterity. Add a new line in the `extends` parameter of the main `[buildout]` section:

```
[buildout]
parts =
    ...
extends =
    ...
    http://good-py.appspot.com/release/dexterity/1.0a2
...
```

6. Build your instance again to fetch and install new versions as defined in Steps 4 and 5:

```
./bin/buildout
```

7. Add more **functional tests** in the existing pox/browser/browser.txt file:

```
Adding a new Banner content item
--------------------------------


We use the 'Add new' menu to add a new content item.

    >>> browser.getLink('Add new').click()


Then we select the type of item we want to add. In this case we
select 'Banner' and click the 'Add' button to get to the add form.

    >>> browser.getControl('Banner').click()
    >>> browser.getControl(name='form.button.Add').click()
    >>> 'Banner' in browser.contents
    True


Now we fill the form and submit it.
```

```
>>> browser.getControl(name='form.widgets.title').value =
'Sample Banner'
>>> browser.getControl(name='form.buttons.save').click()
>>> browser.url
'http://nohost/plone/sample-section/sample-banner/view'
>>> 'Sample Banner' in browser.contents
True
```

```
Default view
```

```
>>> browser.open(portal_url + '/sample-section/sample-banner')
>>> browser.url
'http://nohost/plone/sample-section/sample-banner'
>>> 'Sample Banner' in browser.contents
True
```

8. Test the package by running:

    ```
    ./bin/instance test -s pox.banner
    ```

 You may need to uncomment Zope Functional test and install `pox.banner` product in the Plone Site in `tests.py` as explained in the last steps of *Creating the user interface for Zope 3 content types*.

How it works...

Notice how, unlike the `ISection` interface developed in *Creating a folderish content type*, which was based on `zope.interface.Interface`, `IBanner` of Step 1 inherits from `plone.directives.form.Schema`. This `form.Schema` is actually based on `Interface` but it's improved with extra functionality, such as default values for its fields.

We have highlighted several properties in the `Banner.xml` file of Step 2:

▶ `global_allow` is set to `False`. Banners will be created within sections so they won't appear in the **Add new** menu everywhere. If you open the `Section.xml` file, you can set `filter_content_types` and `allowed_content_types` properties to complement this decision.

▶ `schema`: Observe how we have used a general `plone.dexterity.content.Item` class. We don't need to create any custom class. Instead, by specifying the `IBanner` interface in the `schema` property, Dexterity will take care of creating an **add form**, an **edit form**, and a **view page** by using `z3c.form` with all the fields mentioned in `IBanner`.

▸ `behaviors`: They are reusable bundles of functionality that can be enabled or disabled on a per-content type basis. In this case, we added the same `INameFromTitle` that we used in the `Section` class earlier to set the IDs of Banners based on their titles.

In Step 3, we added these directives in `configure.zcml`:

▸ `<includeDependencies />`: This will tell Zope to process the configuration files (`configure.zcml`) of the dependencies included in `setup.py` of the current package (denoted by a dot).

▸ `<grok:grok />` directive will make **grok** process the current package and register all components found in it. That's why we didn't register anything else in the `configure.zcml` file. Grok does it for us.

 Grok is a framework that simplifies the configuration of **Zope 3** packages by emphasizing implicit conventions rather than explicit configuration. More about Grok at: `http://grok.zope.org/documentation`.

See also

▸ *Creating a folderish content type*

▸ *Creating the user interface for Zope 3 content types*

7

Improving Product Performance

In this chapter, we will cover:

- ▶ Installing CacheFu with a policy product
- ▶ Improving performance by tweaking expensive code
- ▶ Testing server load and benchmarking our code

Introduction

CMS Plone provides:

- ▶ A Means of adding, editing, and managing content
- ▶ A database to store content
- ▶ A mechanism to serve content in HTML or other formats

Fortunately, it also supplies the tools to do all these things in an incredibly easy and powerful way. For example, content producers can create a new article without worrying how it will look or what other information will be surrounding the main information.

To do this Plone must compose a single HTML output file (if we are talking from a web browser viewpoint) by joining and rendering several sources of data according to the place, importance, and target they are meant for.

As it is built upon the Zope application server, all these jobs are easy for Plone. However, they have a tremendous impact as far as work and performance goes. If enough care is not taken, then a whole website could be stuck due to a couple of user requests.

In this chapter, we'll look at the various performance improvements and how to measure these enhancements.

We are not going to make a comprehensive review of all the options to tweak or set up a Zope-based web application, like configuring a like configuring a proxy cache or a load balancer. There are lots of places, maybe too many, where you can find information about these topics. We invite you to read these articles and tutorials and subscribe or visit Zope and Plone mailing lists:

- http://projects.zestsoftware.nl/guidelines/guidelines/caching/caching1_background.html

- http://plone.org/documentation/tutorial/buildout/a-deployment-configuration/

- http://plone.org/documentation/tutorial/optimizing-plone

Installing CacheFu with a policy product

When a user requests HTML pages from a website, many things can be expressed about the downloading files by setting special **headers** in the **HTTP response**. If managed cautiously, the server can save lots of time and, consequently, work by telling the browser how to store and reuse many of the resources it has got.

CacheFu is the Plone add-on product that streamlines **HTTP header** handling in order to obtain the required performance.

We could add a couple of lines to the `buildout.cfg` file to download and install CacheFu. Then we could add some code in our end user content type products (`pox.video` and `Products.poxContentTypes`) to configure CacheFu properly to deliver them in an efficient way.

However, if we do so, we would be forcing these products to automatically install CacheFu, even if we were testing them in a development environment.

To prevent this, we are going to create a **policy product** and add some code to install and configure CacheFu.

 A policy product is a regular package that will take care of general customizations to meet customer requirements. For information on how to create a policy product see *Creating a policy product*.

Getting ready

To achieve this we'll use `pox.policy`, the policy product created in *Creating a policy product*.

How to do it...

1. Automatically fetch **dependencies** of the policy product: Open `setup.py` in the root `pox.policy` folder and modify the `install_requires` variable of the `setup` call:

```
setup(name='pox.policy',
    ...
    install_requires=['setuptools',
                      # -*- Extra requirements: -*-
                      'Products.CacheSetup',
                      ],
```

2. Install dependencies during **policy product** installation. In the `profiles/default` folder, modify the `metadata.xml` file:

```
<?xml version="1.0"?>
<metadata>
 <version>1</version>
 <dependencies>
  <dependency>profile-Products.CacheSetup:default</dependency>
 </dependencies>
</metadata>
```

> You could also add here all the other products you plan to install as dependencies, instead of adding them individually in the `buildout.cfg` file.

3. Configure products during the policy product installation. Our policy product already has a `<genericsetup:importStep />` directive in its main component configuration file (`configure.zcml`). This import step tells **GenericSetup** to process a method in the `setuphandlers` module (we could have several steps, each of them with a matching method). Then modify the `setupVarious` method to do what we want, that is, to apply some settings to **CacheFu**.

```
from zope.app.component.hooks import getSite
from Products.CMFCore.utils import getToolByName
from config import *


def setupVarious(context):

    if context.readDataFile('pox.policy_various.txt') is None:
        return
```

```
portal = getSite()

# perform custom operations
# Get portal_cache_settings (from CacheFu) and
# update plone-content-types rule
pcs = getToolByName(portal, 'portal_cache_settings')
rules = pcs.getRules()
rule = getattr(rules, 'plone-content-types')
rule.setContentTypes(list(rule.getContentTypes()) +
CACHED_CONTENT)
```

 The above code has been shortened for clarity's sake. Check the accompanying code bundle for the full version.

4. Add or update a `config.py` file in your package with all configuration options:

```
# Content types that should be cached in plone-content-types
# rule of CacheFu
CACHED_CONTENT = ['XNewsItem', 'Video',]
```

5. Build your instance up again and launch it:

```
./bin/buildout
```

```
./bin/instance fg
```

6. After installing the `pox.policy` product (it's automatically installed during buildout as explained in *Creating a policy product*) we should see our content types—Video and XNewsItem—listed within the cached content types.

The next screenshot corresponds to the following URL: `http://localhost:8080/plone/portal_cache_settings/with-caching-proxy/rules/plone-content-types`.

The with-caching-proxy *part of the URL matches the* **Cache Policy** *field; and the* plone-content-types *part matches the* **Short Name** *field.*

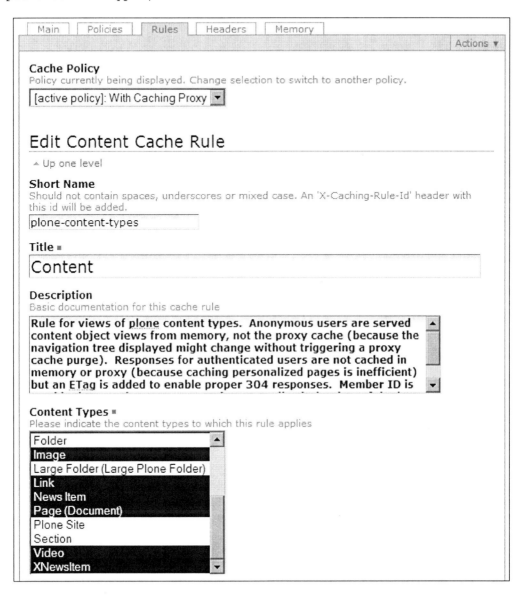

As we added Python code, we must test it.

1. Create this **doctest** in the `README.txt` file in the `pox.policy` package folder:

    ```
    Check that our content types are properly configured
    >>> pcs = getToolByName(self.portal, 'portal_cache_settings')
    >>> rules = pcs.getRules()
    >>> rule = getattr(rules, 'plone-content-types')
    >>> 'Video' in rule.getContentTypes()
    True
    >>> 'XNewsItem' in rule.getContentTypes()
    True
    ```

2. Modify the `tests` module by replacing the `ptc.setupPloneSite()` line with these ones:

    ```
    # We first tell Zope there's a CacheSetup product available
    ztc.installProduct('CacheSetup')
    # And then we install pox.policy product in Plone.
    # This should take care of installing CacheSetup in Plone also
    ptc.setupPloneSite(products=['pox.policy'])
    ```

3. And then uncomment the `ZopeDocFileSuite`:

    ```
    # Integration tests that use PloneTestCase
    ztc.ZopeDocFileSuite(
        'README.txt', package='pox.policy',
        test_class=TestCase),
    ```

4. Run this **test suite** with the following command:

    ```
    ./bin/instance test -s pox.policy
    ```

How it works...

In the preceding steps, we have created a specific procedure to install and configure other products (CacheFu in our case). This will help us in the final production environment startup as well as on installation of other development environments we could need (when a new member joins the development team, for instance).

In Step 1 of the *How to do it...* section, we modified `setup.py` to download and install a **dependency package** during the installation process, which is done on instance buildout. Getting dependencies in this way is possible when products are delivered in **egg** format thanks to Python eggs repositories and distribution services.

If you need to get an old-style product, you'll have to add it to the `[productdistros]` part in `buildout.cfg` (check *Installing Plone on Linux* in Chapter 1 for a warning about these kinds of products).

`Products.CacheSetup` is the package name for CacheFu and contains these dependencies: **CMFSquidTool**, **PageCacheManager**, and **PolicyHTTPCacheManager**.

There's more...

For more information about CacheFu visit the project home page at `http://plone.org/products/cachefu`.

You can also check for its latest version and release notes at Python Package Index (PyPI, a.k.a. The Cheese Shop): `http://pypi.python.org/pypi/Products.CacheSetup`.

The first link that we recommended in the *Introduction* is a great help in understanding how CacheFu works: `http://projects.zestsoftware.nl/guidelines/guidelines/caching/caching1_background.html`.

See also

- ▸ *Creating a policy product*
- ▸ *Installing and configuring an egg repository*

Improving performance by tweaking expensive code

Not all performance problems will be solved by installing and configuring CacheFu. Sometimes there are serious issues in the very code because it could have been coded in a different and more efficient way, or just because of some job that takes too long.

Let's leave the inefficiency problem aside. Many times we perform expensive tasks like searching objects in the catalog, getting images, accessing external relational databases, or accessing web services, and we know in advance that they will be necessary again and again. How to deal with them? Or at least, how to make them more efficient?

In this section, we will see three alternative approaches to tackle this problem:

1. `@view.memoize` decorators.
2. `@ram.cache` decorators.
3. Volatile variables.

Getting ready

The example below will perform a simple catalog query to get all banners located inside a specific section of our portal.

The final classes and methods won't be used anywhere else in our site. They are just dummy examples. However, we will reuse part of their code in *Customizing a new portlet according to our requirements*.

How to do it...

1. Open the `browser` sub-package inside the `pox.banner` product and create this `sectionBanners.py` file:

```python
from Products.Five.browser import BrowserView
from Products.CMFCore.utils import getToolByName
from pox.banner.content.banner import IBanner
from Acquisition import aq_inner
import logging
from plone.memoize import ram, view
from time import time


logger = logging.getLogger('pox.banner')

class ISectionBanners(Interface):
    """
    Retrieve section's contained banners
    """

    def banners():
        """
        Get contained banners
        """

    def banners_count():
        """
        Get banners count
        """


class SectionBanners( BrowserView ):
    """
    Helper view to test code caching techniques
    """
```

```
def banners(self):
    """
    The actual search
    """
    logger.log(logging.DEBUG, 'calling banners')
    context = aq_inner(self.context)
    catalog = getToolByName(context, 'portal_catalog')
    query = dict(object_provides = IBanner.__identifier__)
    query['path'] = {
                'query': '/'.join(context.getPhysicalPath()),
                'depth': 1 }
    brains = catalog(query)

    return brains

def banners_count(self):
    """
    Tells how many banners we found
    """
    logger.log(logging.DEBUG, 'calling banners_count')
    return len(self.banners())
```

We'll use this method for the examples later.

2. Add an adapted class based on the preceding SectionBanners but decorated with @view.memoize:

```
class SectionBannersMem( SectionBanners ):
    """
    Alternative implementation of the SectionBanners class
    """

    @view.memoize
    def banners(self):
        """
        Decorated. It just calls SectionBanners' banners().
        """
        return super(SectionBannersMem, self).banners()
```

3. Add another class based on `SectionBanners` but decorated with `@ram.cache` this time:

```
RAM_CACHE_SECONDS = 10


def _banners_cachekey(method, self, **args):
    """
    Returns key used by @ram.cache.
    """
    the_key = list(self.context.getPhysicalPath())
    the_key.append(time() // RAM_CACHE_SECONDS)
    return the_key


class SectionBannersRam( SectionBanners ):
    """
    Alternative implementation of the SectionBanners class

    """
    @ram.cache(_banners_cachekey)
    def banners(self):
        """
        Decorated. It just calls SectionBanners' banners().

        """
        return super(SectionBannersRam, self).banners()
```

4. Add a third `SectionBanners`-based class, this time without any decorator but using **volatile** variables.

```
class SectionBannersVol( SectionBanners ):
    """
    Alternative implementation of the SectionBanners class

    """

    def banners(self):
        """
        It just calls SectionBanners' banners() when needed.

        """
        the_banners = getattr(self.context, '_v_banners', None)
        if the_banners is None:
            the_banners = super(SectionBannersVol, self).banners()
            self._v_banners = the_banners
        return the_banners
```

5. Modify `configure.zcml` in the browser sub-package to enable the above code as browser views:

```
<browser:page
    for="..interfaces.ISection"
    name="banners"
    class=".sectionBanners.SectionBanners"
    permission="zope2.View"
    allowed_interface=".sectionBanners.ISectionBanners"
/>

<browser:page
    for="..interfaces.ISection"
    name="banners_mem"
    class=".sectionBanners.SectionBannersMem"
    permission="zope2.View"
    allowed_interface=".sectionBanners.ISectionBanners"
/>

<browser:page
    for="..interfaces.ISection"
    name="banners_ram"
    class=".sectionBanners.SectionBannersRam"
    permission="zope2.View"
    allowed_interface=".sectionBanners.ISectionBanners"
/>

<browser:page
    for="..interfaces.ISection"
    name="banners_vol"
    class=".sectionBanners.SectionBannersVol"
    permission="zope2.View"
    allowed_interface=".sectionBanners.ISectionBanners"
/>
```

How it works...

In Step 1, we created the `sectionBanners` module (with all the imports required for the following steps), the interface, and the base class (that we will use), where:

- we first inform there's a call to the banners method by using `logger.log(...)`.
- then we perform the actual search. We are interested in objects providing the `IBanner` interface located right inside the section we are (denoted by `context`). The usage of `'depth': 1` tells `portal_catalog` not to search in the sub-sections.

 `logger` is a handle to output debug information in the instance log (or console when running Zope in foreground mode).

In Step 2, we have only decorated the inherited `banners` method with `@view.memoize`. This decorator, from `plone.memoize`, caches the result of the decorated method. In this way, if we call it several times in the very same request, it will be executed just once. Current context, request, and method's arguments are used to key the values in this short-time cache.

 Alternatively, you can use `@instance.memoize` (from the same package) which caches on the instance and is useful in adapters and other transient components.

Step 3 is similar to the previous one, but the `banners` method this time is decorated with `@ram.cache`. Note how, unlike in the `@view.memoize` decorator, we must state specifically the caching key when using `@ram.cache`. In the case above, we created a special `_banners_cachekey` module-level method to return an interesting caching key. By using `time() // RAM_CACHE_SECONDS`, we ensure that the returned value will be stored in cache for the specified time. We can also use other parameters like context, authenticated user, or any other value that might be helpful.

The next approach (Step 4) is the usage of **volatile** variables (they must be named with a `v_` preffix). This method is the cheapest and a more direct way of caching values. There's no certainty on how long they will be kept in memory. That's why we must always check if the volatile variable is still there.

 Before using any volatile variable inside a method's body, we must check if it is still there, as you can see in the highlighted code in the highlighted code of Step 4.

The last step is to register one **Zope 3 view** (`<browser:page />` directive) for every `SectionBanners` alternative.

Notice how we used `allowed_interface` to state which attributes or methods will be available in the outside world. We could have used the `allowed_attributes` parameter instead, like this:

```
<browser:page
    for="..interfaces.ISection"
    name="banners_vol"
    class=".sectionBanners.SectionBannersVol"
    permission="zope2.View"
    allowed_attributes="banners banners_count"
/>
```

Attributes are separated with whitespaces.

Using `allowed_interface` is preferable when you are planning to add a new method or attribute or when all of them are protected by the same permission. You should just add it in the interface rather than changing every `<browser:page />` directive. However, if you want to limit the access of attributes or methods (by changing the `permission` value) you might need to create different browser pages with different `allowed_attributes` values.

Caching always carries penalties as increasing memory usage, but it also brings obvious benefits. How, when, and where to use any of these options is up to you and your code.

As a rule of thumb, it's advisable to cache methods only when retrieving information, like in our example from the catalog, and not for operations with side effects, like modifying the database.

The shown code won't be used in any production environment, it was created just for learning purposes. We have also included a test inside the `README.txt` file in the accompanying code, not copied here, to see how every kind of caching mode works.

We kindly invite you to have a look at it to fully understand the approaches described in this section. On top of that, we have incorporated some new techniques you may find interesting for testing:

▸ Performing different operations within the same request by means of `zope.publisher.browser.TestRequest`:

```
>>> from zope.publisher.browser import TestRequest

New request
    >>> request = TestRequest()
...
    >>> banners = getMultiAdapter((self.portal.first_section,
request), name=u'banners')
...
```

```
Another new request
    >>> request = TestRequest()
    >>> banners = getMultiAdapter((self.portal.first_section,
request), name=u'banners_ram')
```

▶ Testing what Zope logs (or puts out in the console) by redirecting it to the standard output (`sys.stdout`).

The only piece of test code we'll mention here is the way we can use a **browser view** from outside a **Zope Page Template** (that is, without using the `@@` notation):

```
>>> from zope.component import import getMultiAdapter
>>> banners = getMultiAdapter((self.portal.first_section,
request), name=u'banners')
>>> banners.banners()
```

If we were in a page template, we'd call the `banners` method above like this:

```
<tal:view define="view context/@@banners;
                  banners view/banners">
...
  <!-- do something with the banners -->
</tal:view>
```

If we wanted to check the `banners` method by calling it directly from the URL we could use:

`http://localhost:8080/plone/<some_section>/@@banners/banners`

In the last two cases, the call to the `@@banners` browser view has two implicit arguments: context and request. These two are explicit, however, when calling it from inside Python code. The context is `self.portal.first_section` and the request is an instance of `TestRequest` (in production code we generally use the same `request` parameter used in the `__init__` method).

There's more...

Luckily, yes, there's even more! Consider having a look at the `plone.memoize` package to see what the other alternatives are.

See also

▶ *Customizing a new portlet according to our requirements*

Testing server load and benchmarking our code

In the previous recipes, we have seen how to improve the general performance of our website by setting the proper **HTTP** headers for server responses (*Installing CacheFu with a policy product*) and by adding caching facilities to the underlying Python code (*Improving performance by tweaking expensive code*).

It's now time to verify if those changes really worked.

In this section, we will introduce and work with **FunkLoad**, a functional and load web tester.

 Unfortunately, at the time of writing, FunkLoad doesn't work in Windows. This is because of the lack of support for os.fork(), which is a core function used by FunkLoad: one thread for every concurrent user. However, a fix for it is expected to be applied soon.

Getting ready

To install FunkLoad we will need to make several changes to the original bulidout.cfg file. Thanks to the extendible capability provided by **buildout**, we can separate those modifications in a different file and merge the entire configuration when building the instance up.

How to do it...

1. Create this funkload.cfg file in the instance root folder:

 The real funkload.cfg can be found in the available code for download. We have shortened it here to highlight some interesting options.

```
[buildout]

extends =
    buildout.cfg
parts +=
    tcpwatch-source
    tcpwatch-install
    funkload
    fl-tests
    site-pox banner tests
...
[instance]
```

```
eggs +=
    collective.funkload

[site-pox.banner.tests]
recipe = collective.recipe.plonesite
site-id = pox.banner.tests
instance = instance
site-replace = True
products = pox.banner
```

2. Build your instance again and empower it with FunkLoad. Inside your buildout folder run:

   ```
   ./bin/buildout -c funkload.cfg
   ```

    The `-c` option above is to specify an alternative configuration file. The default is `buildout.cfg`, but you can use whatever you want.

3. Launch the FunkLoad recorder. Like with **zope.testrecorder** and **Selenium**, we can record FunkLoad test cases by navigating and clicking on a live website. So start your instance:

   ```
   ./bin/instance fg
   ```

   Go inside the tests sub-package where you want to store the new test file:

   ```
   cd ./src/pox.banner/pox/banner/tests
   ```

   And launch the **FunkLoad recorder**:

   ```
   ../../../../../bin/fl-record CreateSectionBanner
   ```

   Of course, you can replace all the double dots above with the absolute route of your instance folder. The point here is that you must run the `fl-record` command with the name of the module you want to create in the folder in which you want it to be stored.

   You'll get an output like this:

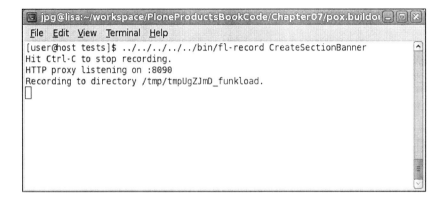

4. Edit proxy settings in the web browser:

FunkLoad recorder is actually a proxy running in port 8090. To record all our interactions, we must edit our web browser network settings:

- Add `localhost:8090` as the **HTTP proxy**.
- Make sure the proxy above will be used even when browsing our Plone site located in `http://localhost:8080/`.

For Firefox in Linux, go to the **Edit | Preferences** menu, **Advanced | Network** tab, **Settings** button.
For Firefox in Windows, use the **Tools | Options** menu instead.

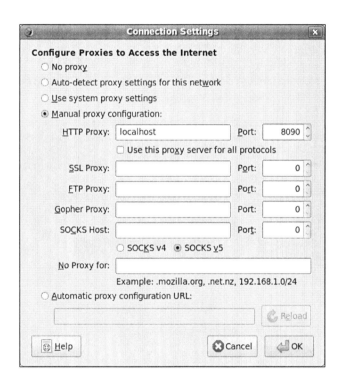

We may choose another port number if we run the `fl-record` command with the `-p` option:

```
../../../../../bin/fl-record -p 9090 CreateSectionBanner
```

5. Record the very test. For testing purposes, we have created a new `pox.banner.tests` Plone site during instance buildout. So go to `http://localhost:8080/pox.banner.tests` and start recording the test:

   ❑ Log in as a manager with the **Log in** left-hand portlet (admin: admin).

   ❑ Click on the **Add new** drop-down menu and then click on the **Section** option.

   ❑ Type **Section1** in the **Section title** field and then press the **Save** button.

   ❑ Click again on the **Add new** drop-down menu, but click on the **Banner** option this time.

   ❑ Type **Banner1** in the **Banner title** field and some HTML code in **Banner HTML** field (or just leave the default value) and then click on **Save**.

That's it, the test is finished. Press *Ctrl + C* in the **FunkLoad recorder** console to stop recording. You should see a message like this:

```
[user@host tests]$ ../../../../../bin/fl-record CreateSectionBanner
Hit Ctrl-C to stop recording.
HTTP proxy listening on :8090
Recording to directory /tmp/tmpTj_G83_funkload.
^CTCPWatch finished.
Creating script: ./test_Createsectionbanner.py.
Creating configuration file: ./Createsectionbanner.conf.
[user@host tests]$
```

6. Modify the just generated `test_CreateSectionBanner.py` test file:

We must first modify the base class of the test to accommodate it to the Zope environment.

Add this import line:

```
from collective.funkload import testcase
```

And change the class definition with this one:

```
#class CreateSectionBAnner(FunkLoadTestCase):
class CreateSectionBanner(testcase.FLTestCase):
```

Unlike **zope.testrecorder** and **Selenium IDE**, FunkLoad doesn't record either mouse clicks or keyboard hits, but HTTP requests. Thus any particular URL that should be dynamic during testing or benching and has been recorded statically must be replaced with Python code to reconstruct the usable URL.

Open the generated `test_CreateSectionBanner` module to make some changes.

The lines:

```
...
self.post(server_url + "/pox.banner.tests /+/addSection",
        params=[['form.title', 'Section1'],
                ['form.actions.save', 'Save']],
        description="Saving Section add form"
)
...
```

should be replaced with

```
...
section = self.post(
        server_url + "/pox.banner.tests /+/addSection",
        params=[['form.title', 'Section1'],
                ['form.actions.save', 'Save']],
        description="Saving Section add form"
)
section_url = server_url + section.url.rsplit('/', 1)[0]
...
```

This way we get a handle to the created section and its URL. *Recall that* `/view` *is added to the section URL after saving it, that's why we* `rsplit` *it.*

Then replace every appearance of

```
server_url + "/pox.banner.tests /section1/+add++Banner"
```

with

```
section_url + "/++add++Banner"
```

We did this because in subsequent tests or benches, the newly created section could be saved with a different ID.

> For **Archetypes** content types, we must make some additional adjustments, given that Archetypes create temporary objects with a very specific ID. See the full `test_CreatSectionBanner.py` file for an example on how to get the correct URLs.

You may also find inline validation requests (performed with AJAX) inside the testing code. Just remove them.

One last important modification is adding a `test_suite` method with a specific level.

```
def test_suite():
    suite = unittest.makeSuite(CreateSectionBanner)
    suite.level = 5
    return suite
```

When running regular tests with Zope test runner, all suites with level 1 are executed by default. If we didn't specify a higher level, this **test suite** might fail because it always needs the instance to be running. By adding a custom `level`, we prevent this from happening.

> Note that the `test_suite` method must be placed outside the `CreateSectionBanner` class.

7. Run the test with Zope test runner:

   This is an optional step.

   As with **Selenium functional tests**, **FunkLoad** needs a live instance for the test suite to be run:

   `./bin/instance fg`

   As we said earlier, FunkLoad test suites can be run with **Zope test runner** as any other kind of test. To do so, use the following command:

   `./bin/instance test -s pox.banner -t CreateSectionBanner -a5`

   The `-t` option sets the specific test we want to run in the `pox.banner` package (`test_` prefix may be omitted, like here).

   The `-a` option specifies the highest level of test suites we want to run (that is, test suites with levels 1 to 5 will be run here).

8. Run the test with FunkLoad test runner:

   This is an optional step.

   Be sure the instance is running. Then run the following command:

   `./bin/fl-run-test pox.banner.tests.test_CreateSectionBanner`

   Unlike with Zope test runner, we must indicate the full module dotted name when using the `fl-run-test` command.

How it works...

We have created a new configuration file for our Zope instance: `funkload.cfg`. Although we have already used the `extends` parameter in previous chapters, we want to identify it here and explain how it works: `buildout.cfg` is extended by `funkload.cfg`. Thus, when building an instance with the last one, every configuration option in the first one will be also considered.

Due to the *extension* nature of this `funkload.cfg` file, we must *add* `parts` and `eggs` by using the `+=` operator. If we had used the regular `parts = ...` line, we would have replaced and missed all other parts defined in `buildout.cfg`.

Finally, we create a new Plone site with the `collective.recipe.plonesite` recipe. This one will be used to test the `pox.banner` product (that's why it is automatically installed). Unlike in `buildout.cfg`, this Plone site will be replaced each time we run the buildout process (`site-replace = True`).

There's more...

We started this chapter with the installation of **CacheFu** and its configuration for our content types to get them better response time. After that we played around with several alternatives for caching expensive code results. However, we didn't test or bench any of those features.

We explicitly wanted to show how to solve some tricky parts of FunkLoad test creation. We expect the example above is clear enough for you to create your own FunkLoad test and bench it, with and without CacheFu configurations.

Bench configuration file

When recording the test earlier, an additional `CreateSectionBanner.conf` file was created inside the `tests` sub-package. Let's see some of its configuration options. Please refer to the accompanying code for the full file.

```
# Main section
#
[main]
...
# the User-Agent header to send default is 'FunkLoad/1.xx' examples:
#user_agent = Opera/8.0 (Windows NT 5.1; U; en)
...
```

We can specify the `user_agent` we wish when running a test or bench.

```
# Monitoring configuration
#
[monitor]
hosts=localhost
```

We can also monitor server performance when running benchmarks: CPU, memory, and network activity.

```
# Configuration for bench mode fl-run-bench
#
[bench]

# cycles = list of cycles with their number of concurrent users
#cycles =  1:2:3
cycles = 1:2:3:5:10

# duration = duration of a cycle in seconds
#duration = 30
duration = 120

# startup_delay = time to wait between starting-up threads in seconds
startup_delay = 0.2

# sleep_time = time to wait between test in seconds
sleep_time = 1

# cycle_time = time to wait between cycle in seconds
cycle_time = 1
```

We have made some changes to the default values. We added two extra `cycles` with 5 and 10 concurrent users (cycles are separated with a colon), and we extended the `duration` of the cycle from 30 to 120 seconds. Consequently, we'll have five cycles: the first one with one user (read: one thread or browser request) that will repeat the test for 120 seconds, the second cycle with two concurrent users that will perform test tasks for 120 seconds, and so on.

Running the bench

We now have a special `pox.banner.tests` Plone site to run our tests and benchmarks, a **test suite** we want to run, and its corresponding configuration file. Just be sure the instance is up before running the following command to start the bench:

```
./bin/funkload bench -s pox.banner -a5
```

This will call the `funkload` script with the `bench` command and two well known other options: `-s`, to specify the package we want to test and `-a` that tells the level of the considered tests suites.

You'll get an output similar to this:

```
Benching
========
Cycle #0 with 1 virtual users
-----------------------------
* Current time: 2009-09-28T00:41:57.559282
* Starting threads: . done.
* Logging for 120s (until 2009-09-28T00:43:57.817400): ...........
done.
* Waiting end of threads: . done.
* Waiting cycle sleeptime 1s: ... done.
* End of cycle, 123.00s elapsed.
* Cycle result: **SUCCESSFUL**, 12 success, 0 failure, 0 errors.
...
Creating html report: ...done:
file:///./var/funkload/reports/2009-09-28-00-44-00/test_create_
section_banner-20090928T004157/index.html
```

As stated in the output, we get an HTML report with lots of information about the load test we have just performed. We include here a few graphics as examples of the information you can find.

This first chart is one of several that show the server's activity during the whole bench:

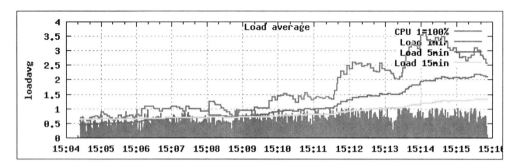

This second graphic shows the response time of a particular web page during the test:

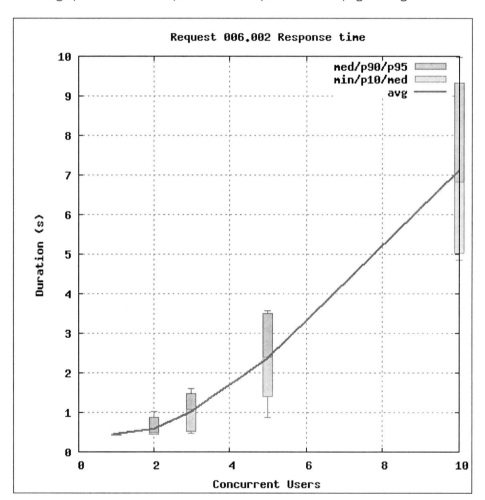

This report is way comprehensive and will help you in identifying possible bottlenecks in your code or configuration. On top of that, after tweaking your code you can run the bench again to get the results of your improvements and you will be able to show your boss nicely colored drawings!

Further reading

FunkLoad is incredibly powerful and it has lots of other features not explained here. To mention just one of them, you can create differential reports based on two situations: before and after your improvements.

 For more information about FunkLoad visit the project's website at `http://funkload.nuxeo.org`.

See also

- ▸ *Using Selenium functional tests*
- ▸ *Zope Functional testing*

8
Internationalization

In this chapter, we will cover:

- ▸ Adding i18ndude support to ArchGenXML
- ▸ Installing i18ndude standalone
- ▸ Using i18ndude
- ▸ Using Placeless Translation Services for i18n support
- ▸ Using the zope.i18n approach
- ▸ Overriding others' translations
- ▸ Using i18n with ArchGenXML
- ▸ Using i18n with paster-created products
- ▸ Adding i18n support to any product
- ▸ Translating content
- ▸ Setting language options

Introduction

We mentioned it in the first page of this book and if you visit Plone's website you'll see it in the home page: Plone is available in more than 40 languages; Plone is internationalized.

What does this mean? It means that you can install Plone and choose one (or several) of the many supported languages and you'll have a full portal in your preferred tongue(s).

However, this was not for free. If Plone is available in many languages, it's because its developers (core and community developers) have coded it in an internationalization-capable fashion.

In this chapter, we'll look at how to do this in Plone: how to prepare our code, beforehand or afterward, to be translatable.

Let's see some short definitions of terms, which we'll use in the following sections:

Term	Definition
Internationalization	Adaptation of *code* so that the *user interface* can be translated. It doesn't refer to translation of data but code.
Domain	A set or collection of related terms to be translated (or already translated).
Message	A term to be translated in a domain context. It might have a default value to be returned if a specific language translation were missing.
Message ID	A unique identifier for every message within a certain domain. A message ID can be a readable or an abstract text like a code.
Message string	The translation of the message in a specific language.
Message catalog	An organization of the above messages that provides setting and getting translations looked up by message ID, language, and domain.
PO file	A text representation of a message catalog. It is parsed by a piece of software that turns it into a compiled MO file.
POT file	A message catalog template. It's not actually used by translation machinery but by programmers or translators to make copies of it for every available language.

Adding i18ndude support to ArchGenXML

Throughout this chapter, we'll use **i18ndude**, a great tool for detecting translatable code and creating the required files for translation.

i18ndude is available as a Python **egg** in **Python package index** (**PyPI**), so we could use easy_install to have it working in a few minutes:

```
$ easy_install i18ndude
```

Nevertheless, in a Plone development environment, this is not advisable because i18ndude has lots of dependencies that will conflict with our Plone installation.

 If you already have **ArchGenXML** installed on your system and think you'll continue using it, it's most likely that you should opt for this configuration, which we are about to explain.

How to do it...

1. Go to your ArchGenXML installation folder and modify the `buildout.cfg` file as follows:

```
[buildout]
parts =
    archgenxml
    agx-profile

[archgenxml]
recipe = zc.recipe.egg:scripts
eggs =
    archgenxml
    i18ndude

[agx-profile]
recipe = iw.recipe.cmd
on_install=true
on_update=false
cmds =
    mkdir ${buildout:directory}/profiles
    cd ${buildout:directory}/profiles
    ${buildout:directory}/bin/agx_argouml_profile
```

2. Build ArchGenXML again: Then rebuild ArchGenXML with this command:

```
$ ./bin/buildout
```

```
neville@hogwarts: ~/archgenxml
File  Edit  View  Terminal  Help
neville@hogwarts:~/archgenxml$ ./bin/buildout
Uninstalling archgenxml.
Installing archgenxml.
Generated script '/home/neville/archgenxml/bin/archgenxml'.
Generated script '/home/neville/archgenxml/bin/agx_argouml_profile'.
Generated script '/home/neville/archgenxml/bin/agx_stereotypes'.
Generated script '/home/neville/archgenxml/bin/agx_taggedvalues'.
Generated script '/home/neville/archgenxml/bin/i18ndude'.
Updating agx-profile.
mkdir: cannot create directory `/home/neville/archgenxml/profiles': File exists
neville@hogwarts:~/archgenxml$
```

You should consider adding `archgenxml/bin` in your PATH environment variable if it's not there yet.

How it works...

Make sure that the `[archgenxml]` recipe ends with `:scripts`. This will create, in the `bin` folder, Python scripts as declared in eggs processed by the **recipe**.

This last part of the buildout configuration file `[agx-profile]` remains the same as the original one.

See also

▸ *Installing ArchGenXML*

Installing i18ndude standalone

If you don't plan either to install or use ArchGenXML, you definitely should use the following installation method.

You might also have ArchGenXML installed but want `i18ndude` to be alone. You certainly can, but you'll miss automatic i18n files generation by ArchGenXML. It's up to you what to do.

How to do it...

1. Create a directory for the target `i18ndude` installation:

    ```
    $ mkdir ~/i18ndude
    $ cd ~/i18ndude
    ```

2. Prepare the **buildout** environment by downloading (or copying from an existing location) the `bootstrap.py` file:

    ```
    $ wget http://svn.zope.org/*checkout*/zc.buildout/trunk/
    bootstrap/bootstrap.py
    ```

Create a `buildout.cfg` file for `i18ndude` like the following one:

```
[buildout]
parts =
    i18ndude

[i18ndude]
recipe = zc.recipe.egg:scripts
eggs =
    i18ndude
```

3. Bootstrap and build `i18ndude`:

    `$ python bootstrap.py`

    `$ ./bin/buildout`

    After this, you'll have a new `i18ndude` command available to be used in the `bin` folder.

 You should consider adding `i18ndude/bin` in your `PATH` environment variable if it's not yet done.

See also

▸   *Installing Python on Linux*

Using i18ndude

In this chapter, we'll use three commands i18ndude comes with:

▸   `find-untranslated`: To identify code where we should add i18n support

▸   `rebuild-pot`: To create the **catalog file** we will use when translating

▸   `sync`: To update translation files with changes that might have been made to the original `pot` file

Getting started

To perform the following actions, we will need a new view template for Video content type:

1. Create a `templates` folder in the `pox.video.browser` package:

   ```
   mkdir ./src/pox.video/pox/video/browser/templates
   ```

2. Create a new view template for Video content type:

 You can find the full version of this template in the source code for this chapter. It is based in the original `file_view.pt` of `Products/CMFPlone/skins/plone_content` in the Plone **egg**.

   ```
   <html xmlns="http://www.w3.org/1999/xhtml" xml:lang="en"
       ...
       xmlns:i18n="http://xml.zope.org/namespaces/i18n"
       metal:use-macro="here/main_template/macros/master"
       i18n:domain="pox.video">
   <body>
   <div metal:fill-slot="main">
       <tal:main-macro metal:define-macro="main"
       ...
           <p id="archetypes-fieldname-file">
               <span>Play video inline:</span>


               ...
           </p>
       ...
       </tal:main-macro>

   </div>

   </body>

   </html>
   ```

3. Update `configure.zcml` in the `pox.video.browser` package with the new browser page.

   ```
   <configure
       xmlns="http://namespaces.zope.org/zope"
       xmlns:browser="http://namespaces.zope.org/browser"
       i18n_domain="pox.video">
       ...
   ```

```
<browser:page
        for="..interfaces.video.IVideo"
        name="video_view"
        permission="zope2.Public"
        template="templates/video_view.pt"
        />
</configure>
```

4. Reinstall the product.

How to do it...

1. The `find-untranslated` command will search inside **Zope Page Templates** (**ZPT** files only, no `py` files) for tags that lack `i18n:translate` or `i18n:attributes` tag attributes.

   For example, if we change to the `pox/video/browser/template` folder, we can run this command to get the following output:

   ```
   $ i18ndude find-untranslated -n ./video_view.pt

   video_view.pt:42:8:

   -ERROR- - i18n:translate missing for this:

   " " "

   Play video inline:

   " " "
   ```

    To fix these errors, we must add i18n attributes in the reported template files as we will do in *Adding i18n support to any product*.

2. The `rebuild-pot` command: Given a **pot file** (a message catalog template) and a list of directories, `i18ndude` will parse all **Zope Page Templates** (`*.pt`), Python source files (`*.py`), import steps profile files (`*.xml`) and configuration files (`*.zcml`) and will add, in the `pot` file, a message for every *marked-for-translation* text.

   You can also provide a `--create <domain>` parameter to create a new template file.

   In the `pox/video` folder, you can run this command:

   ```
   $ i18ndude rebuild-pot --pot ./locales/pox.video.pot --create
   pox.video ./*
   ```

The following file will be created:

```
# --- PLEASE EDIT THE LINES BELOW CORRECTLY ---
# SOME DESCRIPTIVE TITLE.
# FIRST AUTHOR <EMAIL@ADDRESS>, YEAR.
msgid ""
msgstr ""
"Project-Id-Version: PACKAGE VERSION\n"
"POT-Creation-Date: 2009-10-03 05:35+0000\n"
"PO-Revision-Date: YEAR-MO-DA HO:MI +ZONE\n"
"Last-Translator: FULL NAME <EMAIL@ADDRESS>\n"
"Language-Team: LANGUAGE <LL@li.org>\n"
"MIME-Version: 1.0\n"
"Content-Type: text/plain; charset=utf-8\n"
"Content-Transfer-Encoding: 8bit\n"
"Plural-Forms: nplurals=1; plural=0\n"
"Language-Code: en\n"
"Language-Name: English\n"
"Preferred-Encodings: utf-8 latin1\n"
"Domain: pox.video\n"

#: .\content\video.py:24
msgid "Date this video was recorded"
msgstr ""

#: .\content\video.py:23
msgid "Original Date"
msgstr ""

#. Default: "Play video inline:"
#: .\browser\templates\video_view.pt:38
msgid "Play video inline:"
msgstr ""

#: .\content\validators.py:27
msgid "Uploaded file is not FLV"
msgstr ""

#. Default: "Video"
#: .\profiles\default\types\Video.xml
msgid "Video"
msgstr ""

#. Default: "You can also download it!"
```

```
#: .\browser\templates\video_view.pt:56
msgid "You can also download it!"
msgstr ""

#. Default: "It's about ${size} KB."
#: .\browser\templates\video_view.pt:69
msgid "file_size"
msgstr ""

#. Default: "pox Video"
#: .\profiles\default\types\Video.xml
msgid "pox Video"
msgstr ""
```

As you can see, i18ndude automatically extracted not only message IDs, but references of their appearances in source code, and—when applicable—default values.

> In the examples so far, we didn't add any translatable text to the configuration (component registration) files. That's why there's no message taken from zcml files in the po file above.

3. The sync command: with this command, i18ndude synchronizes message catalog templates with a final language message catalog. This means that, for every new message that was added to the pot file, it will create the corresponding entry into the po file. Additionally, i18ndude will remove any line from the translation file that is not a real message (not present in the template).

   This command is particularly useful when first creating language files because they are empty, and we can skip copying and pasting.

   We first create the empty file, and then synchronize it with the original catalog:

   ```
   $ touch poxContentTypes-es.po
   ```

   In Windows, use:

   ```
   > echo:>poxContentTypes-es.po
   ```

   ```
   $ i18ndude sync --pot poxvideo.pot poxvideo.po
   poxvideo.po : 6 added, 0 removed.
   ```

> In *Using Placeless Translation Services for i18n support,* we will cover which headers must be changed at the top of every translation po file you'll create.

There's more...

If you run `i18ndude` without options, you'll get its usage and all available commands.

See also

> ▸ *Adding i18n support to any product*

Using Placeless Translation Services for i18n support

Zope translation services are based in the GNU internationalization and localization `gettext` library (`http://www.gnu.org/software/gettext`).

In a nutshell, Zope fetches all registered catalog (`po`) files and compiles them at startup time, creating `mo` files so that it can get proper translations for requested **message IDs**.

For a long time, **Placeless Translation Services** (**PTS**) has been commonly used for these tasks. Although there's a new approach recommended by the community (covered in the next section) most Plone out-of-the-box products still use PTS.

This section won't produce any usable code at all, but it will show how to organize and register internationalization catalogs in our products.

How to do it...

1. Create catalog files. For PTS to register and use our message catalogs, we must create an `i18n` directory inside the product's main folder and drop all required catalog files. It's a good practice to use filenames like `<domain>-<lang_code>.po`, for instance `plone-eu.po`, for Basque translations, in `plone` domain.

2. Modify header information. There is one important thing to bear in mind to make PTS properly recognize translations: we must provide extra header data—which are not part of `gettext` specification: `Language-Code`, `Language-Name` (optional to be displayed in Zope's Control Panel), and `Domain`:

```
# Translation of plone.pot to Basque
# Gazte Abertzaleak <...@gazteabertzaleak.org>, 2005
# Gari Araolaza <...@codesyntax.com>, 2006
msgid ""
msgstr ""
"Project-Id-Version: Plone\n"
...
```

```
"Language-Code: eu\n"
"Language-Name: Basque\n"
"Preferred-Encodings: latin1 utf-8\n"
"Domain: plone\n"
...
```

 Beware that PO file editors like Poedit (http://poedit.net) or gted (http://gted.org) don't add these headers by default.

Here's a screenshot of Poedit's very intuitive interface:

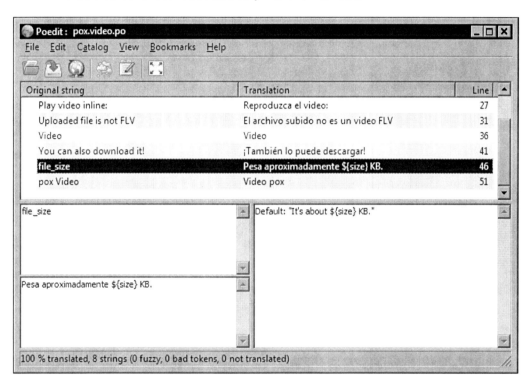

3. Keep your catalog files organized. You should store the original message catalog template (pot file) in the i18n folder: it's a good place and it will help you to find it in case you need to add support for a new language.

4. Test PTS messages. If you want a quick test to know if your **PTS** messages were properly configured, point your browser to: http://localhost:plone:8080/translate?msgid=<your_message_id>&domain=<your_domain>&target_language=<lang_code>.

See also

▶ *Using zope.i18n approach*

Using zope.i18n approach

In previous versions of Plone, **Placeless Translation Services** was the only internationalization manager. In current versions, we can also use all the benefits of Zope 3's zope.i18n library with improved support for i18n.

In Plone 3, we can take advantage of any of these two flavors. However, in spite of PTS being the most widespread option used up to now, you are strongly recommended to use zope.i18n.

How to do it...

zope.i18n is stricter than PTS regarding file organization. It follows the gettext specification:

1. Create a locales folder hierarchy. Add a locales folder in your product main folder.

   ```
   $ mkdir locales
   ```

   Then inside this folder, create a new one for every language you plan to support.

   ```
   $ mkdir locales/es
   $ mkdir locales/en
   ```

   Add a new LC_MESSAGES directory for each of these.

   ```
   $ mkdir locales/es/LC_MESSAGES
   $ mkdir locales/en/LC_MESSAGES
   ```

2. Store catalog files in this structure. Drop your po files inside these last folders (LC_MESSAGES). Message catalog files *must* follow this filename structure: <domain>.po. Unlike with **PTS**, we don't need any special header information to make them work. Language codes are taken from the directory hierarchy and domain names are taken from the filename.

   > When we say *language codes,* we are speaking about ISO 639 standard: http://en.wikipedia.org/wiki/List_of_ISO_639-1_codes.

3. Register available translations. There's one last step we must take to complete i18n support for our product, which is registration. Modify the `configure.zcml` file in the package's main folder according as follows:

```
<configure
    ...
    xmlns:i18n="http://namespaces.zope.org/i18n"
    i18n_domain="pox.video">
    ...
    <i18n:registerTranslations directory="locales"/>
    ...
</configure>
```

We added a new `i18n` namespace and then we used it with its `registerTranslations` directive.

How it works...

When the instance starts, all `locales` folders are registered into the `zope.i18n` machinery to set their corresponding message catalog files. This is organized according to the order in which packages were registered with **ZCML slugs**.

For example, the `buildout.cfg` has a configuration like this:

```
[buildout]
...
[instance]
...
zcml =
    package.one
    package.two
```

Two ZCML slugs are created in the `parts/instance/etc/package-includes` folder: `001-package.one-configure.zcml` and `002-package.two-configure.zcml`.

> From Plone 3.3 onwards, we can use `z3c.autoinclude` as we did in _Zope Functional Testing_ (Chapter 4) and _Creating an Archetypes product with paster (Chapter 5)_, which takes care of registering ZCML slugs for packages outside the `Products` namespace even if they are not listed in the `zcml` parameter. However, in this case, as we want to give an order of their registration, we must explicitly add them.

In this way, message catalogs from `package.one` are registered first, followed by the ones from `package.two`.

PTS processes `i18n` folders in Zope 2 products, though there's no guarantee of the order in which they will be examined.

Any other package that is registered by Zope during startup (via `z3c.autoinclude`, for instance) will be then searched for its i18n support declaration.

 This order is extremely important. if two products or packages have translations for the same message ID, domain, and language, the one first retrieved will take precedence.

There's more...

Unfortunately, for `zope.i18n` catalogs, there's no quick test available. Nevertheless, you can still manually check the resulting translation for a certain message:

Run `ipzope` (if available) or `zopepy` in your **Zope instance** folder:

```
./bin/ipzope
```

And execute this code:

```
>>> from zope.component import queryUtility
>>> from zope.i18n.interfaces import ITranslationDomain
>>> td = queryUtility(ITranslationDomain, name='plonelocales')
>>> td.translate('weekday_sun', target_language='en')
u('Sunday')
>>> td.translate('weekday_sun', target_language='de')
u'Sonntag'
```

There's a named utility for every domain.

See also

▶ *Using Placeless Translation Services for i18n support*

▶ *Zope Functional Testing*

▶ *Creating an Archetypes product with paster*

Overriding others' translations

Suppose we don't like the wording chosen in a certain text of a different product and we'd like to change it. It's definitely not wise to modify the source code or catalog files of the product in question.

As we mentioned in sections above, there's no problem at all in loading several po files for the same domain and language (there used to be problems; thankfully, not anymore). What could be an issue is how to be sure that our customizations will take precedence over the original product translations.

How to do it...

1. Overriding PTS' translations: If the product to override uses the PTS approach (an i18n folder), we can just create a parts/instance/i18n folder and place there all the catalog files we need. In this way, we make sure that all their messages will gain priority.

   To perform these overrides automatically, let's add a new part in buildout.cfg like the following:

   ```
   [buildout]
   ...
   parts =
       ...
       instance-i18n
   ...

   [instance-i18n]
   recipe = plone.recipe.command
   on_install=true
   command =
       ln -s
   ${buildout:directory}/src/pox.policy/pox/policy/instance-i18n/
   ${instance:location}/i18n/
     echo "Custom translations file copied to instance GlobalCatalog"
   ```

   The plone.recipe.command recipe executes arbitrary commands. In the code above, we create a symlink from instance/i18n to the directory where we store translation overrides.

   If you are working in a Windows environment, you should use junction or mklink commands instead. Check their availability for your Windows version.

You can also use the specific `collective.recipe.` `i18noverrides` recipe to create an instance-level `i18n` folder. More about it at: `http://pypi.python.org/` `pypi/collective.recipe.i18noverrides`.

2. Overriding `zope.i18n`'s translations: If the product to override uses the more modern `zope.i18n` techniques (a `locales` folder), we can use a custom package (a policy product would work) with a `locales` folder and place it at the top of the `zcml` parameter in the `instance` part in `buildout.cfg` so that it will be read first and be preferred when translating:

```
[buildout]

...
[instance]

...

zcml =
    translations.package
    other.packages
```

Using i18n with ArchGenXML

In *Creating a model* (Chapter 3), we saw how to create **Archetypes**-based content types with a code generator named **ArchGenXML**. When we did this, we omitted, knowingly, any reference to automatic internationalization support, which this tool supplies.

Let's look at it now.

Getting ready

We are going to use the `poxContentTypes.zargo` file which is available for download, corresponding to the **UML** model we created in the aforementioned recipe. So, if you didn't create it, get it from this book's web page.

In this section, we'll use the PTS approach by using an `i18n` folder.

How to do it...

We could actually leave our **UML** model as it is and still enjoy the benefits of ArchGenXML regarding i18n support. However, let's add some options to the `XNewsItem` content type to supply a better example.

1. Add tagged values for i18n support: As you can see in the following screenshot, we can define the `widget:label` and `widget:description` tagged values, which are already available with AGXProfile.

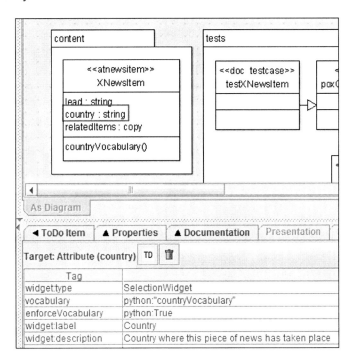

There's a list of other i18n-related tagged values we could use to make better use of ArchGenXML.

Tag	Description
`label`	We can associate a label to the attribute directly without the `widget:` prefix. ArchGenXML will add a `widget:label` element anyway.
`description`	A descriptive text that will be shown as a short help just above the field.
`widget:label`	Just like `label`. However, if specified, ArchGenXML won't duplicate its value in the generated schema.
`widget:description`	Just like `description` with some comments as `widget:label`.
`widget:label_msgid`	The message ID to use for widget's `label`. If not specified, ArchGenXML will automatically assign one.
`widget:description_msgid`	The message ID to use for `description`. If not specified, ArchGenXML will automatically assign one.
`widget:i18n_domain`	The domain to use for translating widget's `label` and `description`. If left blank, the default model name will be used.

2. Run ArchGenXML to get translation-aware code: After saving your model inside the `models` folder, go to this directory and run this to generate the code:

```
$ ../bin/archgenxml ./poxContentTypes.zargo
```

3. Create message catalog files for supported languages: When generating code, two folders are automatically created by ArchGenXML—`locales` (empty) and `i18n` with a `generated.pot` file. As we saw earlier, `pot` files are message catalog templates. We need to create an associated `po` file for every language we plan to add support for.

Rename `generated.pot` with a sensible name:

```
$ mv generated.pot poxContentTypes.pot
```

In Windows, use:

```
> ren generated.pot poxContentTypes.pot
```

The `i18ndude sync` command doesn't create `po` files but synchronizes them (even if they're empty) with the catalog template. That's why we must first create them in `i18n` folder:

```
$ touch poxContentTypes-es.po
```

Then synchronize the `pot` and `po` files by running:

```
$ i18ndude sync --pot ./poxContentTypes.pot ./poxContentTypes-
es.po
./poxContentTypes-es.po: 5 added, 0 removed
```

`i18ndude` tells us how many entries were added and removed from the language file based on the catalog template.

4. Translate messages for every supported language: Use Poedit, gted plugin for Eclipse, a plain text editor, or any other `po` file editor you want. Just be sure not only to provide translations for every message but to update the header information:

```
msgid ""
msgstr ""
...
"Language-Code: es\n"
"Language-Name: Spanish\n"
"Preferred-Encodings: utf-8 latin1\n"
"Domain: poxContentTypes\n"
```

5. We can drop this sentence. After these changes, you must restart your Zope instance to let it know there's a new translation available.

How it works...

We've already seen the results of running the `archgenxml` command against a **UML** model. However, let's go through some snippets of the code to spot where the so-called **i18n** support is.

The following is an excerpt of the schema in the `content/XNewsItem.py` file:

```
StringField(
    name='lead',
    widget=StringField._properties['widget'](
        label='Lead',
        label_msgid='poxContentTypes_label_lead',
        i18n_domain='poxContentTypes',
    ),
    required=True,
),
StringField(
    name='country',
    widget=SelectionWidget(
        label="Country",
        description="Country where this piece of news has taken
place",
        label_msgid='poxContentTypes_label_country',
```

```
                    description_msgid='poxContentTypes_help_country',
                    i18n_domain='poxContentTypes',
            ),
            enforceVocabulary=True,
            vocabulary="countryVocabulary",
        ),
```

If we added a `label`, we would also get a `label_msgid`. If we added a `description`, a `description_msgid` would be also created.

In this way, ArchGenXML has created an internationalized content type by providing these `_msgids` attributes for us.

Placeless Translation Services (**PTS**) will automatically discover language message catalog files inside the `i18n` folder and register all messages to use them when required.

From now on, when viewing your Plone site in Spanish, you'll see all the labels and descriptions we specified in the `po` file.

 Go to the **Languages** option in **Site setup** to turn your portal into a Spanish-speaking one.

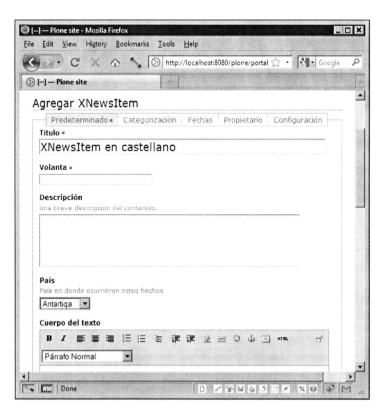

Notice that, even though we haven't set any translation for the remaining fields in XNewsItem, Plone already knows how to show them. This is because XNewsItem is based on ATNewsItem, which uses a different translation domain for its texts. In this way, only new fields with new domains need internationalization.

This is a fragment of the XNewsItem class where we (ArchGenXML actually) set the translation domain:

```
StringField(
    name='lead',
    widget=StringField._properties['widget'](
        label='Lead',
        label_msgid='poxContentTypes_label_lead',
        i18n_domain='poxContentTypes',
    ),
    required=True,
),
```

There's more...

We could have also modified an existing field's label by copying it in the same way we did with the **Related Items** field.

Modifying an existing field's label

Consider the following code where we change the domain for a copied field:

```
copied_fields['relatedItems'] = ATNewsItemSchema['relatedItems'].
copy()
copied_fields['relatedItems'].schemata = "default"
copied_fields['relatedItems'].widget.i18n_domain = "poxContentTypes"
```

If we didn't want to add a new label, we could use the original one and then add it in all message catalog files:

```
msgid = "label_related_items"
msgstr = "Other related news items"
```

The example above uses ArchGenXML tagged values that are converted into Archetype's widget properties in turn.

There's another way to get the same results, as we can see in the `schemata` module of the `Products.ATContentTypes.content` package.

```
relatedItemsField = ReferenceField('relatedItems',
        ...
    widget = ReferenceBrowserWidget(
        ...
        label = _(u'label_related_items', default=u'Related
Items'),
        description = '',
        ....
        )
    )
```

We'll cover this approach in *Using i18n with paster-created products*.

See also

 ▸ *Setting language options*

 ▸ *Using i18n with paster-created products*

Using i18n with paster-created products

In *Creating an Archetypes product with paster*, we covered how to create **Archetypes** content types with **paster** help.

We'll now see how to internationalize content types created in this way.

Getting ready

To perform the following task, we'll use the `pox.video` product available in the accompanying code.

How to do it...

1. Collect translatable text in the `paster`-created code: All `paster`-generated code is already i18n aware, so let's create the message catalog template straight.

    Go to the `pox/video` folder and run:

    ```
    $ i18ndude rebuild-pot --pot ./locales/pox.video.pot --create
    pox.video ./*
    ```

    i18ndude (or any other translation tool) recognizes and extracts translatable text if it's surrounded by `_(u"...")`.

2. Create message catalog files for supported languages. Unlike with XNewsItem (see _Using i18n with ArchGenXML_), we'll use a locales folder in our pox.video package to tell zope.i18n to manage translations in it.

 Be sure that the pox.video.pot file just created is in the locales folder. This is optional but recommended.

Create one language-code folder for every supported language inside the locales directory and an LC_MESSAGES folder inside them:

```
$ mkdir ./locales/es
$ mkdir ./locales/en
$ mkdir ./locales/es/LC_MESSAGES
$ mkdir ./locales/en/LC_MESSAGES
```

Create blank pox.video.po files for every catalog file we need (this file name is mandatory):

```
$ touch ./locales/es/LC_MESSAGES/pox.video.po
$ touch ./locales/en/LC_MESSAGES/pox.video.po
```

Synchronize these po files with the original catalog template:

```
$ i18ndude sync --pot ./locales/pox.video.pot locales/es/
LC_MESSAGES/pox.video.po


./locales/es/LC_MESSAGES/pox.video.po: 8 added, 0 removed


$ i18ndude sync --pot ./locales/pox.video.pot locales/es/
LC_MESSAGES/pox.video.po


./locales/en/LC_MESSAGES/pox.video.po: 8 added, 0 removed
```

3. Translate messages for every supported language: Unlike with **PTS**, there's no need to add custom headers in `po` files when using `zope.i18n`. Just provide proper translations.

English translations

You can leave English message catalog files untouched to use text available in code as default. This is, of course, if you have coded in English.

However, do not forget to add an English option for your translation domains (an `en/LC_MESSAGES` folder). If not present, there will be no English version of the translated text.

If, for any reason, you wanted to modify at a later stage some wording, you could write the corresponding `msgstr` in the catalog file instead of changing your code.

4. Register translations in the configuration file: Open `configure.zcml` in the `pox.package` and modify it as follows:

```
<configure
    xmlns="http://namespaces.zope.org/zope"
    xmlns:five="http://namespaces.zope.org/five"
    xmlns:genericsetup="http://namespaces.zope.org/genericsetup"
    xmlns:i18n="http://namespaces.zope.org/i18n"
    i18n_domain="pox.video">

  <five:registerPackage package="." initialize=".initialize" />

  <i18n:registerTranslations directory="locales"/>

  . . .

</configure>
```

5. Restart your instance: For these changes to take effect, we must restart our instance.

We can also use `plone.reload` to start using the Spanish translation of `pox.video` by going to `http://localhost.8080/@@reload` and clicking on **Reload Code and ZCML** button.

How it works...

Let's go through the code created with `paster` paying attention to what we want.

1. Check the `content/video.py` file:

```
...
from pox.video import videoMessageFactory as _
...

VideoSchema = file.ATFileSchema.copy() + atapi.Schema((

    # -*- Your Archetypes field definitions here ... -*-

    atapi.DateTimeField(
        'originalDate',
        widget=atapi.CalendarWidget(
            label=_(u"Original Date"),
            description=_(u"Date this video was recorded"),
        ),
        validators=('isValidDate'),
    ),


))
```

Everywhere we need a translatable piece of text, `paster` has surrounded it with a special call `_(u"...")`: the text we entered when requested by `paster` asked us is turned into a **unicode** object and then passed to a method named _ (underscore).

If we check the imports at the top of the file, _ (underscore) is an alias for `pox.video.videoMessageFactory`.

2. Open `pox/video/__init__.py`:

```
from zope.i18nmessageid import MessageFactory
...


# Define a message factory for when this product is
internationalised.
# This will be imported with the special name "_" in most modules.
Strings
# like _(u"message") will then be extracted by i18n tools for
translation.

videoMessageFactory = MessageFactory('pox.video')
```

`MessageFactory` is a helper class that turns `strings` (`unicode` objects actually) into `Messages` in a declared domain.

After reading the comment we understand why the underscore is used for this.

Besides, it helps while reading code. If you don't think so, consider for a moment something like this:

```
...
label=videoMessageFactory(u"Original Date"),
...
```

The following screenshot shows a Spanish Video:

There's more...

Testing your translations. For this chapter, we have appended a new test in README.txt for the pox.video package. We first create a Video in an English interface and check that the **Original Date** field has an English label and help text:

```
    ...
    >>> browser.getLink('Add new').click()
    >>> browser.getControl('Video').click()
    >>> browser.getControl(name='form.button.Add').click()

Add form in English.
    >>> '<label class="formQuestion" for="originalDate">Original
Date</label>' in browser.contents
    True
    >>> '<div class="formHelp" id="originalDate_help">Date this video
was recorded</div>' in browser.contents
    True
```

Then we change Portal's default language to Spanish:

```
Add form in Spanish.
    >>> portal.portal_languages.setDefaultLanguage('es')
    >>> portal.portal_languages.use_cookie_negotiation=False
    >>> portal.portal_languages.setLanguageBindings()
    '...'
```

And create a Video again (we didn't save the first one). Now the **Original Date** field has a different label and description, a Spanish one:

```
    >>> browser.open(portal_url)
    >>> browser.getLink('Add new').click()
    >>> browser.getControl('Video').click()
    >>> browser.getControl(name='form.button.Add').click()
    >>> '<label class="formQuestion" for="originalDate">Fecha
original</label>' in browser.contents
    True
    >>> '<div class="formHelp" id="originalDate_help">Fecha de
grabación del video</div>' in browser.contents
    True
```

After saving the Video, we also check that a Spanish legend is shown to play video inline:

```
>>> browser.getControl(name='file_file').add_file(file(os.path.
join(samplesdir, 'video.flv')).read(), 'application/x-flash-video',
'video.flv')
>>> browser.getControl('Save').click()
>>> '<span>Reproduzca el video:</span>' in browser.contents
True
```

See also

▸ *Using i18n with ArchGenXML*

Adding i18n support to any product

From what we have seen so far, we can now add translation facilities to any product as long as the text is in Python code. Using `MessageFactory` we can mark text as translatable.

Getting ready

The following example will modify the `pox.banner` package developed in *Chapter 6*. It's also available in this book's downloadable code.

How to do it...

The following steps should have been taken during `pox.banner` package development. However, we waited to introduce them until now for clarity's sake.

From now on, every code we produce will be i18n-aware from scratch.

1. Create a `MessageFactory` to be used in the whole package.
   Open `pox/banner/__init__.py` file to add the following lines:

   ```
   from zope.i18nmessageid import MessageFactory
   # Define a message factory for when this product is
   # internationalised.
   # This will be imported with the special name "_" in most
   # modules. Strings
   ```

```
# like _(u"message") will then be extracted by i18n tools for
# translation.
```

bannerMessageFactory = MessageFactory('pox.banner')

You can skip the comment.

2. Modify the interfaces module to use translatable text:

```
...
from pox.banner import bannerMessageFactory as _

class ISection(Interface):
    """A Section
    """
    title = schema.TextLine(
                            title=_(u"Title"),
                            description=_(u"Section title."),
                            required=True)


class IBanner(form.Schema):
    """A Banner
    """
    title = schema.TextLine(
                            title=_(u"Title"),
                            description=_(u"Section title."),
                            required=True)
    body = schema.Text(
                        title=_(u"Banner HTML"),
                        default=_(u"<h1>Banner code goes here</h1>"),
                          required=True)
```

These changes are really straightforward. After importing `bannerMessageFactory`, we just have to surround every text legend with `_(u"...")`.

3. Modify `profiles/default/types/Section.xml` and adjust some properties. Highlighted properties have been modified with respect to the original non-translatable version.

```
<?xml version="1.0"?>
<object name="Section"
    meta_type="Factory-based Type Information with dynamic views"
    xmlns:i18n="http://xml.zope.org/namespaces/i18n"
    i18n:domain="pox.banner">

  <!-- Basic information -->
```

```
    <property name="title" i18n:translate="">Section</property>
    <property name="description" i18n:translate="">
      Section container for banners
    </property>
    ...
  </object>
```

4. Apply the same changes in `profiles/default/types/Banner.xml`:

```
<?xml version="1.0"?>
<object name="Banner" meta_type="Dexterity FTI"
    xmlns:i18n="http://xml.zope.org/namespaces/i18n"
    i18n:domain="pox.banner">

  <!-- Basic information -->
  <property name="title" i18n:translate="">Banner</property>
  <property name="description" i18n:translate="">HTML code for
banner ads</property>
  ...
  </object>
```

5. Use `i18ndude` to build message catalog files: Go to `pox/banner` and create the `locales` folder with its well known structure: `<lang_code>/LC_MESSAGES/pox.banner.po`.

   Call `i18ndude`'s `rebuild-pot` command:

```
i18ndude rebuild-pot --pot ./locales/pox.banner.pot --create pox.
banner ./*
```

   Use `i18ndude` again to synchronize the `pot` file with language-specific catalog files.

```
i18ndude sync --pot ./locales/pox.banner.pot ./locales/es/
LC_MESSAGES/pox.banner.po
```

   Supply translations for every message entry in the `po` files, which we have just updated.

6. Register translations in the configuration file: Open `configure.zcml` in the `pox.package` and modify it as follows:

```
<configure
    ...
    xmlns:i18n="http://namespaces.zope.org/i18n"
    i18n_domain="pox.banner">

    ...

    <i18n:registerTranslations directory="locales"/>
    ...
</configure>
```

This tells Zope that our translation files can be found in the `locales` directory.

7. Restart your instance or use `plone.reload` to apply the above changes.

How it works...

As in the `pox.video` example (see *Using i18n with paster-created products),* after these steps have been taken, our `pox.banner` package will supply an internationalized user interface. It's all up to Zope's translation services.

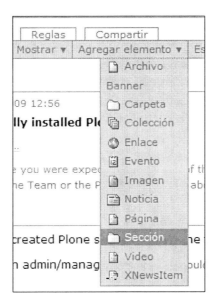

There's more...

Supplying i18n support in templates: Up to now we have hardly mentioned anything about **Zope Page Templates**.

The following are great references concerning **Template Attribute Language** (**TAL**) and **TAL Expression Syntax** (**TALES**), both online and printed:

- ▸ Plone 3 Theming: `http://www.packtpub.com/plone-3-theming-create-flexible-powerful-professional-templates`.

- ▸ Zope Page Template reference: `http://docs.zope.org/zope2/zope2book/source/AppendixC.html`.

- ▸ The Definitive Guide to Plone (first edition): `http://plone.org/documentation/books/definitive_guide_to_plone.pdf`.

- ▸ The Definitive Guide to Plone (second edition): `http://redomino.com/plonebook`.

- ▸ Internationalization (i18n) For Developers: `http://plone.org/documentation/how-to/i18n-for-developers`.

You should perhaps look at the last one first because it's exclusively about i18n support in page templates.

You can check the `video_view.pt` file in the `pox/video/browser/templates` folder to see techniques used to display translated text inside a `pt` file, as shown here:

```
<span i18n:translate="">Play video inline:</span>


<a  href=""
    title="You can also download it!"
    tal:attributes="href string:${here/absolute_url}/at_download/file"
    i18n:attributes="title">
  ...
</a>


<span class="discreet"
      i18n:translate="file_size">
    It's about
    <tal:size content="python:'%s' % (size / 1024)"
              i18n:name="size">
        0
    </tal:size> KB.
</span>
```

See also

► *Using i18n with paster-created products*

Translating content

As stated at the beginning of this chapter, internationalization concerns translation of user interface, not data or content. Thus we have looked at several ways of providing language alternatives to user interfaces.

However, providing translations of content is also a very common requirement and, thank goodness, a star feature of Plone.

Getting started

In this section, we'll install and use **LinguaPlone**—*the* multilingual/translation solution for Plone—as a new dependency of our already used **policy product**: `pox.policy`.

LinguaPlone works only for **Archetypes** content types. Although this is not perfect, it's really good given that most of the content types that come with Plone are delivered by the community that are based on the Archetypes framework. In our particular case, it won't affect us because Banners and Sections developed as Zope 3 **content components** are for administration purposes only, not for end users, and we'll never want to translate them.

However, if we wanted to show banners in different languages, instead of adding the Archetypes + LinguaPlone overhead to the lightweight Banner content type, we'd create a new section for every language.

How to do it...

1. Installing LinguaPlone: There are two ways to install a new product:
   - Adding it in the `eggs` parameter of our `buildout.cfg` file.
   - Adding it as a dependency of a policy product.

   We like the second option better. Modify the `setup.py` file in the `pox.policy` folder and append a new line in the `install_requires` list:

```
setup(name='pox.policy',
      version=version,
      description="Policy product for PloneOpenX website",
      ...
```

```
install_requires=[
    'setuptools',
    # -*- Extra requirements: -*-
    'Products.CacheSetup',
    'Products.LinguaPlone',
],
)
```

This will download LinguaPlone and make it available for use by Zope.

To automatically install it in Plone, we can add it in `profiles/default/metadata.xml` as a dependency of `pox.policy`:

```
<?xml version="1.0"?>
<metadata>
 <version>1</version>
 <dependencies>
  <dependency>profile-Products.CacheSetup:default</dependency>
  <dependency>profile-Products.LinguaPlone:default</dependency>
 </dependencies>
</metadata>
```

2. When LinguaPlone is installed, all `ATContentTypes` automatically recognize it and are turned into translatable.

   This is done in the `Products.ATContentTypes.content.base` module:

```
from Products.ATContentTypes.config import HAS_LINGUA_PLONE
if HAS_LINGUA_PLONE:
    from Products.LinguaPlone.public import BaseContent
    from Products.LinguaPlone.public import BaseFolder
    from Products.LinguaPlone.public import OrderedBaseFolder
    from Products.LinguaPlone.public import BaseBTreeFolder
    from Products.LinguaPlone.public import registerType
else:
    from Products.Archetypes.atapi import BaseContent
    from Products.Archetypes.atapi import BaseFolder
    from Products.Archetypes.atapi import OrderedBaseFolder
    from Products.Archetypes.atapi import BaseBTreeFolder
    from Products.Archetypes.atapi import registerType
```

`ATContentTypes` are based in one of the base classes above. So, if LinguaPlone is present, these content types will inherit all its features.

That's why our `XNewsItem` and `Video` content types are now already translatable:

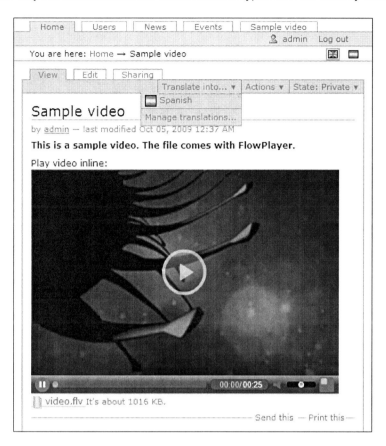

To be honest, before taking the previous screenshot, we edited the video and modified the **Language** field in the **Categorization** tab with the **English** value.

3. Preventing ATContentTypes from being affected by LinguaPlone. If you, for any reason, need LinguaPlone not to turn your ATContent-based Archetype, you can add these few lines in it to remove the `ITranslatable` interface from the original list of implemented interfaces:

```
from zope.interface import implementedBy, implementsOnly
...
class XNewsItem(ATNewsItem):
    """
    """
    ...
    # implements(interfaces.IXNewsItem)
```

```
# Get all original interfaces but ITranslatable
base_interfaces = [i for i in list(implementedBy(ATNewsItem))
    if i.__name__ != 'ITranslatable']
implementsOnly(interfaces.IXNewsItem, base_interfaces)
...
```

Thanks to Taito Horiuchi for this very useful tip, adapted from his original at `http://plone.org/documentation/how-to/make-at-content-type-untranslatable-with-products.linguaplone-installed`.

4. Telling other content types to support translation: If you have any content type that is not based on ATContentTypes but in **Archetypes**' BaseContent, BaseFolder, OrderedBaseFolder, or BaseBTreeFolder classes, you can slightly change your code to benefit from LinguaPlone.

   If your class inherits from BaseContent, you probably have an import line like this:

```
from Products.Archetypes.atapi import *
```

   Change it with these lines:

```
try:
    from Products.LinguaPlone.public import *
except ImportError:
    # No multilingual support
    from Products.Archetypes.atapi import *
```

5. Setting special properties to fields: In LinguaPlone-powered content types, we can use a special languageIndependent property to tell Archetypes which fields must remain intact between translations, and which fields may change. Examples of its use are the Country for a piece of news or an uploaded file in a File object.

   Change the XNewsItem module in the Products.poxContentTypes.content package like this:

```
    ...
    StringField(
        name='country',
        widget=SelectionWidget(
            label="Country",
            description="Country where this piece of news has
            taken place",
            label_msgid='poxContentTypes_label_country',
            description_msgid='poxContentTypes_help_country',
            i18n_domain='poxContentTypes',
        ),
        enforceVocabulary=True,
        vocabulary="countryVocabulary",
        languageIndependent=True,
    ),
    ...
```

Modify the `video.py` file in `pox/video/content`:

```
...
atapi.DateTimeField(
    'originalDate',

    widget=atapi.CalendarWidget(
        label=_(u"Original Date"),
        description=_(u"Date this video was recorded"),
    ),
    validators=('isValidDate'),
    languageIndependent=True,
),
...
```

How it works...

When LinguaPlone is installed, a new **Translate into** drop down menu becomes available beside **Action**, as we shown earlier in an illustration.

In the following screenshot, we can see how the **Title** and **Description** fields are available for translation and the remaining fields (**File** and **Original date**) aren't.

There's more...

For a more detailed study of LinguaPlone, visit its home page at `http://pypi.python.org/pypi/Products.LinguaPlone`. We strongly recommend reading the FAQ section.

There are several LinguaPlone add-on products available on Plone's website. We'd like to specially mention `icSemantic.LangFallback`, a member of the icSemantic family. This product has a special view for translated content that detects missing fields (fields without translation) and shows other translations in place. Although it is not a perfect solution, it's one of the few means of providing language fallback currently available. More about it at: `http://plone.org/products/icsemantic-langfallback`. Both the authors have worked on this project, by the way.

See also

- ▶ *Creating a policy product*
- ▶ *Installing CacheFu with a policy product*

Setting language options

Having installed LinguaPlone, in *Translating content*, which lets us show the same content in different languages, we are now going to set which languages will be available in our portal.

In previous chapters, we have already configured the tools and properties of a Plone site or an installed product.

Getting ready

Given that these preferences are explicit from customer requirements or project needs, it is advisable to add them in a **policy product**.

We'll use the `pox.policy` package we created in *Creating a policy product*.

How to do it...

1. Add an import step for GenericSetup in the `pox.policy` product: Just drop this file named `portal_languages.xml` inside the `profiles/default` folder:

```
<?xml version="1.0"?>
<object name="portal_languages">
 <default_language value="en"/>
 <supported_langs>
  <element value="en"/>
```

```
    <element value="es"/>
  </supported_langs>
</object>
```

With this file, **GenericSetup** will recognize an import step to process and it will set the above properties (default and supported languages) in the `portal_languages` tool.

2. Reinstall the `pox.policy` product for these changes to take effect.

3. Check new language options: With the new language settings, if we point our browser to `http://localhost:8080/plone/@@language-controlpanel`, we'll see the **Language Settings** control panel form improved by LinguaPlone with our just added preferences.

    All translatable content will now show a list of available languages in the **Translate into** drop-down menu.

There's more...

Have we already said that Plone comes with lots of languages at its disposal? What we haven't said—but could be concluded from the above—is that every language catalog file adds memory and process overhead in Zope: The more available catalogs, the longer it will take to tell which is the right translation.

Fortunately, as we can set which languages will be available in Plone's user interface, we can also restrict the languages Zope has to consider during translation resolution.

With **Placeless Translation Services**, we can use a `PTS_LANGUAGES` environment variable with a space-separated list of the languages we want Zope to manage. After setting this, you should go to **Control Panel**'s **Placeless Translation Services** in your instance ZMI (`http://localhost:8080/Control_Panel/TranslationService/manage_main`), delete all catalogs, and restart Zope.

On the other hand, for `zope.i18n` (its 3.5.0 version onwards), the environment variable name is `zope_i18n_allowed_languages`. As `zope.i18n` doesn't supply a user interface, for these changes to take effect you'll have to manually delete all `mo` files inside every `locales` folder. Although it sounds scary, you can just remove all `mo` files inside your instance folder. After that, restart Zope.

```
$ rm -f `find . -name *.mo`
```

In Windows, use:

```
> del /d *.mo
```

Modify the [instance] part in buildout.cfg by adding a new environment-vars parameter with the following lines:

```
[buildout]
...
[instance]
...
environment-vars =
    PTS_LANGUAGES es en
    zope_i18n_allowed_languages es en
...
```

See also

For other examples on how to use **GenericSetup** import steps, please refer to the following recipes:

- *Improving performance of our products*
- *Translating content*
- *Creating a policy product*
- *Creating a custom content type with paster*

9
Adding Security to your Products

In this chapter, we will cover:

- ▶ Creating a new permission
- ▶ Adding a new role
- ▶ Adding user groups
- ▶ Testing security customizations
- ▶ Protecting operations with permissions
- ▶ Managing security with workflows
- ▶ Adding configuration options in the Plone control panel

Introduction

The following excerpt is taken from `AccessControl.txt` located in Zope's `AccessControl` package (`zope2/lib/python/AccessControl`):

> A "permission" is the smallest unit of access to an object, roughly equivalent to the atomic permissions seen in [Windows] NT: R (Read), W (Write), X (Execute), etc. In Principia [former name for Zope], a permission usually describes a fine-grained logical operation on an object, such as "View Management Screens", "Add Properties", etc.
>
> Different types of objects will define different permissions as appropriate for the object.

When users try to perform restricted actions in Zope, its security machinery will check first if they have the right authorization by testing the operation's restrictions against the user's permissions.

However, in Zope, permissions are never assigned directly to users, but to roles. Thus, if we want to give users the freedom to access restricted operations, roles must be assigned to them, or even better, to the groups to which users belong.

Looking at the customer requirements listed in the preface, we are now going to focus on the sixth one: *Commercial (and non-technical) staff should be able to modify the location of the banners.*

For this to happen, we'll add security controls by means of permissions, roles, and groups to one of the products we've been developing throughout this book: `pox.banner`.

After that, we'll add a new workflow, which will let us control security in content objects at certain stages within processes.

By the end of the chapter, we will create a new restricted area in Plone's control panel so that only users with the correct permissions will be able to work with it.

Creating a new permission

Typical Plone permissions are `View`, `Modify portal content`, and `Manage portal` (defined in the `Products.CMFCore.permissions` module), and often we'll just use them as we've been doing so far instead of creating new ones. However, we are free to add as many restrictions as we need, if really required. One example of a product-specific permission is `Add portal topics` from `Products.ATContentTypes.permission`.

Getting started

The following code changes will be made in the `pox.banner` product. If you don't have it, you can just download it from this book's web page.

How to do it...

1. Register the permission: To add a new permission, we must register it in a component configuration file. Open `configure.zcml` in the `pox.banner` package and add the following lines:

```
<configure ...>
    ...

    <permission
        id="pox.ManageBanners"
```

```
            title="Manage banners and sections"
    />

    ...
    <include package=".browser" />
</configure>
```

2. Use the permission to guard Zope 3 views: In the `configure.zcml` file of the `pox.banner.browser` package, change `cmf.AddPortalContent` and `cmf.ModifyPortalContent` permissions for the one created in the previous step:

```
<configure
    xmlns="http://namespaces.zope.org/zope"
    xmlns:browser="http://namespaces.zope.org/browser"
    i18n_domain="pox.banner">

    <browser:page
        for="zope.app.container.interfaces.IAdding"
        name="addSection"
        class=".section.Add"
        permission="pox.ManageBanners"
        />

    <browser:page
        for="..interfaces.ISection"
        name="edit"
        class=".section.Edit"
        permission="pox.ManageBanners"
        />
    ...
</configure>
```

3. Create the permission programmatically: If we need to protect any other piece of code other than Zope 3 views, then we *must* create the permission with Python code.

   In the `pox.banner` package, modify `__init__.py` like this:

```
...
from Products.CMFCore.permissions import setDefaultRoles
...

def initialize(context):
    """Initializer called when used as a Zope 2 product."""
    setDefaultRoles('Manage banners and sections', \
                    ('Manager', ))
```

4 You must restart your Zope instance for these changes to take effect.

How it works...

After Step 1, a new permission will be ready to be used wherever we need. However, Zope won't really *create* it until it is used to protect a **browser view**. So if we reference the above permission from a **GenericSetup** `rolemap.xml` file, for instance (as we'll do in *Adding a new role*), we'll get a `ValueError` exception.

In Step 2, we therefore use the permission in order for Zope to really create it. However, if we didn't have anything to protect at that point, we could skip that step and go straight to the next one.

Notice that we are using the ID of the permission created in Step 1.

 It's important to protect a `<browser:page />` directive so that **Five** can create the permission. If you protect any other component, it won't work, at least in the 1.5.6 version of Five.

Given that the **Zope 3 view** uses the new permission, we must be sure that the `browser` package configuration file is processed after the permission definition; refer to the order of the directives in `configure.zcml` in Step 1.

If you need to protect any other component, you'll need to use Python code to programmatically create it in Zope; this is what Step 3 is about to. The `setDefaultRoles` second argument should be a tuple with role names.

 Convention is to grant full access rights to `('Manager',)` only and then manage everything else on the site level with `rolemap.xml` as depicted in *Adding a new role*.

Unlike in the `ZCML` directives seen in Step 2, we must use a permission *title* instead of its ID. This step is optional and can be used together with the previous one. But you *must* use it if you don't plan to protect Zope 3 browser views.

With these changes, Zope creates the new permission on start up and leaves it ready to be used. Actually, we are already using it as a security restriction for two Zope 3 views.

If you browse to `http://localhost:8080/manage_access` (Zope root **Security** tab) you'll see the new `Manage banners and sections` permission listed and assigned to the `Manager` role.

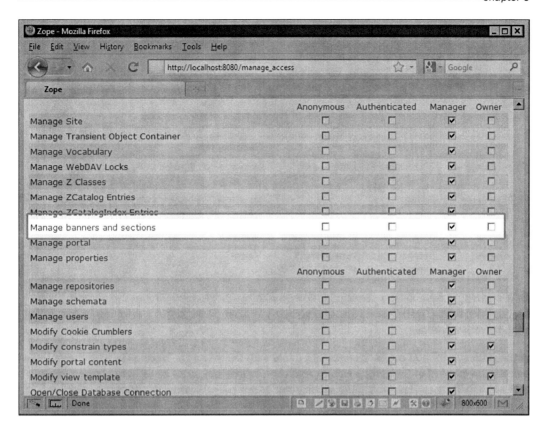

In *Adding a new role*, we'll see how to give access rights to existing and new roles.

There's more...

There exists a package named `collective.autopermission` that performs the Step 3 automatically. In other words it creates a Zope 2 permission from a Zope 3 `<permission />` directive. For information and how to use it, visit `http://pypi.python.org/pypi/ collective.autopermission`.

See also

▶ *Adding a new role*

Adding a new role

As we said in the previous section, permissions are never given directly to users but to their roles. Think of roles as collections of permissions given to users in a specific context.

The following table shows some examples of typical roles in a Plone site:

Role	Context	Permissions
Manager	Plone site (site-wide)	Manage properties, Add portal content, Modify portal content
Manager	Folder	Manage properties, Add portal content, Modify portal content
Owner	Specific object in private state	Modify portal content
Owner	Specific object in published state	View

As you can see, even for the same role, access rights change according to the context (Plone site, specific folder, workflow status, and so on). We'll see more about **workflows** in *Managing security with workflows*.

In this recipe, we'll add a new `Commercial` role with the `Manage banners and sections` permission created in *Creating a new permission*. In this way, we'll be able to allow users to add and modify `Section` and `Banner` objects for our `pox.banner` product.

Getting ready

Although the following instructions are straightforward and can be easily applied to any product, if you want to follow our exact example, you should get a copy of `pox.banner` in the book's accompanying code.

How to do it...

Thanks to **GenericSetup** machinery, we can create new roles and assign permissions to them in a really simple way.

1. Create a `rolemap.xml` file inside the `profiles/default` folder of the `pox.banner` package with the following contents:

```
<?xml version="1.0"?>
<rolemap>
  <roles>
    <role name="Commercial"/>
  </roles>
  <permissions>
```

```
<permission name="Manage banners and sections"
              acquire="True">
  <role name="Commercial"/>
  <role name="Manager"/>
</permission>
  </permissions>
</rolemap>
```

2. Restart your instance and reinstall the product to apply this change.

How it works...

When the `pox.banner` product is installed (or re-installed), GenericSetup will create a new `Commercial` role.

Apart from that, two roles will be assigned to the already created (as detailed in *Creating a new permission*) `Manage banners and sections` permission: `Commercial` and `Manager`. Note that we are using the permission *title* instead of its ID (`pox.ManageBanners`).

 If you plan to give existing permissions to any role, you must include the whole list of roles that should enjoy the benefits. If not, only the new roles will end up with the access rights you were modifying.

If you now go to `http://localhost:8080/plone/manage_access` (Plone site **Security** tab), you'll see the permission associated with the two roles above.

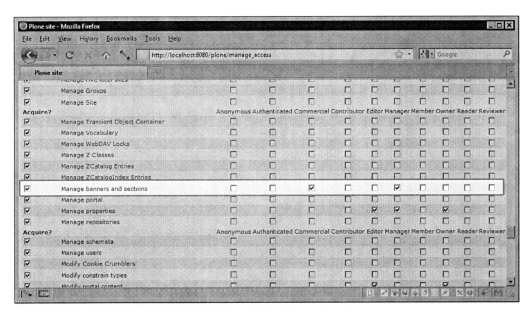

There's more...

Automatic roles

Anonymous and **Authenticated** are two automatic roles that cannot be given to any user or group, but are assigned by Plone according to the users' status: if they are not logged in, users share the **Anonymous** role. On the other hand, every user that has correctly logged in will gain the **Authenticated** role in addition to other roles which that particular member might have.

In this way, by granting, for example, View permission to the **Anonymous** role, every regular visitor of a Plone website will be able to see its public content.

Local roles

For information about **local roles**, please refer to:

- The *Roles* section in Chapter 6, *Security and Workflow* of *Professional Plone Development* by Martin Aspeli
- The *Workflow* section in *Dexterity Developer Manual* at `http://plone.org/products/dexterity/documentation/manual/developer-manual/advanced/workflow`.

See also

- *Creating a new permission*
- *Managing security with workflows*

Adding user groups

When dealing with applications security, it is often wiser to give power to groups instead of users. Why is this? Because groups let us add or remove users as they come and go to a certain position or responsibility in an organization, which is reflected in the group itself.

In this way, if new people join the editors' crew of our website, then we can add their member IDs to the matching Editors' group in Plone and they will automatically have all their required roles and permissions.

On the other hand, if our security strategy were based on plain users, we'd have to manually add or remove every role to each and every member. In addition, there's no way in Plone to list all members for a specific role, so it would be difficult to know who can do what.

Furthermore, there is also a significant performance advantage when **local roles** are involved: adding a local role to a folder re-indexes the entire folder tree, which can be extremely costly if we added several users. On the other hand, if we manage folder security with groups, adding a user to a folder that already has a local role won't require any re-indexing.

How to do it...

Unfortunately, there's no **GenericSetup** import step we can take advantage of when creating user groups; we must add them programmatically.

1. Tell GenericSetup to call some methods when installing the product.

    Modify `configure.zcml` in the `pox.banner` package:

```
<configure
  . . .
    xmlns:genericsetup=
              "http://namespaces.zope.org/genericsetup"
  >
  . . .
   <genericsetup:importStep
       name="various"
       title="Sections and Banners: miscellaneous import steps"
       description=" "
       handler="pox.banner.setuphandlers.setupVarious"
   >
<!--    <depends name="other step's name"/>  -->
   </genericsetup:importStep>
   . . .
</configure>
```

This will tell GenericSetup to call `setupVarious()` in the `pox.banner.setuphandlers` module when installing the product.

2. Add code for group creation in `setuphandlers` module:
    Modify (or create) a `setuphandlers.py` file in `pox.banner` main package's folder with the following code:

```
from zope.app.component.hooks import getSite
from Products.CMFCore.utils import getToolByName

def setupVarious(context):

    if context.readDataFile('pox.banner_various.txt') is None:
        return
```

```
portal = getSite()
acl_users = getToolByName(portal, 'acl_users')
portal_groups = getToolByName(portal, 'portal_groups')

if not acl_users.searchGroups(id='Commercials'):
    portal_groups.addGroup('Commercials')
    portal_groups.setRolesForGroup('Commercials',
['Commercial'])
```

3. Create a new `pox.banner_various.txt` file in the `pox/banner/profiles/default` folder so that the `setupVarious` method can find it. This **flag file** is used to ensure that this step is processed only when (re)installing the `pox.banner` product.

4. Given that we have changed the installation procedure of the product, we must restart Zope and reinstall it for the above changes to be applied.

How it works...

Notice that in Step 1, we added a `<genericsetup:importStep />` directive as well as its corresponding namespace in the main `<configure />` tag.

The group creation code of Step 2 is very easy to understand: we create a new `Commercials` group (if it doesn't exist). After that, the `Commercial` role is automatically applied to the group so that its member users will be able to `Manage banners and sections` (the only permission available for that role).

Having installed (or reinstalled) the `pox.banner` product, the new `Commercials` group will be available as seen in the following screenshot taken from **Users and Groups** settings in Plone control panel:

Group name	Roles							Remove Group
	Commercial	Contributor	Editor	Member	Reader	Reviewer	Manager	
Administrators	☐	☐	☐	☐	☐	☐	☑	☐
Commercials	☑	☐	☐	☐	☐	☐	☐	☐
Reviewers	☐	☐	☐	☐	☐	☑	☐	☐
Authenticated Users (Virtual Group)	☐	☐	☐	☐	☐	☐	☐	☐

You can now enter the **Commercials** group link and add or remove users according to your needs.

See also

- ▸ *Managing security with workflows*
- ▸ *Adding configuration options in Plone control panel*
- ▸ *Installing CacheFu with a policy product*

Testing security customizations

In this section, we will focus on testing changes in permissions, roles, and groups.

Although this will be a very short recipe, we want to show some useful functions that you may need when testing them.

How to do it...

Open README.txt—with all the tests written in **doctest** syntax—of pox.banner package and add the following **test cases** at the end of the file:

1. Test new permissions:

   ```
   >>> len(portal.permission_settings('Manage banners and
   sections')) > 0
   True
   ```

   The permission_settings method returns a list of dictionary elements containing the name of the permission, its associated roles, and whether or not it's acquired from the object's parent.

2. Test new roles:

   ```
   >>> 'Commercial' in self.portal.validRoles()
   True
   ```

   The validRoles() method lists all available roles.

3. Test permissions on roles:

   ```
   >>> [x['selected'] for x in portal.permissionsOfRole('Commercial')
   if x['name'] == 'Manage banners and sections']
   ['SELECTED']
   ```

   When we call the permissionsOfRole method, we get a list with a dictionary for all available permissions in the site. If the permission is enabled for the passed role-argument (Commercial in this example) the selected item is 'SELECTED'.

4. Test groups:

```
>>> acl_users = getToolByName(portal, 'acl_users')
>>> len(acl_users.searchGroups(name='Commercials'))
1
>>> group = acl_users.getGroupById('Commercials')
>>> 'Commercial' in group.getRoles()
True
```

In this test, we search for a group named Commercials. Then we get it and ask for its roles.

Protecting operations with permissions

The whole point of creating permissions and roles in a Plone site is, at the end of the day, to add security restrictions to certain methods, operations, or information within the portal.

Although we've been doing this in previous chapters, we'll now pinpoint how to do it.

How to do it...

1. Control who can create objects of a certain class: Modify the configure.zcml file in the pox.banner package by changing the cmf.AddPortalContent permission with pox.ManageBanners.

```
<configure ... >
    ...
    <permission
        id="pox.ManageBanners"
        title="Manage banners and sections"
    />
    ...
    <five:registerClass
        class=".content.section.Section"
        meta_type="Section"
        permission="pox.ManageBanners" />
    ...
</configure>
```

With this change, we allow the creation of Section objects to users with the pox. ManageBanners permission.

As you might have already noticed, we must sometimes refer to permissions by their `id` and at other times by their `title`. In most Python code (typically `checkPermission` and `declareProtected` calls) and in the **ZMI**, we must use the permission title. On the other hand, in **ZCML** files and some **Zope 3** code, we must use the permission `id`.

2. Add security restrictions to other operations: The following is a copy of Step 2 of the earlier *Creating a new permission* recipe. If you have already done this, just skip the changes but read the comments below.

    In the `configure.zcml` file of the `pox.banner.browser` package, change `cmf.AddPortalContent` and `cmf.ModifyPortalContent` permissions for `pox.ManageBanners`:

```
<configure
    xmlns="http://namespaces.zope.org/zope"
    xmlns:browser="http://namespaces.zope.org/browser"
    i18n_domain="pox.banner">

    <browser:page
        for="zope.app.container.interfaces.IAdding"
        name="addSection"
        class=".section.Add"
        permission="pox.ManageBanners"
        />

    <browser:page
        for="..interfaces.ISection"
        name="edit"
        class=".section.Edit"
        permission="pox.ManageBanners "
        />
    ...
</configure>
```

Unlike with Dexterity, *Add* and *Edit* actions for formlib-based Plone content components are declared in ZCML files, where we also have to define their corresponding permissions.

How it works...

Zope and Plone user interfaces only show actions for which the user has the required permissions. Thus, if the logged in user has the Contributor role for instance, he or she would be able to create regular content types (all the enabled ones for the Contributor role's permissions) but won't even see the **Banner** and **Section** options in the **Add new** drop-down menu.

Adding security restrictions to Dexterity content types

To restrict the use of **Dexterity** content types, such as `Banner`, with custom permissions, there's no configuration file to change but an XML one. Open `profiles/default/types/Banner.xml` and modify the `add_permission` property and `Edit` action with this:

```xml
<?xml version="1.0"?>
<object name="Banner" meta_type="Dexterity FTI"
   xmlns:i18n="http://xml.zope.org/namespaces/i18n"
   i18n:domain="pox.banner">
 <!-- Basic information -->
 <property name="title" i18n:translate="">Banner</property>

 ...

 <property name="add_permission">pox.ManageBanners</property>

 ...

<action title="Edit" action_id="edit" category="object"
condition_expr=""
   url_expr="string:${object_url}/edit" visible="True">
  <permission value="Manage banners and sections"/>
 </action>
 ...
</object>
```

Given that default **add and edit forms** for Dexterity content types are protected with default Plone permissions—`cmf.AddPortalContent` and `cmf.ModifyPortalContent` respectively—if we plan to change restrictions by using other permissions, we have two options:

▶ Grant custom permission as well as a default one to the corresponding roles

▶ Create new add and edit forms with a new restriction guard

The first choice can be achieved by using `rolemap.xml` as we did in *Adding a new role*.

To accomplish the second alternative, create this `banner.py` file in the `pox.banner.browser` package:

```python
from five import grok
from plone.directives import dexterity
from pox.banner import interfaces
```

```
class AddForm(dexterity.AddForm):
    grok.name('Banner')
    grok.require('pox.ManageBanners')

class EditForm(dexterity.EditForm):
    grok.context(interfaces.IBanner)
    grok.require('pox.ManageBanners')
```

Testing restricted operations

To see how our permission guards are applied, let's go through the following test cases we've added in the README.txt **doctest** file of the pox.banner package:

```
>>> portal.acl_users.userFolderAddUser('commercial', 'secret',
['Commercial'], [])
>>> self.login('commercial')
```

We first create a new member with the Commercial role. In this way, he or she will automatically receive Manage banners and sections permissions to perform the next operations. Once the user is created we log in as this *commercial* user.

```
>>> portal.invokeFactory('Section', 'commercial_section1')
'commercial_section1'
>>> portal.invokeFactory('Banner', 'commercial_banner1')
'commercial_banner1'
```

Yes, we were able to create not only Sections but also Banners.

```
>>> portal.acl_users.userFolderAddUser('contributor', 'secret',
['Contributor'], [])
>>> self.login('contributor')
```

In this case, we ensure there's a *contributor* user by creating it, and then, we log in with this new member.

```
>>> portal.invokeFactory('Section', 'commercial_section2')
Traceback (most recent call last):
...
Unauthorized: Cannot create Section

>>> portal.invokeFactory('Banner', 'commercial_banner2')
Traceback (most recent call last):
...
Unauthorized: Cannot create Banner
```

Oops! Although we tried, this time we created neither Sections nor Banners because the Contributor role has no ability to add them.

Checking paster and ArchGenXML permissions

ArchGenXML and **paster** automatically create new permissions for adding content objects. You can find them in the `config` module of their main package folders.

For more information about explicitly defining permissions in ArchGenXML, please refer to the online manual at `http://plone.org/documentation/manual/archgenxml2` and look for `_permissions` suffixed tagged values.

See also

▶ *Creating content types with Dexterity*

Managing security with workflows

One of the main advantages of binding documents (of any kind or content type) to a **workflow**, and moving them from stage to stage, is to allow or ban operations or interactions that can be performed on the objects in certain statuses. Examples of these actions are:

▶ Changing the status of the document to a new one

▶ Modifying document contents

▶ Including the document in lists

▶ Showing the document

If we stare intently at the examples above, they are all related to security: who can do what (like editing a document or viewing it at all).

In this section, we'll create a new simple workflow and bind it to `Section` and `Banner` content types to automatically apply it to objects of those classes.

The following diagram shows what the workflow will look like: what states and transitions it will have and who will be able to do which operation (basically only Commercial staff and Managers will do everything).

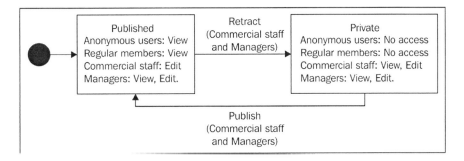

How to do it...

1. Copy an existing workflow: Although we could have written workflow code straight into the XML syntax required by **GenericSetup**, we liked the idea of copying an existing workflow and modifying it in Zope's UI, given the similarity of our requirements to the `simple_publication_workflow` Plone comes with.

    Go to the `portal_worklflow` tool in your Plone site by opening your browser at `http://localhost:8080/portal_workflow/manage`, and then click on the **Contents** tab to display the list of already registered workflows. Select one (in our case `simple_publication_workflow`), click on the **Copy** button at the bottom, and then **Paste** it.

2. Adjust the just copied workflow to your needs: We won't go through the whole process of converting an existing workflow to our `pox.banner_workflow`. However, here is a summarized list of what we have done:

    ❏ Renamed the copied workflow with `pox.banner_workflow` by selecting it and clicking on **Rename** in the **Contents** tab.

    ❏ Modified `title` and `description` by clicking on it to open its **Properties** tab.

    ❏ Removed unnecessary states (`pending` in our case) displayed in the **States** tab.

    ❏ Set the new initial state (`published` in our example) by selecting it and pressing the **Set Initial State** button of the **States** tab.

    ❏ Removed unnecessary transitions (`reject` and `submit` here) displayed in the **Transitions** tab.

    ❏ Modified the remaining states and transitions by changing description fields and their permissions. Remember that we are using the `Manage banners and sections` permission.

The following screenshot is of the **States** tab of `pox.banner_workflow` once finished:

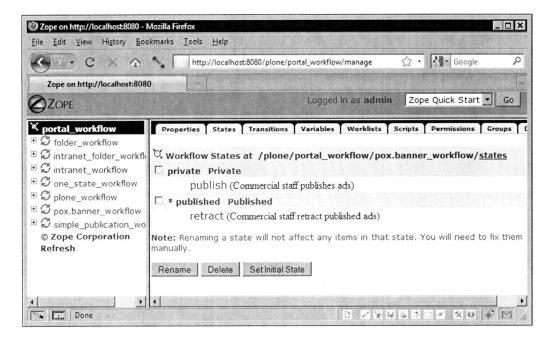

3. Get the XML code of the workflow: **GenericSetup** doesn't only turn XML files into configuration options (Python code actually), but it can also do it the other way around.

Go to the `portal_setup` tool by visiting `http://localhost:8080/plone/portal_setup/manage` and open the **Export** tab. Then select the **Workflow Tool** checkbox and click on the **Export selected steps** button at the bottom of the page.

This will make Zope download a tarball with all the XML configuration files corresponding to the `portal_workflow` tool, its settings, and the already registered workflows. Just keep the `definition.xml` file from the `workflows/pox.banner_workflow` folder, the one we are interested in.

4. Add a new workflow to your product installation script: To add a workflow step in the installation routine, performed by **GenericSetup**, place this new `workflows.xml` file in the `profiles/default` folder of the `pox.banner` package:

```
<?xml version="1.0"?>
<object name="portal_workflow" meta_type="Plone Workflow Tool">
 <object name="pox.banner_workflow" meta_type="Workflow"/>

 <bindings>
  <type type_id="Banner">
   <bound-workflow workflow_id="pox.banner_workflow"/>
  </type>
  <type type_id="Section">
   <bound-workflow workflow_id="pox.banner_workflow"/>
  </type>
 </bindings>

</object>
```

This will create a new `pox.banner_workflow` entry in the **Contents** tab of `portal_workflow` tool. It will also bind `Banner` and `Section` content types to the new workflow. This means that whenever a new `Banner` or `Section` object is created in the Plone site, `pox.banner_workflow` will be applied to them by assigning the default `published` state and showing its available transitions when possible.

However, we haven't told GenericSetup what the name of the default state is yet, or anything at all about `pox.banner_workflow`. To do that, create a `workflows/pox.banner_workflow` folder (this name must be the same as used in the `workflows.xml` file above) inside `profiles/default` and drop the `definition.xml` file, which we kept apart in the previous step.

Here is a shortened version of that file:

```
<?xml version="1.0"?>
<dc-workflow workflow_id="pox.banner_workflow"
             title="Banners and Sections workflow"
             description=" - Simple workflow that is used by
pox.banner ..."
             state_variable="review_state"
             initial_state="published">
```

This is descriptive information about `pox.banner_workflow` and the status ID of the initial state.

```
<permission>View</permission>
```

Above is the list of permission names that our workflow will handle (just `View` in our case).

 At every stage, these permissions will be granted or revoked to available roles to allow (or prevent) users with those roles to perform restricted operations. This is the key of security in workflows.

```
<state state_id="private" title="Private">
  <description>Can only be seen and edited by the
  commercial staff.
  </description>
  <exit-transition transition_id="publish"/>

  <permission-map name="View" acquired="False">
   <permission-role>Commercial</permission-role>
   <permission-role>Manager</permission-role>
  </permission-map>
</state>
```

For `private` state there's just one possible transition (`publish`, defined later). Only commercial staff (`Commercial` role) and managers (`Manager` role) will be able to view objects with this status. Modification access is given, not here by workflow, but with the permissions specified when registering their edit actions in the `configure.zcml` file (see *Protecting operations with permissions*).

```
<state state_id="published" title="Published">
  <description>Visible to everyone.
  </description>
  <exit-transition transition_id="retract"/>

  <permission-map name="View" acquired="False">
   <permission-role>Anonymous</permission-role>
  </permission-map>
</state>
```

Content in the `published` state will be viewable by everybody.

If you give permission to the Anonymous role, all the other roles will automatically gain it too.

```
<transition transition_id="publish"
          title="Commercial staff publishes ads"
          new_state="published" trigger="USER"
          before_script="" after_script="">
 ...

 <guard>
   <guard-permission>Manage banners and sections
   </guard-permission>
 </guard>
</transition>

<transition transition_id="retract"
          title="Commercial staff retract published ads"
          new_state="private" trigger="USER"
          before_script="" after_script="">
 ...

 <guard>
   <guard-permission>Manage banners and sections
   </guard-permission>
 </guard>
</transition>
```

There are just two transitions, `publish` and `retract`, that are available only to users with `Manage banners and sections` permission.

The rest of the `definition.xml` file is common for almost every workflow in Plone. You can see the whole file in the book's accompanying source code.

5. We must reinstall the `pox.banner` product to see these changes. Don't forget to remove the manually created workflow to let GenericSetup do its job.

There's more...

ArchGenXML can help us in the creation of content types as well as in the generation of workflows. For more information about this, visit `http://plone.org/documentation/manual/developer-manual/using-archgenxml/basics/workflows`.

See also

▸   *Protecting operations with permissions*

Adding configuration options in Plone control panel

Most of Plone's configuration options can be managed via the control panel. To see what it looks like, just click on the **Site Setup** link in the top-right corner of a freshly installed Plone site. This will lead you to `http://localhost:8080/plone/plone_control_panel`.

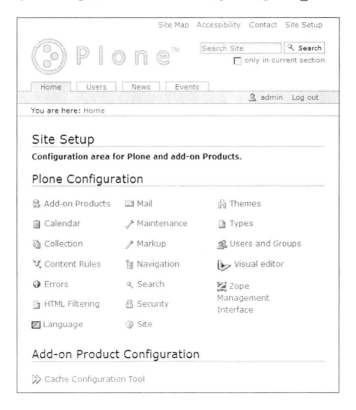

In this recipe, we will add a new link in the **Add-on Product Configuration** section to access a restricted area where Managers and Commercial people will be able to create and organize Sections and Banners.

   Options available in Plone Control Panel are called **configlets**.

Getting ready

Just for clarity's sake, we have put this configuration functionality in a different package named pox.controlpanel. Given that we definitely won't explain every single item of its anatomy, just the essential steps to create a configlet, please get this Plone product from the downloadable source code of this book.

To get an idea of what we are going to do, please consider the following screenshot of our configlet-to-be and read the next list:

- ▶ Sections and banners won't be created anywhere in the site except in a new pox-root Section that will be automatically created on product installation.
- ▶ Sections will be displayed with a new @@pox.controlpanel browser view and they will look like the previous screenshot, a combo box to select the type of object we want to add, and a table with all the sections and banners available in the current section level.

How to do it...

1. Create a *root* Section during installation. This is done with a `setupVarious` method in the `setuphandlers` module. In this chapter, we have already seen how to add a new import step to call arbitrary code—we created a new group in the *Adding user groups* recipe. Refer to that recipe for more details and check the `configure.zcml` and `setuphandlers.py` files to see the handler code.

2. Define the interface for the new configlet form: Our **configlet** will not only show a table of Sections and Banners but it will also display a combo box with two options to create more objects (that is, it will be a form). So we need to define its interface.

   Create an `interfaces` module in `pox.controlpanel` main's package:

```
from zope import schema
from zope.interface import Interface

from pox.controlpanel import message_factory as _

class IControlPanel(Interface):
    """ Defines ControlPanel schema
    """
    type = schema.Choice(title=_(u"Type"),
        description=_(u"Content type."),
        vocabulary='pox.controlpanel.vocabularies.allowed_types',
        required=True,)
```

3. Create a vocabulary for the form combo box: The interface above (and the configlet form) needs a vocabulary to populate the combo box's options.

   Create this `vocabularies.py` file in `pox.controlpanel` main's package:

```
from zope.schema.vocabulary import SimpleVocabulary, SimpleTerm
from pox.controlpanel import message_factory as _

def AllowedTypes(context):
    """ Allowed types Vocabulary.
    """
    subjects = (SimpleTerm(u'Section', title=_(u'Section')),
                SimpleTerm(u'Banner', title=_(u'Banner')),
                )

    return SimpleVocabulary(subjects)
```

Register the `AllowedTypes` method as a vocabulary in the main `configure.zcml` file:

```
<configure
    xmlns="http://namespaces.zope.org/zope"
    . . .
    i18n_domain="pox.controlpanel">

    . . .

    <utility
        component=".vocabularies.AllowedTypes"
        name="pox.controlpanel.vocabularies.allowed_types"
        provides="zope.schema.interfaces.IVocabularyFactory"
        />

    . . .
</configure>
```

4. Add a browser view to manage configlet's form operations: Here is a piece of the actual code intended to create Sections and Banners from the configlet's form:

```
class ControlPanelForm(form.Form):
    fields = field.Fields(IControlPanel)
    label = "Manage sections and banners"

    @button.buttonAndHandler(_(u'Add'))
    def handleApply(self, action):
        data, errors = self.extractData()

        type_id = data['type']
        . . .
        url = calculate the url for adding a Section or
        Banner depending on type_id above
         self.request.response.redirect(url)
```

Please see the whole code in the `manage.py` file of the `browser` sub-package. We specially recommend reading how to get the add form URL, which is not included here due to its length.

5. Register the browser page into component architecture: In the `pox.controlpanel.browser` package, add this `configure.zcml` file:

```
<configure
    xmlns="http://namespaces.zope.org/zope"
    xmlns:browser="http://namespaces.zope.org/browser"
    i18n_domain="pox.controlpanel">

    <browser:page
        for="pox.banner.interfaces.ISection"
        name="pox.controlpanel"
        class=".manage.ControlPanelView"
        permission="pox.ManageBanners"
        />

</configure>
```

6. Ensure everything is available in main `configure.zcml`:

```
<configure
    xmlns="http://namespaces.zope.org/zope"
    ...
    i18n_domain="pox.controlpanel">


    ...

    <include package="pox.banner" />
    <include package=".browser" />


    ...
</configure>
```

7. Change the default view for Sections: If we want Section objects to be displayed using the `@@pox.controlpanel` browser view, then we must change its default view (as defined in `pox.banner`).

   To keep the `pox.banner` product independent of `pox.controlpanel`, we can override this property without touching the original code.

   Create a `types` folder inside `profiles/default` and drop this `Section.xml` file into it:

```
<?xml version="1.0"?>
<object name="Section"
    meta_type="Factory-based Type Information with dynamic views"
    xmlns:i18n="http://xml.zope.org/namespaces/i18n"
    i18n:domain="pox.banner">
```

```
<alias from="(Default)" to="@@pox.controlpanel"/>
<alias from="@@folder_contents" to="@@pox.controlpanel"/>
<alias from="folder_contents" to="@@pox.controlpanel"/>
<alias from="view" to="@@pox.controlpanel"/>
```

```
</object>
```

8. Add the very configlet to Plone's control panel: To include a new option in site setup, we can use an import step of **GenericSetup**.

   Create this `controlpanel.xml` file in the `profiles/default` folder of the `pox.controlpanel` package:

```
<?xml version="1.0"?>
<object name="portal_controlpanel" meta_type="Plone Control
Panel Tool">
 <configlet
    title="PloneOpenX Config"
    action_id="pox.controlpanel"
    appId="pox.controlpanel"
    category="Products" condition_expr=""
    url_expr="string:${portal_url}/pox-root/@@pox.controlpanel"
    visible="True">
  <permission>Manage banners and sections</permission>
 </configlet>
</object>
```

   As you can see, the new `PloneOpenX Config` link will be available for users that can `Manage banners and sections`, and it will point to the automatically created `pox-root` section.

How it works...

Once the interface (Step 2) and its required vocabulary (Step 3) is defined, we can focus on the creation of the actual configlet view in Step 4. As a matter of fact, we need more than a browser view, we need a form manager. From the final developer's standpoint, the only difference between the two is the base class we have to use: instead of `Products.Five.browser.BrowserView`, we will use `z3c.form.Form`:

- We first populate the form with the fields defined in the `IControlPanel` interface above. We can also add a title via the `label` attribute.

- Then a new submission button is created with an `Add` label. When this button is pressed the `extractData` method will return all the submitted data accessible in a dictionary fashion. Based on the selected type, we redirect the user to the corresponding **add form**.

After Step 5, the new browser view (form actually) will be available for `Sections`, by appending `@@pox.controlpanel` to their URL, when accessed by users with `pox.ManageBanners` permission. However, this permission is not defined in this product but in `pox.banner`. What if Zope processes this package first and doesn't know anything about `pox.banner`? To ensure this does not happen, we can tell Zope to process another package first (if not done yet) so that we can be sure nothing will break. This is done in Step 6 by adding the `<include package="pox.banner" />` directive.

There's more...

Unfortunately, in Plone 3, the **Site Setup** action (the top-right link we mentioned at the beginning of this recipe) and Plone control panel page are only available for users with the `Manage portal` permission.

Consequently, if Commercial staff don't have that permission, which is most likely, they won't be able to access the configlet at all.

However, on the user preferences page, a list of available configlets are shown even if the user is not Manager (see next screenshot). The problem is that the **Preferences** link is not included by default. So let's make it visible by adding this `actions.xml` file to `profiles/default` folder to let **GenericSetup** do what it knows.

```
<?xml version="1.0"?>
<object name="portal_actions" meta_type="Plone Actions Tool"
    xmlns:i18n="http://xml.zope.org/namespaces/i18n">
 <object name="user" meta_type="CMF Action Category">
   <object name="preferences" meta_type="CMF Action" i18n:
domain="plone">
    <property name="visible">True</property>
   </object>
 </object>
</object>
```

In the above file, we simply included the line to be changed (`visible` property). In spite of this, regular `actions.xml` files have more contents such as description, URL, permissions, and so on.

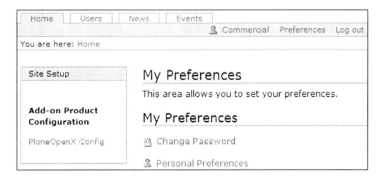

See also

In this section, we have worked with several import steps from GenericSetup, manual setup handlers, and form managers. You can find more examples of them in these recipes:

- *Adding user groups*
- *Creating a folderish content type*
- *Setting language options*

As we have already said, this recipe has lots of code not included here. We encourage you to navigate the whole pox.controlpanel package to find useful examples, tests, and the remaining code.

10

Improving User Interface with KSS

In this chapter, we will cover:

- ▶ Preparing a form to take full advantage of KSS
- ▶ Changing end user pages with client-side KSS
- ▶ Submitting data via AJAX

Introduction

Since the birth of **JavaScript** back in 1995, web applications hadn't really used this scripting technology at its very limits. Typical examples of JavaScript application were image rollovers, changing `<select />` options after other user selections, form client-validations, auto-complete in combo-boxes, and so on.

However, five years ago, new widgets appeared in browser web pages that caught everybody's attention, being Google suggests one of the most remarkable examples.

After a while, a new term was coined that gave a name to this new approach: **AJAX**, after Asynchronous JavaScript and XML. Although neither of these two are strictly necessary to create an AJAX application they are commonly used.

 The AJAX concept is easy to explain. While viewing a web page, the browser communicates with the server, posting or retrieving information, without leaving the original page. Then the user is told what has happened, usually based on the server response.

With the AJAX boom, several JavaScript frameworks sprang into developers' communities to make work easy when creating new web applications: Ext JS, jQuery, Prototype + Scriptaculous, and Yahoo! UI.

Nevertheless they are not only aimed to help client-server communication but, taking advantage of CSS, to provide new widgets or visual effects, like auto-complete, and drag-and-drop, among others.

Many times **Web 2.0** term is often misused for websites with rich user interfaces and AJAX-based communication. Web 2.0 actually refers to the information sharing and collaboration approach, which many websites have been offering for several years.

Customers' reviews in online stores, social networks, search suggestions—as they show results of previous user searches—and most notably Wikipedia, are examples of Web 2.0 applications. The confusion over the name is down to the technologies these kinds of websites frequently use to provide these services. More information about Web 2.0 can be found in Wikipedia at `http://en.wikipedia.org/wiki/Web_2.0`.

In the current chapter, we'll focus on **KSS** (**Kinetic Style Sheets**), whose main purpose is AJAX, although other functionalities, like effects, can be incorporated as plugins.

This excerpt, taken from the KSS home page at `http://kssproject.org`, describes the technology:

KSS, Ajax with style

*KSS is an Ajax framework that allows UI development without writing any Javascript. It uses style sheets with CSS-compliant syntax to declare and bind dynamic behaviors in the browser. The [KSS] engine supports a set of generic **DOM**-like commands; they are computed on the server and sent back to manipulate the HTML page.*

KSS is the preferred AJAX framework for Plone 3.0. Although **jQuery** has been gradually incorporated in Plone core and third-party products and is one of the most widespread JavaScript libraries, using it is just a matter of JavaScript, which is not covered in this book. KSS in Plone, on the other hand, already comes with server-side support (provided by the `kss.core` and `plone.app.kss` packages) to translate client **requests** into Python objects and give proper feedback by turning Python code into **XML responses**.

You can see an example of using jQuery in Plone and registering a new **JavaScript** source file in *Modifying the view of a content type with jQuery*.

In the following tasks, we will use KSS to create from simple client-side visual changes to server-side objects manipulation. All our work will use the **PloneOpenX configlet**, which we created in *Adding configuration options in Plone control panel*. However, we'll change it significantly.

Preparing a form to take full advantage of KSS

This task is actually the explanation of how we have modified the already developed configlet so that we can enrich it with KSS in the next recipes. If you are merely seeking KSS details, just skip this. However, we introduce here several form-related concepts that you might find very useful.

Before making any code change, let us explain what we want to achieve. Our **PloneOpenX** configlet so far has just a combo box with two options: **Section** and **Banner**. Once users select either of these and click on the **Add** button, they will be automatically redirected to the **add form** for the chosen content type.

We are going to change that. Instead of opening a new URL, we will let users create Sections or Banners straight there, in the same form. To do this, we must add new fields: **Title** and **Body**, the latter just for **Banner** objects. You can see the final configlet in the following screenshot (when the **Section** radio button is selected, the **Body** field is hidden):

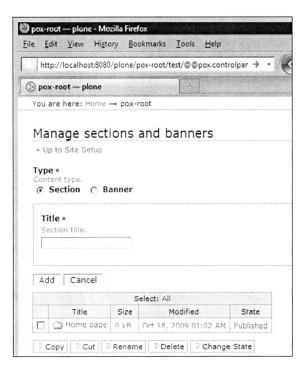

Getting started

The following changes will be applied to the `manage` module in the `pox.controlpanel.browser` package developed in *Adding configuration options in Plone control panel*. If you don't have it, get a fresh copy from the book's accompanying code.

To achieve the desired results, we could simply add two new field definitions (the aforementioned `Title` and `Body` ones) in the `IControlPanel` interface of the `interfaces.py` file. However, they are already included in two existing interfaces: the ones for Section and Banner in the `pox.banner` package. Moreover, if for some reason we were to modify any of the above schemas in the future, we wouldn't have to worry about changing any other piece of code because we are relying now on the original interfaces.

Fortunately, `z3c.form` library, the Zope 3 community alternative to the original `zope.formlib` package, lets us literally *add* schema fields in one single form.

How to do it...

1. Create forms with fields from several interfaces. Create two helper classes in the `manage` module of `pox.controlpanel`:

    ```
    . . .
    from pox.banner.interfaces import ISection, IBanner
    from z3c.form import form, field, button, group
    . . .
    class SectionGroup(group.Group):
        label = _(u'Section')
        fields = field.Fields(ISection, prefix='section')

    class BannerGroup(group.Group):
        label = _(u'Banner')
        fields = field.Fields(IBanner, prefix='banner')
    ```

    Once we have these new field groups, let's put everything together to create the desired form. In the same `manage.py` file, modify the base class for `ControlPanelForm` and add this:

    ```
    . . .
    from z3c.form.browser.radio import RadioFieldWidget
    . . .

    class ControlPanelForm(group.GroupForm, form.AddForm):
        fields = field.Fields(IControlPanel)
        fields['type'].widgetFactory = RadioFieldWidget
        groups = (SectionGroup, BannerGroup)
    ```

```
    # don't use context to get widget data
    ignoreContext = True
    label = "Manage sections and banners"
```

With these changes, we have now a form with all the fields we need.

2. Define code to process submitted data:

```
class ControlPanelForm(group.GroupForm, form.AddForm):
    form.extends(form.AddForm) # copy buttons and handlers


    . . .


    @button.buttonAndHandler(_(u'Cancel'))
    def handleCancel(self, action):
        """Just an empty new button as an example
        """
        pass


    def extractData(self):
        """Custom extractData method for our dual
        purpose form.
        Shared fields and selected group fields are considered
        """
        data, errors = super(form.AddForm, self).extractData()
        for group in self.groups:
            if group.label == data['type']:
                groupData, groupErrors = group.extractData()
                data.update(groupData)
                if groupErrors:
                    if errors:
                        errors += groupErrors
                    else:
                        errors = groupErrors
        return data, errors
```

3. Wrap up our configlet form: Modify the `create` method:

```
def create(self, data):
    container = aq_inner(self.context)
    fti = getattr(getToolByName(container, 'portal_types'),
    data['type'])
    content = createObject(fti.factory)

    if hasattr(content, '_setPortalTypeName'):
        content._setPortalTypeName(fti.getId())
```

```
        # Acquisition wrap temporarily to satisfy things like
        vocabularies
        # depending on tools
        if IAcquirer.providedBy(content):
            content = content.__of__(container)

        for group in self.groups:
            if group.label == data['type']:
                form.applyChanges(group, content, data)

        return content

    def add(self, object):
        container = aq_inner(self.context)
        object.id=''
        object.id= INameChooser(container).\
                  chooseName(None, object)
        newName = container._setObject(object.id, object)
        return container._getOb(newName)

    def nextURL(self):
        return self.context.absolute_url()
```

How it works...

In Step 1, we created two new classes: SectionGroup and BannerGroup. They are field groups (which are rendered as <fieldsets /> in the final HTML) with all field definitions found in the ISection and IBanner interfaces. Note that we added a prefix argument to the Fields() method to prevent naming collisions in the final form (both interfaces have a title field).

After that, we modified the ControlPanelForm class, where there are a few things to take note of:

- The new base classes are GroupForm and AddForm. The first one lets us add groups of fields, the latter comes with built-in methods to create new content types.
- We can change default field widgets by specifying a widgetFactory attribute. Check the z3c.form.browser package for more available widgets.
- The groups variable populates the form with a list of fieldsets.
- To prevent the form from automatically filling with data from the context object, we can use the ignoreContext variable.

The existing **Add** button (the one developed in *Adding configuration options in Plone control panel*) had just the job of getting the **add form** URL of the selected content type and opening it. However, we now want to create objects in place, so we have to replace the full code. This is carried out in Step 2.

As we said earlier, the `AddForm` base class comes with various methods for creating new objects. It also has an **Add** button that submits all fields and creates a new object with *all submitted data*. So that's it? Actually not.

If we wanted to create another button, a **Cancel** button for instance, our buttons' definition would override the `AddForm` ones. To prevent this, instead of just inheriting original buttons, we copy them—by calling `form.extends(form.AddForm)`—and then add as many as we need.

There's still another problem. We don't want to create a single object with all submitted data. We need to create a **Section** (just a `title` field) or a **Banner** (`title` and `body`), without a `type` field but choosing the content type based on its value. Furthermore, every field is `required` in the `ISection` and `IBanner` interfaces. Thus, if we submitted a partially filled form, we would get a validation error. To skip this obstacle, we overrode the original `extractData` method to be sure that only the desired fields will be considered for validation and creation.

 Every time we create a class which inherits from `AddForm`, like here, we must define three of its methods, as they are not implemented in the original base class: `create` (to create the object), `add` (to add the object to an existing container), and `nextURL` (to load a URL after the object creation).

The two (highlighted) differences between the `create` method in Step 3 and the original **Dexterity** code (`plone.dexterity.browser.add`) are the way we get the **Factory Type Information** (**FTI**) and the selection of the group fields we want to use when creating the new object.

There's more...

More examples and `z3c.form` documentation is available at `http://docs.zope.org/z3c.form/form.html`.

See also

- *Creating a folderish content type*
- *Creating the user interface for Zope 3 content types*
- *Creating content types with Dexterity*
- *Adding configuration options in Plone control panel*

Changing end user pages with client-side KSS

Up to now we have a full configuration form that works perfectly well, but the purpose of this chapter is to introduce KSS and show how to improve the final user interface with JavaScript and AJAX functionalities.

One of Plone's main characteristics and objectives is to comply with **accessibility** standards. We must not forget this when using KSS or any other JavaScript feature: things *have to work* also for a non-JavaScript browser. Furthermore, things must work *first* in a non-JavaScript fashion; if we can then improve the user experience with any advanced technique, we should incorporate it unobtrusively. Find more information about this at `http://en.wikipedia.org/wiki/Unobtrusive_JavaScript`.

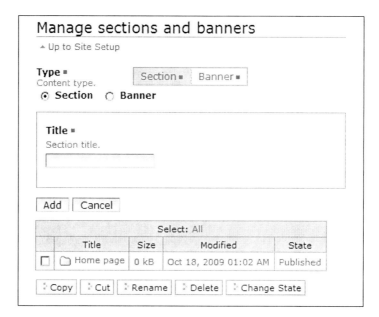

The preceding screenshot shows what our configlet form looks like with the work done so far, where we can spot at least these problems:

1. There are two **Section-Banner** controls, We could click on the **Banner** tab and select the **Section** radio button as well.

2. The top tabs show red squares to make us aware of required fields. Even if we wanted to create a Section, the **Banner** tab would still show the required-fields indicator.

3. Tabs are used to group logically-related fields for the *same* object. This is not the case here.

What can we do to solve this?

If we hid the radio buttons, we should add _intelligence_ to the tabs to set the **Type** value. This would only _partially_ solve the problem because the red spots would still be there.

On the contrary, if we hid the tabs, we would still see the red squares next to required fields, like always. In addition, the grouping-fields tabs would disappear and the unusual behavior of the fieldsets would vanish from the end user standpoint. However, we would be missing the show/hide benefit of top tabs.

Let's hide the tabs and then add show and hide functionalities to the **Type** radio buttons.

How to do it...

1. Creating a KSS file: In the `pox.controlpanel.browser` sub-package, create a new `kss` folder and drop this `pox.controlpanel.kss` file:

```
ul.formTabs:load {
    action-client: setStyle;
    setStyle-name: display;
    setStyle-value: none;
}

#form-widgets-type-0:click(show) {
    action-client: setStyle;
    setStyle-kssSelector: htmlid(fieldset-0);
    setStyle-name: display;
    setStyle-value: block;
}

#form-widgets-type-0:click(hide) {
    action-client: setStyle;
    setStyle-kssSelector: htmlid(fieldset-1);
    setStyle-name: display;
    setStyle-value: none;
}

#form-widgets-type-1:click(show) {
    action-client: setStyle;
    setStyle-kssSelector: htmlid(fieldset-1);
    setStyle-name: display;
    setStyle-value: block;
}
```

```
#form-widgets-type-1:click(hide) {
    action-client: setStyle;
    setStyle-kssSelector: htmlid(fieldset-0);
    setStyle-name: display;
    setStyle-value: none;
}
```

2. Registering a KSS resource: For the above KSS file to be *consumed* by user agents (web browsers), we must register it as an available resource component.

    Modify the `configure.zcml` file in the `browser` sub-package by adding these lines:

```
<configure
    xmlns="http://namespaces.zope.org/zope"
    xmlns:browser="http://namespaces.zope.org/browser"
    i18n_domain="pox.controlpanel">

    . . .

    <browser:resource
        file="kss/pox.controlpanel.kss"
        name="pox.controlpanel.kss"
        />

</configure>
```

3. Installing a new KSS file to be automatically included in web pages: As with JavaScript source files (see *Modifying the view of a content type with jQuery* in Chapter 5) and CSS resources, KSS style sheets can also be registered in a Plone tool (**portal_kss**) to be automatically referenced in HTML.

    The straightforward and recommended method to do this is by using **GenericSetup** import steps. Given that we have already configured the `pox.controlpanel` product to be installed as an extension profile (check `configure.zcml` in the `pox/controlpanel` folder), we simply need to create a new `kssregistry.xml` file in the `profiles/default` folder with the following XML declarations:

```
<object name="portal_kss" meta_type="KSS Registry">
 <kineticstylesheet cacheable="True" compression="safe"
 cookable="True" enabled="1"
    expression="nocall:here/@@pox.controlpanel|nothing"
    id="++resource++pox.controlpanel.kss"/>
</object>
```

Note the `expression` property: this is used to decide whether the stylesheet should be included or not when rendering the HTML page.

Given that there are lots of places in a Plone site that are affected by the `ul.formTabs:load` statement above, we have chosen to add this KSS resource only when `pox.controlpanel` **Zope 3 view** is available for the current context (denoted by the `here` variable).

How it works...

We are now going to explain in detail the aforementioned first KSS rule and then give some hints about the following ones.

Manipulating DOM elements on document load

Check the following KSS statement:

```
ul.formTabs:load {
    action-client: setStyle;
    setStyle-name: display;
    setStyle-value: none;
}
```

 As you can see, KSS rules are very similar to CSS regular rules.

Let's go through the whole KSS rule to identify and explain its parts:

`ul.formTabs:load` is the KSS selector. It is composed of a regular CSS selector but it's always followed by a colon and an event name, in this case `load`. This could be read like this: find all `<ul />` elements with the `formTabs` class attribute and bind to their `load` event the following KSS statements.

The first KSS statement is `action-client: setStyle;` that tells the KSS engine that the `setStyle` action, performed when the `load` event is fired, will be run in the client (that is, in the web browser).

The KSS means of passing arguments is like: `method-argument: passed-value`. The `setStyle` client action expects two arguments: `name` (the name of the style property we want to set) and `value`. That's why there are two other statements:

```
setStyle-name: display;
setStyle-value: none;
```

Once the KSS engine executes this rule, all `<ul />` HTML elements with the `formTabs` class name will be hidden after they are loaded (rendered) in the browser.

Dynamically adding user interactions

The second task we wanted to do with KSS was to show and hide `<fieldsets />` after user clicks. Given that we have hidden form tabs, we must mimic their behavior.

We can use the same technique as used above with the `setStyle` client-side action, but there are some caveats:

> ► We can't use the same action (`setStyle`) more than once in the same KSS statement. It would be like overriding a previously set property in CSS.

> ► The selector **DOM** elements, radio buttons, are not the same as the target elements—fieldsets—(as with the `ul.formTabs` element in the previous rule). We should somehow tell the KSS engine what to show or hide explicitly.

To get around these problems, we have created two KSS statements, one to show and the other one to hide. Adding a unique identifier in parentheses next to the event part in the selector won't do any harm (it will still match the same DOM elements), but it will let us perform the same `action-client` in the same objects without the overriding issue.

On the other hand, to specify a target DOM element, we can use the `-kssSelector` property with a regular CSS selector. In our case, we have used the `htmlid` function to create an ID selector, but we could have used the `css` function as well.

```
#form-widgets-type-0:click(show) {
    action-client: setStyle;
    setStyle-kssSelector: htmlid(fieldset-0);
    setStyle-name: display;
    setStyle-value: block;
}

#form-widgets-type-0:click(hide) {
    action-client: setStyle;
    setStyle-kssSelector: htmlid(fieldset-1);
    setStyle-name: display;
    setStyle-value: none;
}
```

But this is not the full KSS file we created earlier. There are two other statements left. You might have noticed that they are a copy of these preceding two except for the selectors. As you can see, KSS has this kind of limitations: while it is very easy to *create* JavaScript functions, it is also limited due to its very strict syntax. So we have to repeat full blocks of code that could have been more easily done with a simple JavaScript loop statement.

There's more...

I think it is worth showing you how the approach used in this chapter can produce perfectly **usable** and **accessible** HTML. The following screenshots are from a JavaScript-disabled Firefox and a Lynx text-only browser session:

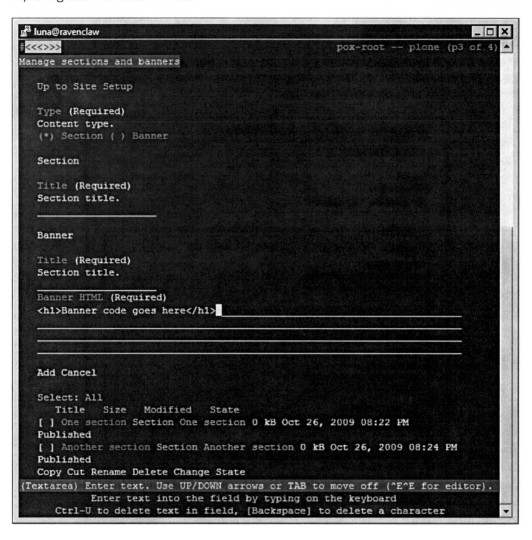

▶ *Modifying the view of a content type with jQuery*

Submitting data via AJAX

One of the most exciting features of web application nowadays is the ability to send data to, and retrieve from, the server without the painful task of reloading the whole page.

This is not only *cool* but very useful and can help us incredibly with regards to overall site performance. As an example, think of a document rating system: do we really have to reload a web page after clicking on a **Yeah, I like it** button? Couldn't we just update a small portion of the rendered HTML to tell users that their ratings have been recorded?

We won't speak at length about the well known benefits of AJAX, we just wanted to emphasize how positive its implementation in Plone can be.

How to do it...

1. Add a KSS rule to replace the standard submitting action. Open `pox.controlpanel.kss` in the `browser/kss` folder and add this KSS statement at the bottom:

```
#form-buttons-add:click {
    evt-click-preventdefault: True;
    action-server: kssHandleAdd;
    kssHandleAdd-kssSubmitForm: currentForm();
}
```

2. Create a server method to handle the new KSS action. To see the whole `ControlPanelKSSView` class we added in the `browser.manage` module, refer to this chapter's source code. The main `kssHandleAdd` method will be explained in the *How it works...* section.

3. Register the new browser view. Modify the `configure.zcml` file in `browser` package as follows:

```
<configure
    xmlns="http://namespaces.zope.org/zope"
    xmlns:browser="http://namespaces.zope.org/browser"
    i18n_domain="pox.controlpanel">

    ...

    <browser:page
        for="pox.banner.interfaces.ISection"
        name="kssHandleAdd"
        class=".manage.ControlPanelKSSView"
        attribute="kssHandleAdd"
        permission="zope2.View"
        />

</configure>
```

Unlike with the previous `<browser:page />` directives, we are using here the `attribute` property to tell Zope which attribute (it can certainly be a method like here) to use when the view is called, instead of using a `template` (if specified) or the default `__call__` method.

How it works...

The first two steps in the preceding procedure deserve a full description.

Replacing standard button's behavior

Let's have a look again at the KSS rules:

```
#form-buttons-add:click {
    evt-click-preventdefault: True;
    action-server: kssHandleAdd;
    kssHandleAdd-kssSubmitForm: currentForm();
}
```

We first tell KSS to stop the button's default action. In other words, after clicking the button, do not submit the form (because we will do it via AJAX).

Then we call a server action (the same one registered in the component configuration file) with all the data contained in the form. This is done with the special `-kssSubmitForm` parameter together with the `currentForm()` function.

Server side KSS actions

We will explain the `kssHandleAdd` method here, which is responsible for the creation of the selected object. The rest of the `ControlPanelKSSView` class can be found in the book's accompanying code.

Note that we have to entirely rewrite the code of the regular form submission especially for KSS: getting data, validating it, creating objects and, finally, giving feedback to the user who is waiting for a server response.

```
@kssaction
def kssHandleAdd(self):
    z2.switch_on(self, request_layer=self.request_layer)
    self.form_instance.update()
    data, errors = self.form_instance.extractData()
```

The `@kssaction` decorator will force all KSS commands in this method to be properly sent back to the client.

The `z2.switch_on` call is required before rendering `z3c.forms` in a Zope 2 instance.

By using the `update()` method of `form_instance` (the submitted form), we can later make an `extractData` call, although this is not a standard form submission.

```
ksscore = self.getCommandSet('core')
kssplone = self.getCommandSet('plone')
```

KSS works with server-side command sets. They are collections of methods that can be rendered as XML instructions to be executed by the KSS engine in the client.

Plone already comes with three command sets: `core`, `plone`, and `zope`. In this example we use the first two.

```
fieldset = [i for i in \
                range(len(self.form_instance.groups)) \
                if self.form_instance.groups[i].label ==
    data['type']][0]
```

Now, we get the fieldset that we are interested in; the one that matches the selected content type in the **Type** radio button.

```
ksscore.removeClass('#form-buttons-add', 'submitting')
for group in self.form_instance.groups:
    for name,widget in group.widgets.items():
        fieldname = widget.name
        fieldId = '#fieldset-%s #formfield-%s' % (str(fieldset),
                                        fieldname.replace('.', '-'))
        errorId = '#fieldset-%s #formfield-%s
        div.fieldErrorBox' % \ (str(fieldset),
        fieldname.replace('.', '-'))
        field_div = ksscore.getCssSelector(fieldId)
        error_box = ksscore.getCssSelector(errorId)
        ksscore.clearChildNodes(error_box)
        ksscore.removeClass(field_div, 'error')
        kssplone.issuePortalMessage('')
```

All this code simply cleans the user interface from previous submissions and validation errors:

- By removing the `submitting` class from the **Add** button, we skip the prompt message shown when clicking the submit button twice.

- Then we loop through groups (fieldsets) and their widgets, removing previous errors and pending messages.

```
if errors:
    for error in errors:
        validationError = error.message
        validate_and_issue_message(ksscore, validationError,
            error.widget.name, fieldset, kssplone)
    return
```

If we find a validation error, we stop the execution of the method and send a message back to the user.

```
obj = self.form_instance.createAndAdd(data)
if obj is not None:
    kssplone.issuePortalMessage(_(u"Item created"), "info")
    self.update_table()
```

If everything goes well, we are now able to create the object, inform the user, and update the folder contents table below the form.

Remember that we are using a custom `extractData` method to get just the field values we need for the selected content type.

```
for group in self.form_instance.groups:
    for name,widget in group.widgets.items():
        ksscore.setAttribute(ksscore.getHtmlIdSelector(
        widget.name.replace('.', '-')), "value", "")
```

Finally, we clean submitted fields by setting their `value` attribute to an empty string (actually we are cleaning all form fields).

There's more...

You can find beginner and intermediate tutorials on the KSS website: `http://kssproject.org/documentation/tutorials`.

There's also a KSS manual available at plone.org: `http://plone.org/documentation/kb/kss-manual`.

For a comprehensive KSS guide and reference (events, command sets, `action-client` available functions, and so on) please refer to Chapter 14, *Rich User Interfaces with KSS,* of Martin Aspeli's book: *Professional Plone Development*.

As for **testing**, the best way to test KSS is with **Selenium**. Nevertheless the `kss.core` package comes with useful classes (test layer, test cases, and **functional test** cases) in its `tests.base` module that can be used to replace usual XML responses with regular Python dictionaries. Check the chapter source code for examples of this.

See also

▶ *Using Selenium functional tests*

11
Creating Portlets

In this chapter, we will cover:

- ▶ Creating a portlet package
- ▶ Customizing a new portlet according to our requirements
- ▶ Testing portlets
- ▶ Assigning portlets automatically

Introduction

One of the major changes from Plone 2.5 to Plone 3.0 was the complete refactoring of its portlets engine. In Plone 2.5, left and right side portlets were managed from **Zope Management Interface** (**ZMI**) by setting two special properties: `left_slots` and `right_slots`.

This was not so hard but was cumbersome. Any **TALES** path expression—**ZPT** macros typically—could be manually inserted in the above two properties and would be displayed as a bit of HTML to the final user.

The major drawback for site managers with the old-style approach was not just the uncomfortable way of setting which portlets to display, but the lack of any configuration options for them. For example, if we wanted to present the latest published news items, we wouldn't have any means of telling how many of them to show, unless the portlet itself were intelligent enough to get that value from some other contextual property. But again, we were still stuck in the ZMI.

Fortunately, this has changed enormously in Plone 3.x:

- Portlets can now be configured and their settings are mantained in **ZODB**.

- Portlets are now managed via a user-friendly, Plone-like interface. Just click on the **Manage portlets** link below each of the portlets columns (see the following screenshot).

In the above screen, if we click on the **News** portlet link, we are presented with a special configuration form to choose the **Number of items to display** and the **Workflow state**(s) we want to consider when showing news items.

If you have read previous chapters, you might be correctly guessing that **Zope 3** components (`zope.formlib` mainly) are behind the portlets configuration forms.

In the next sections, we'll look again at the customer's requirements listed in this book preface:

- ▶ Advertisement banners will be located in several areas of every page
- ▶ Advertisement banners may vary according to the section of the website

Creating a portlet package

Once again, **paster** comes to the rescue. As in *Creating a product package structure* (Chapter 6) and *Creating an Archetypes product with paster* (Chapter 5), we will use the `paster` command here to create all the necessary boilerplate (and even more) to get a fully working portlet.

Getting ready

As we are still at the development stage, we should run the following commands in our **buildout**'s `src` folder:

```
cd ./src
```

How to do it...

1. Run the `paster` command: We are going to create a new egg called `pox.portlet.banner`. The pox prefix is from PloneOpenX (the website we are working on) and it will be the namespace of our product.

> Portlets eggs usually have a nested `portlet` namespace as in `plone.portlet.collection` or `plone.portlet.static`. We have chosen the `pox` main namespace as in the previous eggs we have created, and the `banner` suffix corresponds to the portlet name.
>
> For more information about eggs and packages names read `http://www.martinaspeli.net/articles/the-naming-of-things-package-names-and-namespaces`.
>
> If you want to add portlets to an existing package instead of creating a new one, the steps covered in this chapter should tell you all you need to know (the use of `paster addcontent portlet` local command will be of great help).

In your `src` folder, run the following command:

```
paster create -t plone3_portlet
```

This `paster` command creates a product using the `plone3_portlet` template. When run, it will output some informative text, and then a short wizard will be started to select options for the package:

Option	Value
Enter project name	pox.portlet.banner
Expert Mode?	easy
Version	1.0
Description	Portlet to show banners
Portlet Name	Banner portlet
Portlet Type	BannerPortlet

After selecting the last option, you'll get an output like this (a little longer actually):

```
Creating directory ./pox.portlet.banner

  ...

  Recursing into +namespace_package+
    Recursing into +namespace_package2+
      Recursing into +package+
        Recursing into profiles
          Creating ./pox.portlet.banner/pox/portlet/banner/
          profiles/
          Recursing into default
            Creating ./pox.portlet.banner/pox/portlet/banner/
            profiles/default/
            Copying metadata.xml_tmpl to ./pox.portlet.banner/pox/
            portlet/banner/profiles/default/metadata.xml
            Copying portlets.xml_tmpl to ./pox.portlet.banner/pox/
            portlet/banner/profiles/default/portlets.xml
```

This tells us that even the **GenericSetup** extension profile has also been created by `paster`. This means that we can install the new *Banner portlet* product (as entered in the `portlet_name` option above).

2. Install the product: To tell our **Zope instance** about the new product, we must update the `buildout.cfg` file as follows:

```
[buildout]
...
eggs =
...
    pox.portlet.banner
...
develop =
 src/pox.portlet.banner
```

We can automatically install the product during buildout. Add a `pox.portlet.banner` line inside the `products` parameter of the `[plonesite]` part:

```
[plonesite]
recipe = collective.recipe.plonesite
...
products =
...
 pox.portlet.banner
```

3. Build your instance and, if you want to, launch it to see the new empty Banner portlet:

```
./bin/buildout
./bin/instance fg
```

4. Check the new portlet: After implementing the changes above, if you click on the **Manage portlets** link in the site's home page (or anywhere in the Plone site), you will see a new **Banner portlet** option in the drop-down menu. A new box in the portlet column will then be shown.

The **Header/Body text/Footer** box shown above matches the **template** definition in the `bannerportlet.pt` file the way paster created it.

How it works...

Let's have a look at the different folders and files `paster` has just created:

Portlet component configuration file

In the `pox.portlet.banner` main folder, open `configure.zcml`. It contains the `<genericsetup:registerProfile />` directive for this product to be listed in the `portal_quickinstaller` tool and in the **Add-on Products** configlet in Plone Control Panel.

Most important is the `<plone:portlet />` directive used to register the generated portlet and to let it available to be used everywhere we can add portlets (left and right columns or user's dashboard, for instance):

```
<!-- If the portlet has no configurable parameters, you
can remove the EditForm declaration in bannerportlet.py
and delete the 'editview' attribute from this statement.
-->

<plone:portlet
    name="pox.portlet.banner.BannerPortlet"
    interface=".bannerportlet.IBannerPortlet"
    assignment=".bannerportlet.Assignment"
    view_permission="zope2.View"
    edit_permission="cmf.ManagePortal"
    renderer=".bannerportlet.Renderer"
    addview=".bannerportlet.AddForm"
    editview=".bannerportlet.EditForm"
    />
```

Portlet registration has several properties which are explained in this table:

Property	Description
name	The name of the portlet. Think of it as the name of a browser (Zope 3) view.
interface	The actual class—used for this portlet display logic—will be the one implementing this interface. `IBannerPortlet` in our example.
assignment	The implementing class.
view_permission/edit_permission	Zope 3-like **permissions** to guard the viewing and editing of the portlet.

Property	Description
renderer	A class with a special `render` method to tell what to show in the user interface (generally a **ZPT** file). Other helper methods can be created and they will all be available via the `view` variable inside the template.
addview	An **add form** class, pretty much like previous add form examples we already saw.
editview	Same as above. If the portlet had no configuration options, we could just skip this property.

Portlet module

In the automatically created source files, open the `bannerportlet.py` file to find:

Element	Description
The interface (`IBannerPortlet` in our case)	It's empty for the time being, which means that no configuration settings can be applied to the portlet.
An `Assignment` class	The interface implementation class with a `@property` decorated `title` method to tell how to call this portlet within the management screen.
An `AddForm` class with a special `create` method	If our portlet had no settings, `AddForm` could inherit from `base.NullAddForm` instead.
An `EditForm` class	A class to handle edition of the portlet configuration options. If the portlet had no settings, we could skip this class.

GenericSetup import step

As we said before, there's also a `profiles/default` folder with this `portlets.xml` file to tell **GenericSetup** to register the portlet:

```
<?xml version="1.0"?>
<portlets>

  <!-- Portlet type registrations -->

  <portlet
    addview="pox.portlet.banner.BannerPortlet"
    title="Banner portlet"
    description="Portlet to show banners"
    />

</portlets>
```

Note that the `addview` property matches the `addview` in the `configure.zcml` file described earlier.

See also

- ► *Creating an Archetypes product with paster*
- ► *Creating a product package structure*
- ► *Creating the user interface for Zope 3 content types*
- ► *Creating a policy product*
- ► *Protecting operations with permissions*

Customizing a new portlet according to our requirements

In the previous recipe, we covered how to create a new portlet package and then we examined some of its most remarkable pieces of code.

In this task, we will modify some of the previously explained classes and modules to achieve the desired results: to display several Banners inside a single portlet.

How to do it...

1. Add a schema to the portlet interface: In the `bannerportlet` module, change the `IBannerPortlet` interface definition for the following block of code:

```
...
from pox.banner.interfaces import ISection
from plone.app.vocabularies.catalog import \
SearchableTextSourceBinder
...

class IBannerPortlet(IPortletDataProvider):
    section = schema.Choice(
            title=_(u"Section"),
            description=_(u"Base section where banners will be
fetched from."),
            required=True,
            source=SearchableTextSourceBinder(
            {'object_provides': ISection.__identifier__,}))

    initial = schema.Int(
            title=_(u"Initial Banner"),
```

```
                description=_(u"First banner to show from the above
Section."))

        final = schema.Int(
                title=_(u"Final Banner"),
                description=_(u"Last banner to show. Leave it empty to
show all banners."),
                required=False)
```

2. Initialize data in the `Assignment` class: In the same file, change the `Assignment` class with the following lines:

```
class Assignment(base.Assignment):
    implements(IBannerPortlet)

    section = u""
    initial = 1
    final = 0

    def __init__(self, section=u"", initial = 1, final = 0):
        self.section = section
        self.initial = initial
        self.final = final

    @property
    def title(self):
        return "Banner portlet"
```

3. Tweak forms by changing widgets: Modify the `AddForm` and `EditForm` classes to change the default widget used by a `Choice` field with this folder-navigation oriented one:

```
...
from plone.app.form.widgets.uberselectionwidget import \
UberSelectionWidget
...
class AddForm(base.AddForm):
    form_fields = form.Fields(IBannerPortlet)
    form_fields['section'].custom_widget = UberSelectionWidget

    def create(self, data):
        return Assignment(**data)

class EditForm(base.EditForm):
    form_fields = form.Fields(IBannerPortlet)
    form_fields['section'].custom_widget = UberSelectionWidget
```

4. State what and when to show in the portlet: In the same `bannerportlet` module, add these lines:

```
...
from Acquisition import aq_inner
from pox.banner.interfaces import IBanner
from plone.memoize import ram
from time import time

RAM_CACHE_SECONDS = 60
...
def _banners_cachekey(method, self):
    """
    Returns key used by @ram.cache.
    """
    the_key = [self.data.section,
               self.data.initial,
               self.data.final]
    the_key.append(time() // RAM_CACHE_SECONDS)
    return tuple(the_key)

class Renderer(base.Renderer):
    render = ViewPageTemplateFile('bannerportlet.pt')

    @property
    def available(self):
        return len(self.banners())

    @ram.cache(_banners_cachekey)
    def banners(self):
        """ Returns banner HTML from selected section
        """
        banners=[]
        context = aq_inner(self.context)
        # Get the catalog
        catalog = getToolByName(context, 'portal_catalog')
        if self.data.section:
            # Is it a min:max or just min: query?
            if not self.data.final:
                position_range = "min:"
                range = (self.data.initial - 1, )
            elif self.data.final == self.data.initial:
                position_range = ""
                range = self.data.initial - 1
            else:
```

```
                    position_range = "min:max"
                    range = (self.data.initial - 1,
                            self.data.final - 1)

            # From the selected section
            # get all the banners
            # in range
            banners = catalog(
             path =
               {"query": '/'.join(portal.getPhysicalPath()) + \
                        self.data.section,
                "depth": 1},
             object_provides = IBanner.__identifier__,
             getObjPositionInParent =
               {"query": range,
                "range": position_range})

            banners = [banner.body for banner in banners]
            return banners
```

5. Modify the **ZPT** file to display the portlet: Change `bannerportlet.pt` with this short TAL-improved XHTML:

```
<dl class="portlet portletBannerPortlet"
    i18n:domain="pox.portlet.banner">

    <dt class="portletHeader">
        <span class="portletTopLeft"></span>
        <tal:title i18n:translate="">Advertisement</tal:title>
        <span class="portletTopRight"></span>
    </dt>

    <dd class="portletItem">
        <tal:banners repeat="banner view/banners">
            <div tal:content="structure banner">
                Banner HTML
            </div>
        </tal:banners>
    </dd>
</dl>
```

6. There's one remaining task that is not related to portlet creation, but to this particular portlet. Banner objects store their HTML code in a `body` field, which is not included by default as metadata (catalog columns) in Plone `portal_catalog`.

To correct this, we have created a `catalog.xml` file in `profiles/default` of the `pox.banner` package to tell us which new metadata columns we need in the catalog:

```
<?xml version="1.0"?>
<object name="portal_catalog" meta_type="Plone Catalog Tool">
 <column value="body"/>
</object>
```

 Although this field's name is `body`, which might be reminiscent of long-formatted text, the contents stored in it are limited: merely the HTML code to render the banner. That's why we included it as metadata in the catalog. Note that it's bad practice to put big fields in catalog.

Once **GenericSetup** has created this new column, we must re-index all existing Banners to update their catalog information. To do this, we have also created a custom import step in `pox.banner` that runs the new `reindexBanner` method in the `setuphandlers` module (available in the accompanying source code).

How it works...

The code in Step 1 is just another schema definition with three fields. For `section`, we are using a `schema.Choice` field, which expects a `source` argument with the vocabulary to be used. In this case, we are using the very useful `SearchableTextSourceBinder` method that returns a vocabulary with all objects found in `portal_catalog` with the passed query. Once we select a Section object, its full path will be stored in the field. You can see how we use it in the `banners` method in Step 4.

The changes to the `Assignment` class in Step 2 provide sensible default values for the three fields in the portlet schema: the highlighted lines show the default values when displaying the **add form**. The `__init__` method is called from the create method in `AddForm` class (when submitting the portlet configuration data for the first time) and sets the values for every field.

In Step 4, inside the `Renderer` class, we created a `@property` decorated `available` method that returns `True` if the portlet should be displayed (that is, has contents to show, is appropriate for the current user, and so on) or `False` if not.

The `render` method is used to tell what to show to the final user, in this case, a **ZPT** file.

The `banners` decorated method is used to get all the Banners to display. Inside the template file, this method will be available via a special `view` variable: `view/banners` will return the tuple of found banners.

In the template in Step 5, the `repeat` tag uses the `banners` method from the `Renderer` class referenced by the `view` variable.

See also

- ▸ *Creating a folderish content type*
- ▸ *Creating content types with Dexterity*
- ▸ *Improving performance by tweaking expensive code*
- ▸ *Adding configuration options in Plone control panel*

Testing portlets

When working with portlets, we can test two things:

- ▸ Whether the portlet is correctly installed and ready to be used
- ▸ Whether the portlet shows what we wanted under the expected conditions

Fortunately, **paster** creates a test suite with these two test cases. Given that it can't know what we want to show in any portlet (`paster` magic doesn't cover Divination, a rather fuzzy discipline), there's a part that we must complete: the `test_render` method in the `test_portlet` module.

If we have a look at `test_portlet` in the `pox.portlet.banner.tests` package, we'll find something that we haven't seen in this book so far: a **PyUnit** test.

We have already talked about our favorite testing approach (**doctest**), so we won't give more details here. Nevertheless, `paster` has done a very good job so we don't need to reinvent the wheel. Let's see our *render* test.

How to do it...

1. Update the `afterSetup` method: Open the `test_portlet.py` file in `tests` sub-package and modify the `afterSetup` method in the `TestRenderer` class with the following:

```
...
from zope.publisher.browser import TestRequest
from zope.annotation.interfaces import IAttributeAnnotatable
from zope.interface import classImplements
...

class TestRenderer(TestCase):
    def afterSetUp(self):
```

```
#log in as manager to install pox.banner product
self.setRoles(('Manager', ))
self.portal.portal_quickinstaller.installProduct(\
'pox.banner')

# create a pox-root Section
self.portal.invokeFactory('Section', 'pox-root')

# Then, 2 Sections with 2 Banners each are created.
folder = getattr(self.portal, 'pox-root')
folder.invokeFactory('Section', 'mars')
folder.invokeFactory('Section', 'earth')
folder.mars.invokeFactory('Banner', 'banner1')
folder.mars.banner1.body = "<span>Good bye</span>"
folder.mars.banner1.reindexObject()
folder.mars.invokeFactory('Banner', 'banner2')
folder.mars.banner2.body = "<span>Mars</span>"
folder.mars.banner2.reindexObject()
folder.earth.invokeFactory('Banner', 'banner1')
folder.earth.banner1.body = "<span>Hello</span>"
folder.earth.banner1.reindexObject()
folder.earth.invokeFactory('Banner', 'banner2', )
folder.earth.banner2.body = "<span>World!</span>"
folder.earth.banner2.reindexObject()
```

2. In the same module and class, update the `test_render` method:

```
def test_render(self):
    classImplements(TestRequest, IAttributeAnnotatable)
    # new portlet with "mars" as the configurable section
    r = self.renderer(
            context = self.portal,
            request=TestRequest(),
            assignment = bannerportlet.Assignment(section=
                                        '/pox-root/mars')
    )
    r = r.__of__(self.folder)
    r.update()
    # render the portlet and start the tests
    output = r.render()
    self.failUnless('<span>Good bye</span>' in output)
    self.failUnless('<span>Mars</span>' in output)
    self.failIf('<span>Hello</span>' in output)
    self.failIf('<span>World!</span>' in output)
```

```
# new portlet with "earth" as the configurable section
r = self.renderer(
        context = self.portal,
        request=TestRequest(),
        assignment = bannerportlet.Assignment(section=
                                        '/pox-root/earth')
)
r = r.__of__(self.folder)
r.update()
# render the portlet and start the opposite tests
output = r.render()
self.failUnless('<span>Hello</span>' in output)
self.failUnless('<span>World!</span>' in output)
self.failIf('<span>Good bye</span>' in output)
self.failIf('<span>Mars</span>' in output)
```

3. Test the portlet: Run this command in your buildout folder:

    ```
    ./bin/instance test -s pox.portlet.banner
    ```

How it works...

The code in Step 1 of the *How to do it...* section creates the correct environment for our test to take place:

▸   We make sure that `pox.banner` is installed in Plone. The `afterSetUp` method is run before any test method is executed. In this way we can do everything we need for the following tests such as creating Sections and Banners.

▸   Then we create a `pox-root` Section in the root of the site. Bear in mind that the `pox.controlpanel` product (covered in *Adding configuration options in Plone control panel* in Chapter 9) has not been installed for this test run, so we don't have any `pox-root` section that is already created.

Step 2 shows the code of the test itself:

▸   We have slightly changed the original paster `Assignment` call to pass the `section` argument our portlet `Assignment` class expects.

▸   The `output` variable contains the HTML snippet rendered from the portlet associated **ZPT** file (`bannerportlet.pt` in our case).

▸   Then the actual tests begin: for a `/pox-root/mars` Section portlet there should be two banners—`Good bye` and `Mars`—and nothing else (neither `Hello` nor `World!`).

▸   After that, a new configuration is set to our portlet—associated to another Section—and we make the opposed test: for a `/pox-root/earth` Section portlet, `Hello` and `World!` banners are shown, unlike `Good bye` and `Mars` that are not displayed.

Note the use of a special `TestRequest` method to create new requests every time we call to `renderer`. This is necessary because the portlet's main method (`banners`) is decorated with `@ram.cache` which keeps a cache of the returned value as long as the `_banners_cachekey` method returns the same value.

See also

▸ *Working with paster generated test suites*

▸ *Adding configuration options in Plone control panel*

Assigning portlets automatically

As we said in the introduction to the chapter, one of the main advantages of Plone 3.x portlets is the great improvement with regards to the portlets management user interface. Portlets can now be assigned very easily in a friendly and typical Plone administration area.

However, as Plone developers, we always want to automate things, and if there's a customer requirement that states there must be a certain portlet under certain conditions, then it is not just a wish but a need.

There are four categories we can use for portlets assignment:

1. **Context**: Portlets created in folders via the **Manage portlets** link.

2. **Group**: Portlets associated to a group will be displayed just for those users belonging to it. These portlets can be created or managed when visiting the Group details page in **Site Setup**.

3. **Content type**: Portlets related to all objects of an explicit content type. They can be managed in the **Types** configlet in Plone Control Panel by choosing the selected content type and then clicking on **Manage portlets assigned to this content type**.

4. **User**: Portlets inserted into a member's dashboard. You can view and manage your personal dashboard at `http://localhost:8080/plone/dashboard`.

In this task, we will automatically associate a new portlet to a specific content type. Nevertheless, the code presented here can be easily changed to work with other portlet categories.

Getting ready

For this task to be more useful, we have created a new portlet inside the `pox.video` package. This portlet displays a Flash player (**FlowPlayer** actually) with every `Video` included as a related item in any object.

Since we haven't explained this portlet anywhere before, first download the chapter's source code. Here is a summarized list of the steps taken to produce the portlet in the `pox.video` package:

1. A new `inlinevideoportlet.py` file was added in the `portlets` sub-package.
2. The matching `inlinevideoportlet.pt` file was also created with the required markup.
3. The new `inlinevideoportlet` portlet was registered in the `configure.zcml` file.
4. Some **JavaScript** (**jQuery** actually) was added to the `video.js` source file inside the `browser/flowplayer` folder.
5. The new portlet was included in the `portlets.xml` file in the `profiles/default` folder as a new import step for **GenericSetup**.

We encourage you to have a look at this new portlet, especially the Python module and the component configuration (**ZCML**) file.

Since the configuration we are going to set involves `XNewsItem` and `Video` content types (they are separate products) and it is very specific to this particular project, we have chosen to add a new installation routine (a **GenericSetup** import step) in the `pox.policy` package. Get an updated copy of it from this chapter's available code.

How to do it...

The following changes will be made in the `pox.policy` package:

1. Create this `portlets.xml` **import step** in the `profiles/default` folder:

```xml
<?xml version="1.0"?>
<portlets>
  <assignment
        category="content_type"
        key="XNewsItem"
        manager="plone.rightcolumn"
        name="inlinevideo"
        type="pox.video.InlineVideoPortlet"
  />
</portlets>
```

2. Create or update `metadata.xml` in `profiles/default` to install dependency products:

```xml
<?xml version="1.0"?>
<metadata>
 <version>1</version>
 <dependencies>

  ...

  <dependency>profile-Products.poxContentTypes:default
  </dependency>
  <dependency>profile-pox.video:default</dependency>
 </dependencies>
</metadata>
```

3. Relaunch and reinstall the `pox.policy` product for these changes to take effect.

   After creating and publishing Video and XNewsItem objects and linking them properly (Video as a related item of XNewsItem) you should get a result like this:

How it works...

The new portlet assignment in the XML file in Step 1 has five properties:

   ▶ Depending on the portlet group we want to deal with, we should use different combinations for **category** and **key**:

Group	category	key
Context, for portlets in a specific path of the site	`context`	The path of the object we want to assign portlets to.
Group, for portlets to be displayed to users in a certain group	`group`	The group ID.
Content type, for portlets associated to every object of a content type	`content_type`	The content meta type.
User, for portlets in user's dashboard	`user`	The user ID. It works just for Dashboard portlet managers.

- ▶ Once we are clear which group of portlets we want to update, we can choose the portlet **manager** that will render the portlet: typically `plone.leftcolumn` and `plone.rightcolumn` (for left and right portlet columns).

- ▶ Plone has a special container for portlets for every combination of `category`, `key`, and `manager`. The `name` property is actually the portlet ID to be uniquely identified in that container.

- ▶ The `type` property matches the `name` of the `<portlet />` directive in its configuration file. In our case, this is `configure.zcml` in the `pox.video.portlets` package:

```
<plone:portlet
    name="pox.video.InlineVideoPortlet"
    interface=".inlinevideoportlet.IInlineVideoPortlet"
    assignment=".inlinevideoportlet.Assignment"
    view_permission="zope2.View"
    edit_permission="cmf.ManagePortal"
    renderer=".inlinevideoportlet.Renderer"
    addview=".inlinevideoportlet.AddForm"
    />
```

There's more...

Assigning portlets programmatically

Martin Aspeli's *Professional Plone Development* shows an example of adding context portlets automatically after content creation. You can find it in the *Creating a New Portlet* section of his book (Chapter 10) or in its accompanying source code at `http://www.packtpub.com/Professional-Plone-web-applications-CMS`.

Portlet managers

We won't cover in this book how to create **portlet managers**, as there's already a great add-on product that can be used to add them in several places in the final web page: ContentWellPortlets.

If you need to place even more portlet managers, you can check `ContentWellPortlets` code and documentation to achieve similar results; consider starting from the `browser/configure.zcml` file.

These online tutorials can be also of great help:

- `https://weblion.psu.edu/trac/weblion/wiki/AddingNewPortletManager`
- `http://plone.org/documentation/how-to/adding-portlet-managers`
- `http://plone.org/documentation/tutorial/customizing-main-template-viewlets/adding-a-viewlet`

See also

- *Modifying the view of a content type with jQuery*
- *Creating a policy product*
- *Adding user groups*

12
Extending Third-Party Products

In this chapter, we will cover:

- ▸ Using skin layers
- ▸ Overriding Zope 3 components
- ▸ Customizing Zope 3 browser templates and files
- ▸ Subscribing to others' events
- ▸ Using the ZCA to extend a third party product: Collage

Introduction

Throughout the book we have focused on the development of Plone add-on products, as stated in the title of the book itself. However, Plone development is concerned not just with new products, but also with interacting with other functionalities: base or core Plone, and third-party products.

In this chapter, we will deal with adjusting community's products to our own requirements, by changing how or what to display in the final web page, or by adding new features to existing components.

All the code produced in the following sections is contained in the same package: `pox.customizations`. To create the package structure:

1. Run this **paster** command in the `src` folder of your buildout directory:

```
$ paster create -t plone pox.customizations
```

2. Enter these options:

Option	Value
Expert Mode?	Easy
Version	1.0
Description	Customizations for PloneOpenX website

3. Create a `MessageFactory` object to provide **internationalization**:

   Open the `__init__.py` file in the `pox.customizations` package and add these lines:

```
from zope.i18nmessageid import MessageFactory
message_factory = MessageFactory('pox.customizations')
```

 More about `MessageFactory` objects and internationalization can be found in *Using i18n with paster-created products* and *Adding i18n support to any product* (both recipes in Chapter 8).

4. Modify your **buildout** configuration file to include this new **egg**:

```
[buildout]
...
eggs =
    ...
    pox.customizations
...
develop =
    ...
    src/pox.customizations
...
[plonesite]
recipe = collective.recipe.plonesite
...
products =
    ...
    pox.customizations
```

   The change in the `products` parameter of the `[plonesite]` part is to auto-install our new product when building the instance.

Using skin layers

CMF Skin layers have been widely used in older versions of Plone to provide end user resources like forms, **page templates**, images and JavaScripts, among others.

Skin layers are the most common and direct way of adding functionalities to a Plone site: register a filesystem directory, drop some files in it, register it as a skin layer, and that's it.

The concept is straightforward: resources available in skin layers are accessible in the Plone site and can be immediately acquired by any object. With this in mind, we could reference to the same image by using two different URLs:

- `http://localhost:8080/plone/news/logo.jpg`
- `http://localhost:8080/plone/logo.jpg`

These two are actually the same Plone logo which is displayed at the top of a fresh Plone site.

As you might have already guessed, this can be a double-edged sword: on the one hand we could use this acquisition benefit by calling a **Controller Page Template** (form) or a **Python Script** wherever we need to perform contextual tasks. This is how Plone's recommendations system works: at the bottom of every page, there's a **Send this** action that invokes the same `sendto_form` form relative to the object we are visiting.

 More about Zope **Acquisition** at: `http://plone.org/documentation/glossary/acquisition` and `http://docs.zope.org/zope2/zope2book/Acquisition.html`.

On the other hand, as we illustrated above, an unaware developer could be forcing a web browser to request the same file several times (one for every different URL it is referenced by) instead of using a cached version. As a rule of thumb, if there is a context-independent resource you want to call to, make sure to anchor its filename to the portal root. Here's an example taken from `main_template.pt` found at `Products/CMFPlone/skins/plone_templates`:

```
<!-- IE6 workaround CSS/JS  -->
<tal:iefixstart replace="structure string:&lt;!--[if lte IE 7]&gt;" />

  <style type="text/css" media="all" tal:condition="exists: portal/
IEFixes.css"
    tal:content="string:@import url($portal_url/IEFixes.css);">
  </style>

  <script type="text/javascript"
    tal:attributes="src string:${portal_url}/iefixes.js">
  </script>

<tal:iefixend replace="structure string:&lt;![endif]--&gt;" />
```

But what happens if two different skin layers have resources sharing the same filename? Well, here is where the magic begins: all skin layers are registered in the `portal_skins` tool—at the root of the Plone site—and the ones that are higher in the list are prioritized over the lower ones.

This is how we can override resources: by creating our own customized versions of them and placing our new layer above the ones we want to override.

 We must always leave the `custom` skin layer at the top: it is not a filesystem directory reference but a special layer that lives in the **ZODB** that allows temporary, through the web customizations of skin files.

In this recipe, we will add a new version of the Plone default contact form (`contact-info.cpt`) without the site description, the bold-faced instructions, and the fieldset legend that you can see in the following screenshot:

Contact form

PloneOpenX is a project to integrate OpenX ads system into Plone

Fill in this form to contact the site owners.

┌─ Feedback details ──────────────────────────────

Name

Please enter your full name

[   ]

Getting ready

Make sure you have the `pox.customizations` **egg** structure mentioned in the introduction to this chapter. If you don't want to perform these tasks but just want to see the code, get a copy of it from the book's accompanying source files.

How to do it...

1. Turn the package into an installable Plone product and register a filesystem directory: Open the `configure.zcml` file in the `pox.customizations` package folder and add these lines:

```
<configure
    xmlns="http://namespaces.zope.org/zope"
    xmlns:five="http://namespaces.zope.org/five"
    xmlns:genericsetup=
            "http://namespaces.zope.org/genericsetup"
```

```
    xmlns:cmf="http://namespaces.zope.org/cmf"
    i18n_domain="pox.customizations">

    <cmf:registerDirectory name="pox.customizations" />

    <genericsetup:registerProfile
        name="default"
        title="pox.customizations"
        description="pox.customizations"
        directory="profiles/default"
        provides="Products.GenericSetup.interfaces.EXTENSION"
        for="Products.CMFPlone.interfaces.IPloneSiteRoot"
    />

</configure>
```

> In latest versions of ZopeSkel, the `<genericsetup:`
> `registerProfile />` directive is automatically added if you
> select `True` to the `Register Profile` option paster has.

2. Add a new skin layer: Once we have created a reference to an existing filesystem directory, we can securely add a skin layer bound to it.

    In the `pox/customizations` folder, create a new `profiles/default` folder structure with this `skins.xml` file:

```
<?xml version="1.0"?>
<object name="portal_skins" meta_type="Plone Skins Tool">
  <object name="pox.customizations" meta_type="Filesystem
  Directory View"
      directory="pox.customizations:skins/pox.customizations" />

  <skin-path name="*">
    <layer name="pox.customizations" insert-after="custom"/>
  </skin-path>

</object>
```

3. Create a new skin layer filesystem folder: In the `pox/customizations` directory, create a `skins/pox.customizations` folder structure.

```
mkdir -p ./skins/pox.customizations
```

4. Create a new resource in the skin layer: Copy `contact-info.cpt` and `contact-info.cpt.metadata` from `Products/CMFPlone/skins/plone_templates` into our `skins/pox.customizations` folder.

    To get the full version of the custom `contact-info` **Controller Page Template**, check this chapter's source code. We have simply removed these lines:

    ```
    <p tal:content="portal/description">Site Description</p>


    ...


    <p class="documentDescription"
       i18n:translate="description_contact_site_owner">
       Fill in this form to contact the site owners.
    </p>
    ```

    We also have omitted the `<fieldset />` and `<legend />` tags:

    ```
    <fieldset tal:omit-tag="">
     <tal:comment replace="nothing">
        <legend i18n:translate="legend_feedback_for_contact_info">
          Feedback details
        </legend>
     </tal:comment>
     ...
    </fieldset>
    ```

5. Reinstall your product: If you haven't done so, reinstall your product to see the changes in the **Contact** form.

> Make sure you have configured an outgoing e-mail server in the control panel in `http://localhost:8080/plone/@@mail-controlpanel`. Alternatively, you can use `PrintingMailHost` available at `http://plone.org/products/printingmailhost`.

How it works...

In Step 1, we have taken two actions:

- We made pox.customizations installable in Plone via portal_quickinstaller by adding a <genericSetup /> directive. Note that to add this directive, we must first include its namespace in the root <configure /> element.

- We registered a filesystem folder as a skin layer: The <cmf:registerDirectory /> directive assumes that pox.customizations is a folder in a skins directory of our package's root folder. If this weren't the case, we could add a directory parameter with the name of the parent folder. Find the complete reference of this directive in the zcml module of the Products.CMFCore package. We have also added the cmf namespace in the root <configure /> element.

The XML file in Step 2 will tell **GenericSetup** two things:

> ▸ To add a new pox.customizations **Filesystem Directory View** object in the portal_skins tool

> ▸ To insert a new pox.customizations layer, just below the custom layer, for every available **skin** (or **theme**).

When overriding resources, it is advisable to copy the existing ones into our skin folder and make the changes there. This is what we did in Step 4.

Skin resources are often accompanied by a metadata file: a file with more information about the page template, the image, or whatever it is that we are customizing. If you are dealing with one of them (like in our example), make sure to also make a copy of it.

As we mentioned in this section's introduction, given that we have placed our skin layer above all the others (except for the custom special layer), we can be sure that all files dropped in the skins/pox.customizations folder will take precedence over the rest.

If you now visit your site's portal_skins tool, you will see a new pox.customizations **Filesystem Directory View**:

Then go to the **Properties** tab to check that the `pox.customizations` skin layer was correctly added just below `custom`.

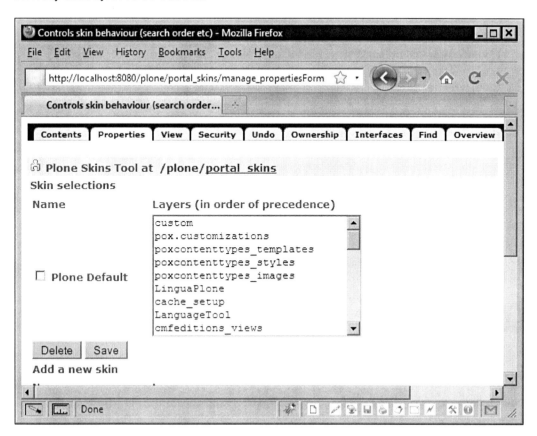

There's more...

In the earlier procedure, we created a skin layer, which is a reference to a filesystem directory in the `DirectoryView` registry. We also created two files in that folder: `contact-info.cpt` and `contact-info.cpt.metadata`. To see how this is managed by Plone, run `ipzope` (if available) in your buildout:

```
./bin/ipzope
```

and execute this code:

```
>>> from Products.CMFCore import DirectoryView
>>> registry = DirectoryView._dirreg
>>> registry.listDirectories()
['Products.ATContentTypes:skins',
...
'pox.customizations:skins/pox.customizations']

>>> customizations = registry.getDirectoryInfo('pox.customizations:
skins/pox.customizations')

>>> customizations.getContents(registry)
({'contact-info': <FSControllerPageTemplate at contact-info>},
({'meta_type': 'Filesystem Controller
 Page Template', 'id': 'contact-info'},))

>>> customizations._filepath
'/home/severus/pox/src/ pox.customizations/pox/customizations/skins/
pox.customizations
```

See also

▶ *Customizing Zope 3 browser resources*

Overriding Zope 3 components

In this section, we will customize Zope 3 components with a new kind of configuration file named `overrides.zcml`. This file works in exactly the same way as regular `configure.zcml` files, but it allows us to override previously registered components.

For our example to be simple, we have chosen to change the usual rendering of the `plone.pathbar` viewlet (the breadcrumbs bar). Although customization of Zope 3 **browser templates and files** can be done in other ways (see *Customizing Zope 3 browser templates and files*) the procedure detailed here can also be applied to other **Zope 3 components**, like **adapters**, **utilities**, and so on.

Note that there can only be one `overrides.zcml` file for any given component. So while this is fine for customer projects, you shouldn't do this in anything you release for general consumption. There's always a way to achieve the same results without `overrides.zcml` but with extra effort, normally by registering components for a more specific interface, as we'll see in the *There's more...* section.

Getting ready

The following changes will be made in the `pox.customizations` package we have been working on in *Using skin layers*. If you don't have it, you can download it from this book's website.

Make sure there's a `browser` sub-package. If not, create it by adding the new folder and placing an empty `__init__.py` file inside it.

How to do it...

1. Create a package level `overrides.zcml` file: In the main `pox.customizations` package folder, add this short `overrides.zcml` file:

```
<configure
    xmlns="http://namespaces.zope.org/zope"
    xmlns:five="http://namespaces.zope.org/five"
    i18n_domain="pox.customizations">

    <include package=".browser" file="overrides.zcml" />

</configure>
```

2. Create the `browser` sub-package `overrides.zcml` file: In the `pox/customizations/browser` folder, add this new `overrides.zcml` file:

```
<configure
    xmlns="http://namespaces.zope.org/zope"
    xmlns:five="http://namespaces.zope.org/five"
    xmlns:browser="http://namespaces.zope.org/browser"
    i18n_domain="pox.customizations">

  <browser:viewlet
     name="plone.path_bar"
     manager="plone.app.layout.viewlets.interfaces.IPortalTop"
     class="plone.app.layout.viewlets.common.PathBarViewlet"
     permission="zope2.View"
     template="templates/path_bar.pt"
  />

</configure>
```

3. Add a customized version of the template: Create a new `templates` folder inside the `browser` sub-package and drop the customized version of the original `path_bar.pt` file (you can copy it from the `plone.app.layout.viewlets` package).

You can get the full version of the template in this chapter's source code. We have removed the **You are here** legend:

```
<span id="breadcrumbs-you-are-here"
      i18n:translate="you_are_here">
  You are here:
</span>
```

Then we replaced all the arrows (`&rarr;` and `&raquo;`):

```
<span tal:condition="view/breadcrumbs"
      class="breadcrumbSeparator">
   <tal:ltr condition="not: view/is_rtl">&rarr;</tal:ltr>
   <tal:rtl condition="view/is_rtl">&raquo;</tal:rtl>
</span>
```

by greater than (`&gt;`) and lower than (`&lt;`) symbols:

```
<span tal:condition="view/breadcrumbs"
      class="breadcrumbSeparator">
  <tal:ltr condition="not: view/is_rtl">&gt;</tal:ltr>
  <tal:rtl condition="view/is_rtl">&lt;</tal:rtl>
</span>
```

4. You need to restart your Zope instance for these changes to take effect.

Now, if you go to `http://localhost:8080/plone/events/aggregator/previous`, the resulting new path bar will look like this:

How it works...

In Step 1, we added a reference to the `overrides.zcml` file inside the `browser` sub-package: it's preferable to make real changes in it to keep things organized.

The registration in Step 2 is an exact copy of the `plone.path_bar` viewlet that you can find in the `plone.app.layout.viewlets` package's `configure.zcml` file; we are using absolute names instead of relative ones though. The most important difference here is that we have added a `template` attribute to the `<browser:viewlet />` directive. Our custom `templates/path_bar` **page template** will be used instead of the original one.

When starting up, Zope will not only process all **component configuration** files but also the `overrides.zcml` files. When found, Zope will override previous components (browser views, file resources, viewlets, and others) that share the same configuration: in our example the viewlet's `name` and `manager` attributes.

Note that ZCML files (`configure.zcml`, `overrides.zcml`, and every other file that is included from them) are always processed at Zope instance startup as long as they are loaded by ZCML `<include />` directives or **ZCML slugs**, even for products that are not installed in the Plone site. Since **z3c.autoinclude** automatically registers packages, even if you don't install the `pox.customizations` product, you will still see the customized version of the breadcrumbs bar.

In short, if you override any kind of Zope 3 component (a **utility** or **adapter**, for instance) make sure that your code will work even when the product is not installed via `portal_quickinstaller`.

There's more...

To override Zope 3 **browser components**, like in the example above, there is a way of registering components based on a special condition named **browserlayer**, which makes customizations available only when the product is installed in Plone. You can see how to use it in Step 7 of the *How to do it...* section in *Customizing Zope 3 browser templates and files*.

See also

- *Using skin layers*
- *Customizing Zope 3 browser templates and files*

Customizing Zope 3 browser templates and files

Zope 2 **skin layers**, covered earlier, have a big drawback: all resources in skin layers are available all over the Plone site, even if they were intended for specific objects.

Besides, and what can be even worse, somebody could create an object (a news item, for instance) in a folder with the exact same ID as a skin resource, preventing it (preventing the skin resource) being available throughout the folder structure: Zope acquisition machinery returns a direct attribute, if it exists (the news item), instead of the skin resource.

Fortunately, with the advent of Plone 3 and its wholesale use of Zope 3 techniques, the use of skin layers has been discouraged in favor of Zope 3 **browser components**: views, templates, files, and so on.

However, with this new approach it has become a bit more difficult—or at least more laborious—to perform customizations of these new types of resources: it would be very tedious if we had to perform all the tasks described in *Overriding Zope 3 components* for every single browser resource we wanted to change for our Plone site.

In the following example, we will use a very straightforward and handy way of customizing Zope 3 browser templates and files with the help of **z3c.jbot** (after "just a bunch of templates"). In this case, we will slightly change the appearance of Plone's default search box (`plone.searchbox` viewlet).

Getting ready

The following changes will be made, again, in the `pox.customizations` package we started in this chapter. If you don't have it, you can download it from this book's webpage.

How to do it...

1. Automatically fetch the `z3c.jbot` package during buildout: Open the `setup.py` file in the root folder of the `pox.customizations` egg and modify the `install_requires` variable of the setup call:

```
setup(name='pox.customizations,
    ...
    install_requires=['setuptools',
                      # -*- Extra requirements: -*-
                      'z3c.jbot',
                      ],
```

2. Be sure to process `browser`'s configuration files: In `pox.customizations`' main `configure.zcml` file, add this line:

```
<configure
    xmlns="http://namespaces.zope.org/zope"

    ...

    i18n_domain="pox.customizations">

    <include package=".browser" />

</configure>
```

3. Register `z3c.jbot` and tell it what to process: In the `browser` sub-package, where we will place our customized resources, add a `configure.zcml` file (or modify it if it already exists) with the following configuration:

```
<configure
    xmlns="http://namespaces.zope.org/zope"
    xmlns:browser="http://namespaces.zope.org/browser"
    i18n_domain="pox.customizations">

    <include package="z3c.jbot" file="meta.zcml" />

    <include package="plone.browserlayer" />

    <browser:jbot
        directory="templates"
        layer="..interfaces.IPoxCustomizations" />

</configure>
```

4. Create a custom template: If you don't already have one, create a new `templates` folder inside the `browser` package folder. Then place into it the adapted version of the `searchbox.pt` file that you can find in the `plone.app.layout.viewlets` package.

   We haven't included the final source code for the template, we have just removed the **only in current section** checkbox:

```
<div class="searchSection">
    <input id="searchbox_currentfolder_only"
        class="noborder"
        type="checkbox"
        name="path"
        tal:attributes="value view/folder_path"
        />
    <label for="searchbox_currentfolder_only"
        i18n:translate="label_searchbox_currentfolder_only"
```

```
                     style="cursor: pointer">
               only in current section
          </label>
     </div>
```

5. Rename the template with its canonical name:

    mv searchbox.pt plone.app.layout.viewlets.searchbox.pt

6. Make the changes product-dependent: In the `pox.customizations` folder, create this `interfaces.py` file:

    ```
    from zope.interface import Interface
    class IPoxCustomizations(Interface):
        """ A layer specific to this product.
            Is registered using browserlayer.xml
        """
    ```

    Finally, create this `browserlayer.xml` file in the `profiles/default` folder for **GenericSetup** to register when our product is installed:

    ```
    <layers>
     <layer name="PoxCustomizations"
        interface="pox.customizations.interfaces.IPoxCustomizations"
     />
    </layers>
    ```

7. Rebuild and reinstall your product to fetch `z3c.jbot` and apply all these changes.

    You should no longer see the **only in this section** checkbox below the search box.

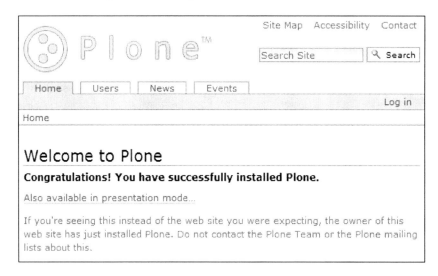

How it works...

The changes made in Step 3 tell the Zope component configuration machinery to:

- Process z3c.jbot's meta.zcml file when configuring the browser sub-package. This will make the <browser:jbot /> directive work.

- Process the plone.browser layer package if not already done so. It will be used in the next directive.

- Find customized versions of Zope browser templates and files in the templates directory.

After the first three steps, we have z3c.jbot installed (we must first build our instance again) and configured. We can start using it now by adding personalized templates, images, or other browser files.

In Step 6, z3c.jbot replaces the original resource with the new one according to the latter's filename. In our example, given that the initial template was located in the plone.app. layout.viewlets package under the searchbox.pt filename, we must rename our own file: plone.app.layout.viewlets.searchbox.pt.

 You might be interested in reading more about z3c.jbot at the package home page at: http://pypi.python.org/pypi/z3c.jbot.

As introduced in *Overriding Zope 3 components*, there is a way to apply <browser /> directives only when the product is installed in portal_quickinstaller: the <browser /> directives expect an optional layer attribute that can take the value of a special marker interface. This interface, if registered as a **browserlayer**, will be applied to the HTTPRequest making our browser configuration more specific than any other existing one and being returned by the Zope Component lookup procedure. More about browserlayer can be found in *There's more...*

The interface attribute in the browserlayer.xml file in Step 7 matches the absolute-dotted path of the interface just defined.

As we said earlier, thanks to z3c.jbot, we can now create new directories inside the browser sub-package (not necessarily there, but it would be a good practice given that z3c.jbot is intended for Zope 3 browser components) and save custom versions of the existing resources we want to override. Just keep in mind that these files need a special name depending on the location of the original file we want to override.

There's more...

z3c.jbot and skin layers

You can also use `z3c.jbot` to override **CMF skin layers** to achieve results similar to those in the *Using skin layers* recipe. Nevertheless, given that `z3c.jbot` doesn't use **skin layers priorities**, there's no easy way to tell whether our package will take precedence or another one will.

Anyway, if you'd like to use it, just follow the procedure above and don't forget to add a `skins` part in the filename mentioned in Step 5. For instance, to override the `contact-info.cpt` form, you should use this filename:

```
Products.CMFPlone.skins.plone_templates.contact-info.cpt
```

Understanding browserlayer

If you have the `iw.debug` package installed in your buildout (if not, read *Taking advantage of an enhanced interactive Python debugger with ipdb* in Chapter 2), open this URL to get an **ipdb** prompt in your console: `http://localhost:8080/plone/ipdb`.

Then run the following commands:

```
>>> from pox.customizations.interfaces import IPoxCustomizations
>>> IPoxCustomizations.providedBy(self.request)
True
>>> from Products.Five.viewlet.manager import ViewletManager
>>> from zope.component import getMultiAdapter
>>> from plone.app.layout.viewlets.interfaces import\
IPortalHeader
>>> PortalHeader = ViewletManager('plone.portalheader',\
                                  IPortalHeader)
>>> the_view = getMultiAdapter((self.context, self.request),\
                                name='plone_portal_state')
>>> header = PortalHeader(self.context, self.request,\
                          the_view)
>>> header.update()
>>> searchbox = header.get('plone.searchbox')
>>> searchbox.update()
>>> 'only in current section' in searchbox.render()
False
>>> from zope.interface import noLongerProvides
>>> noLongerProvides(self.request, IPoxCustomizations)
>>> PortalHeader = ViewletManager('plone.portalheader',\
                                  IPortalHeader)
```

```
>>> header = PortalHeader(self.context, self.request,\
                            the_view)
>>> header.update()
>>> searchbox = header.get('plone.searchbox')
>>> searchbox.update()
>>> 'only in current section' in searchbox.render()
True
```

The above set of commands is to better understand how browser layers work: if `HTTPRequest` provides the layer interface, **ZCA** will find more specific browser components.

There is very helpful online documentation about browser layers at:

- `http://plonemanual.twinapex.fi/serving/layers.html`
- `http://plone.org/documentation/tutorial/customization-for-developers/browser-layers`
- `http://pypi.python.org/pypi/plone.browserlayer`

See also

- *Using skin layers*
- *Overriding Zope 3 components*

Subscribing to others' events

One of the best features of **Zope Component Architecture** is the ability to add functionalities to objects even if their original API (`interface` in Zope's jargon) didn't know about it. This can be done with **adapters**.

We have already seen a special case of adapters in *Adding a custom validator to a content type* (Chapter 5): **subscribers**. They are called when a certain **event** (they are subscribed to) is fired.

In this section, we will explain briefly how to add new subscription adapters to existing objects in order to modify their original behavior.

In this case, we are going to validate the URLs entered in `Event` content types (**Event URL** field).

How to do it...

1. Create the validation routine: In the `pox.customizations` package, create this `validators.py` file:

```python
import urllib2
import urlparse
from pox.customizations import message_factory as _
from pox.customizations.interface import IPoxCustomizations

class ValidateHTTPLink(object):
    """
    Checks if Event URL is a valid http(s) URL
    """
    field_name = 'eventUrl'

    def __init__(self, context):
        self.context = context

    def __call__(self, request):
        # workaround to make this validation
        # browser layer specific
        if not IPoxCustomizations.providedBy(request):
            return None

        # error message
        error_msg = _(u"Event URL not found, please verify URL
        and correct it.")

        # get submitted URL in eventUrl field
        url = request.form.get(self.field_name, \
                            request.get(self.field_name, None))

        # we are interested just in http(s) protocols
        protocol = urlparse.urlparse(url)[0]
        if protocol in ('http', 'https'):
            # open URL: return error if code != 200
            try:
                f = urllib2.urlopen(url)
                if getattr(f, 'code', None) != 200:
                    return {self.field_name: error_msg}
            except:
                return {self.field_name: error_msg}

        # for other protocols skip this validator
        # and use Plone default isURL() validator
        return None
```

2. Register the new validator: Open the `configure.zcml` file in the `pox.customizations` package and add these lines:

```
<subscriber
        factory=".validators.ValidateHTTPLink"
        provides="
            Products.Archetypes.interfaces.IObjectPostValidation"
        for="Products.ATContentTypes.interface.event.IATEvent"
/>
```

3. Restart your instance and reinstall the `pox.customizations` product.

   `./bin/instance fg`

   Then test the validator by creating a new `Event` object and entering a non-valid URL:

Event URL
Web address with more info about the event. Add http:// for external links.
Event URL not found, please verify URL and correct it.
http://localhost:8080/plone/doesnt-exist

Contact Name

How it works...

The code shown in Step 1 is the validation routine. As explained in *Adding a custom validator to a content type*, if the validator fails, a dictionary keyed by field name with an error message is returned. If the validator succeeds, it returns `None`.

Given that `<subscriber />` directives—Step 2—don't allow a `layer` property, as with `browser` components, the validation routine has an initial workaround to check if the browser layer **marker interface** is applied to the `request`. This makes our **subscription adapter** a layer-specific one!

Unlike in the aforementioned recipe, we explicitly declared three properties for the `<subscriber />` configuration:

  ▸ `factory`: To tell the class that should be called to handle the event

  ▸ `provides`: To tell which kind of event this validator should be fired for

  ▸ `for`: To tell the interfaces this validator is bound to

The only required property is `factory`. If we omitted `provides` and `for`, we should have stated them in the validation class:

```
from zope.interface import implements
from zope.component import adapts
from Products.Archetypes.interfaces import IObjectPostValidation
from Products.ATContentTypes.interface.event import IATEvent
...
class ValidateHTTPLink(object):
    ...
    implements(IObjectPostValidation)
    adapts(IATEvent)
    ...
```

See also

 ▸ *Adding a custom validator to a content type*
 ▸ *Customizing Zope 3 browser templates and files*

Using the ZCA to extend a third-party product: Collage

There are some Plone products that take **Zope Component Architecture** a step forward. Products like PloneGetPaid or **Collage** can be categorized as frameworks.

This is because they are pluggable. They were conceived to be extended with new features (PloneGetPaid can be extended with new payment processors, for example).

In the case of Collage, the product we will work with in this section, it is full of places where we can add new functionalities.

Collage comes with four content types:

 ▸ `Collage`: The main object that we use to create the layout of the page. It is a **container** (**folderish**) because it can hold other objects. However, it doesn't expose a **Contents** tab because it implements the `INonStructuralFolder` interface from `Products.CMFPlone`.

 ▸ `Row`: The direct child of a `Collage` object. It is used to create visual horizontal separations in the created layout. It is also an `INonStructuralFolder`.

 ▸ `Column`: The direct child of a `Row` object. It is used to create visual vertical separations and they store the objects that should be displayed in the layout: pages, news items, or aliases.

▸ `Alias`: A special content type used to reference to an existing object. When the user wants to include an object, `Collage` automatically creates an `Alias` object with a reference pointing to the former.

The following is an example of a two-column layout with two `Alias` objects: the left one pointing to an `XNewsItem` and the right one to a `Video`.

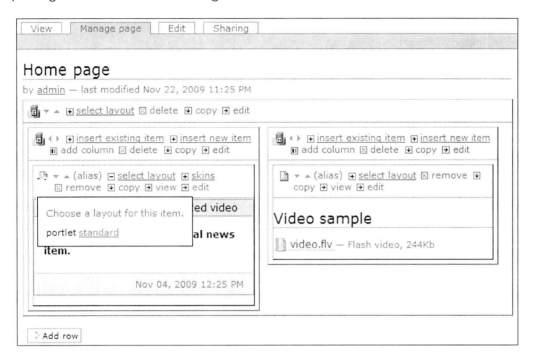

As you can see, on top of every object (`Row`, `Column`, or `Alias`), there is a toolbar with different options: in the left `Alias` object, we can see two arrows, two viewlets (**select layout** and **skins**), and four regular `XNewsItem`'s actions: **remove**, **copy**, **view**, and **edit**.

Let's focus now on the **select layout** viewlet: it can't be appreciated in a still image like the previous one, but the minus icon on the left indicates that the **Choose a layout for this item** box is open. The two options there—**portlet** and **standard**—are two different **browser views** registered for `XNewsItems`. As a matter of fact, they are registered for `ATDocument`, a parent class of `XNewsItem`.

The **skins** viewlet shows a similar box containing all the registered **utilities** providing interfaces related to the above browser views. If this is Greek to you, don't worry, we will cover this a bit later.

This is extraordinary: we can add new **viewlets** (Collage has a custom **viewlet manager**) to perform special operations. We can also register new browser views to display objects according to our needs, and we can even register utilities to apply different skins to those views.

In this recipe, we will add a new browser view to display Section objects so that they show their contained Banners in the same way we show them in the portlet of the pox.portlet.banner package explained in *Customizing a new portlet according to our requirements* (Chapter 11).

How to do it...

1. Add Collage as a dependency: The first thing to do is to fetch automatically an updated version of Collage when building our instance.

   Open the setup.py file in the root folder of the pox.customizations egg and modify the install_requires variable of the setup call:

   ```
   setup(name='pox.customizations,
       ...
       install_requires=['setuptools',
                       # -*- Extra requirements: -*-
                       'z3c.jbot',
                       'Products.Collage',
                       ],
   ```

2. Automatically install Collage when installing pox.customizations: In the profiles/default folder, create or update a metadata.xml file with these contents:

   ```
   <?xml version="1.0"?>
   <metadata>
    <version>1</version>
    <dependencies>
     <dependency>profile-Products.Collage:default</dependency>
    </dependencies>
   </metadata>
   ```

3. Create a **browser view** class (**layouts** in Collage jargon) for Section objects. Add this new views.py file inside the pox.customizations.browser package:

   ```
   from Products.Collage.browser.views import BaseView
   from Acquisition import aq_inner
   from Products.CMFCore.utils import getToolByName
   from pox.banner.interfaces import IBanner
   ```

```
class SectionView(BaseView):
    def banners(self):
        banners=[]
        context = aq_inner(self.context)
        catalog = getToolByName(context, 'portal_catalog')
        # From the selected section
        # get all the banners in range
        banners = catalog(
          path =
            {"query": '/'.join(self.context.getPhysicalPath()),
             "depth": 1},
            object_provides = IBanner.__identifier__)

        banners = [banner.body for banner in banners]
        return banners
```

 Note that this is almost an exact copy of the `banners` method in the `Renderer` class of the `pox.portlet.banner.bannerportlet` module, except that this method returns all banners instead of filtering by position.

4. Register the view: Modify the `browser` sub-package's `configure.zcml` file by adding this browser view configuration:

```
<browser:page
    name="standard"
    for="pox.banner.interfaces.ISection"
    permission="zope.Public"
    template="templates/section.pt"
    class=".views.SectionView"
    layer="Products.Collage.interfaces.ICollageBrowserLayer"
    />
```

5. Create the template to be used for the Collage **layout**: In the `browser/templates` folder, place this `section.pt` **Zope Page Template**:

```
<tal:manager
    replace="structure provider:collage.ContentManager" />

<dl class="portlet portletBannerPortlet"
    i18n:domain="pox.portlet.banner">

    <dt class="portletHeader">
        <span class="portletTopLeft"></span>
```

```
            <tal:title i18n:translate="">Advertisement</tal:title>
        <span class="portletTopRight"></span>
    </dt>

    <dd class="portletItem">
        <tal:banners repeat="banner view/banners">
            <div tal:content="structure banner">
                    Banner HTML
            </div>
        </tal:banners>
    </dd>
</dl>
```

6. Create a skins file: In the `browser` sub-package, create this `skins.py` file:

   ```python
   from pox.customizations import message_factory as _
   from zope.interface import Interface

   class IBannerHeader(Interface):
       pass

   class IBannerNoHeader(Interface):
       pass

   class BannerHeader(object):
       title = _("With header")

   class BannerNoHeader(object):
       title = _("No header")
   ```

7. Register the classes as **utilities**: In the `browser`'s `configure.zcml` file, add these `<utility />` directives:

   ```xml
   <utility
       name="pox-collage-banner-header"
       provides=".skins.IBannerHeader"
       factory=".skins.BannerHeader"
       />

   <utility
       name="pox-collage-banner-noheader"
       provides=".skins.IBannerNoHeader"
       factory=".skins.BannerNoHeader"
       />
   ```

8. Add the interfaces to the view: Open the `views` module in `pox.customizations.browser` and add these lines:

```
...
from skins import IBannerHeader, IBannerNoHeader

class SectionView(BaseView):

    skinInterfaces = (IBannerHeader, IBannerNoHeader, )

    def banners(self):
        ...
```

9. Apply skin to HTML: Modify the `browser/templates/section.pt` file to automatically apply the selected skin as a `class` attribute:

```
...
<dl tal:attributes=
    "class string:portlet portletBannerPortlet ${view/getSkin}"
    i18n:domain="pox.portlet.banner">
...
```

10. Rebuild your instance to fetch `Collage` and reinstall your product to apply all these changes.

The remaining job is creating the corresponding CSS rules to alter the HTML style. We'll leave it as an exercise for the reader.

How it works...

Steps 1 and 2 are to automatically install `Collage` together with the `pox.customizations` product.

Steps 3, 4, and 5 are intended to create Collage **layouts**, which are nothing less than **Zope 3 browser views**:

▶ The `SectionView` class created in Step 3 is not based on regular `BrowserViews`, but on a Collage specific `BaseView` class with helper methods like `isAnon()` and `portal_url()`.

▶ Step 4 registers a new browser view available only for objects providing the `ISection` interface.

The ICollageBrowserLayer interface is added to the request every time a Collage object is called. This makes the browser view available only in the proper context. Collage uses the **browserlayer** approach here, which we explained in *Customizing Zope 3 browser templates and files*. Check the Products.Collage.browser.renderer module to see how the mark_request method is used.

▸ The template file in Step 5 is almost an extract copy of the bannerportlet.pt file in the pox.portlet.banner package. The only difference is the first line which renders the custom Collage's **viewlet manager** (it will be shown only when editing the layout).

You should consider having a look at the getLayouts method in Products.Collage.viewmanager module.

It would be good to have two alternatives when displaying banners inside a Collage: with and without an **Advertisement** title. However, we don't mind if it is rendered, because this is just a matter of visual impact. We achieve this in steps 6, 7, 8, and 9.

Collage BaseView has a skinInterfaces attribute that can take the value of a tuple of **marker interfaces**. If we register **utilities** for them, a **skins** viewlet will allow us to select which skin we want to apply to the view in question.

Be aware of the difference between Collage skins and the **CMF skins** we dealt with in *Using skin layers*: for every available Collage layout, there are several skins defined, which are applied to them in the final rendered HTML. Think of Collage skins as a class attribute in the final HTML element, which, after all, is the usual use for skins.

▸ Step 6 creates the marker interfaces and their implementation classes—those with just a title attribute to be shown as the skin name. Make sure you have a message_factory object in the pox.customizations package, if not, you can copy it from this chapter's introduction.

▸ The name attribute of utilities in Step 7 will be used as a new class attribute for the Collage <dl /> box.

▸ After Step 8, a **skins** option will be available on top of the layout to let us select which skin we want to apply to the box.

The `getSkins` method in `Products.Collage.viewmanager` is a very good example you should really look at to get familiarized with **ZCA**.

▸ The change in the HTML in Step 9 will give the `<dl />` HTML element an extra `class` attribute according to the chosen skin: `pox.collage.banner-noheader` or `pox.collage.banner-header` depending on the chosen skin.

To see the changes we have made, create a `Collage` object and select a `Section` with at least one banner inside it. A **skins** link should be visible to select one of the two options we have created.

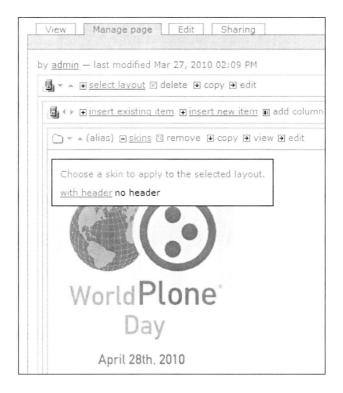

Due to a bug in Collage, we must explicitly select a layout on an object to make the **skins** option available. Given that there's no other existing layout for Section objects except the one we just created, Collage won't show a **select layout** link, thus we won't be able to choose one. To overcome this, create a new dummy layout by repeating Steps 3 to 5 and changing its name as in Step 4.

There's more...

We wanted to take one big step forward by adding a completely new functionality to the just registered `Collage` view: configurable settings. In the same way we can maintain settings in the Plone portlets machinery, we wanted our browser view to be configurable so that we could specify the initial and final banners to be displayed in every `Collage` box.

In the following screenshot, you can see how the layout adds a **configure banners portlet** viewlet that displays a configuration form:

We won't dive into the implementation of these changes, but we'll just mention the techniques we used to tackle this new requirement. They are a good example of how to take advantage of the pluggable nature of `Collage` and even more:

- We registered a new **viewlet** available for the `ISection` interface in `Collage`'s **viewlet manager**.
- The viewlet associated `template` renders an `expandable section` element (like the **select layout** one).
- When this element is expanded, it displays a box with a contained **z3c.form**.
- The form `schema` has two fields: `initial` and `final` to restrict the banners to display.

- ▸ The original `SectionView` **browser view** was modified to filter the banners according to the above settings.

- ▸ Given that `z3c.form` by default reads and writes directly in the `context` object, we had to **adapt** our form to interact with an **Annotation** storage instead of regular `context` attributes.

You can find the code in the `pox.customizations.browser.views` module and in the configuration component file of the same package.

 For more information about Collage and documentation for developers visit `http://pypi.python.org/pypi/Products.Collage`.

See also

- ▸ *Customizing a new portlet according to our requirements*
- ▸ *Installing CacheFu with a policy product*

13

Interacting with other Systems: XML-RPC

In this chapter, we will cover:

- ▶ Creating a configuration form
- ▶ Registering a local utility
- ▶ Registering a global utility

Introduction

This is the penultimate chapter and we wanted to keep something impressive for it. In the following sections, we will focus on creating the required features to communicate to an external **OpenX** server and fetch all their *websites*—formerly known as *publishers*—along with their *zones* (more about this a bit later).

To do that, we need several things:

- ▶ A form to let the manager enter the OpenX server URL, with a username and password so that we can log into the remote service
- ▶ Somewhere to **persist** this data (the above three fields)
- ▶ The import code itself to loop through the OpenX inventory and recreate it in our Plone site

Why do we need that? Since our project is a news website full of ads (check the book's preface for the list of customer requirements), we need a way to store and organize the HTML code to show the banners. That's why, we have created in the previous chapters two new content types (Section and Banner), a configuration option or **configlet** to manage them, and **portlets** and **Collage** views to display them.

Again, why do we need to import the whole inventory already stored in OpenX? Well, that's because of performance. Instead of fetching every banner's HTML code on the fly while rendering a Plone web page, it's better to have them already saved in our own database. There would be advantages in loading banners on demand, however, replicating them within Plone provides clear examples of useful techniques.

Before going on, let's introduce some OpenX concepts we should be familiar with (the following wireframe will illustrate these ideas):

OpenX Term	Description	Plone ad-hoc counterpart
Website/Publisher	A mechanism to group zones. Websites or Publishers are generally related one-to-one with a web site. However, given that OpenX doesn't have any other categorization option, we have chosen to group related zones with them. For example, all the ads to be displayed in the right column of the Economy section in our news website will be stored in the Economy_Right OpenX Publisher.	A hierarchy of `Section` objects (for example, Economy > Right Column). In the previous screenshot, they are represented as grey boxes like **Economy Headlines Section**.
Zone	The placeholder to display banners. Zones have an invocation code (HTML) that is responsible for showing the correct banners. Although this could be confusing now, we think it was easier to talk about Banners throughout the book and then give a thorough explanation in this chapter.	Objects of the `Banner` content type. In the previous screenshot, they are the white boxes like **Headlines Banner 1**.
Banner	The picture, flash movie, or piece of text to be shown as an advertisement. Banners are linked to Zones. A Zone could have no Banner at all (and would be rendered empty) or could have more than one Banner and would show one at a time (a shared Zone).	We don't deal with OpenX Banners directly but with Zones.
Agency/Manager	A special kind of user that can manage a subset of Websites, Zones, and Banners. There is at least one Agency in every OpenX installation.	We will only use Agencies in the code to import OpenX data.

Creating a configuration form

In order to establish communication with the remote OpenX server, we first need at least three pieces of data: the URL to connect to, a username with sufficient rights access to fetch the inventory, and the password.

We could just hard-code them and it would work perfectly well, but that's not even close to the ideal solution. That's why we will now create a general purpose form with the previously introduced z3c.form library.

Getting ready

All the code detailed in this chapter will be added to the existing pox.controlpanel package developed earlier. If you don't have it, you can download it from this book's webpage.

How to do it...

1. Edit the interfaces.py file in the pox.controlpanel package:

```
from zope import schema
from zope.interface import Interface

from pox.controlpanel import message_factory as _

class IImportSettings(Interface):
    """ Defines import form schema
    """
    url = schema.URI(
        title=_(u"URL"),
        description=_(u"The URL you used to log in to OpenX"),
        required=True,)

    user = schema.TextLine(
        title=_(u"Username"),
        description=_(u"An OpenX user with admin rights"),
        equired=True,)

    password = schema.Password(
        title=_(u"Password"),
        description=_(u"OpenX password."),
        required=True,)
```

2. Add the code to be run when submitting the form: Create this new import module in the pox.controlpanel.browser package:

```
from z3c.form import form, field, button
from plone.app.z3cform.layout import wrap_form
from pox.controlpanel.interfaces import IImportSettings
```

```
from pox.controlpanel import message_factory as _

class ImportForm(form.EditForm):
    fields = field.Fields(IImportSettings)
    label = _(u"Import sections and banners from OpenX")
    description = _(u"Import websites (publishers) and zones from
    OpenX into Plone sections and banners")

    @button.buttonAndHandler(_(u'Import'), name=import')
    def handleApply(self, action):
        data, errors = self.extractData()
        if errors:
            self.status = self.formErrorsMessage
            return
        changes = self.applyChanges(data)

        # TODO: Import inventory from OpenX

ImportView = wrap_form(ImportForm)
```

3. Register the form as a browser view (or form): Open the `configure.zcml` file inside the `browser` sub-package and add this `<browser:page />` directive to register the above class as an available resource.

```
<configure
    xmlns="http://namespaces.zope.org/zope"
    xmlns:browser="http://namespaces.zope.org/browser"
    i18n_domain="pox.controlpanel">
    ...
    <browser:page
        for="pox.banner.interfaces.ISection"
        name="pox.import"
        class=".import.ImportView"
        permission="pox.ManageBanners"
        layer="..interfaces.IPoxControlpanelLayer"
        />

</configure>
```

4. Create an adapter for Sections: Modify the `import.py` file created in Step 2 with the following lines:

```
class ImportAdapter(object):
    url = ''
    user = ''
    password = ''

    def __init__(self, context):
        self.context = context
```

5. Register the adapter: Open the `configure.zcml` file inside the `browser` sub-package and add this `<adapter />` directive:

```
<adapter
    for="pox.banner.interfaces.ISection"
    provides="pox.controlpanel.interfaces.IImportSettings"
    factory=".import.ImportAdapter"
    />
```

That's it! We are now ready to see the new form (do not forget that it doesn't have any real import code yet, as we will cover that later):

How it works...

The interface in Step 1, based on `zope.schema` fields, is enough for `z3c.form` to know what fields should be included in the form.

 Notice how we are preparing our code so it can be translated using the special underscore method call to show text strings in the end user's preferred language. There is more about this in *Using i18n with paster-created products (Chapter 8)*.

In Step 2, having included the fields in the form, we added a submit button and its associated code as well as contextual information like a title and description for the form:

- ▸ The `handleApply` decorated method will be called when the **Import** button is pressed. It's a simple method that validates and tries to store the submitted data and then do the import actions, which are not coded yet.

 You could add more submit buttons to the form by adding new methods decorated with `@button.buttonAndHandler`. For instance, you could separate Save and Import logic, which we'll tackle in *Registering a local utility* and *Registering a global utility*.

- ▸ The last line is used to create an `ImportView` class (`wrap_form` method actually returns a class) that will be configured as a **Zope 3 browser view**.

In Step 3, we made the new form available only for `Section` objects (or any other that provides the `ISection` interface). To open it, we add `@@pox.import` to any `Section` URL like `http://localhost:8080/plone/pox-root/@@pox.import`.

 We also added a `layer` restriction to this directive to make the form available only when the `pox.controlpanel` product is installed. Check the rest of the `interfaces.py` file and `profiles/default/browserlayer.xml` to see the necessary code to register the layer. More about registering **browser layers** is in the *Customizing Zope 3 browser templates and files* recipe.

With the previous three steps, we have added a new form to our Plone site that will be valid just for `Section` objects. However, if we tried it right now (before step four), we would get the following error:

```
TypeError: ('Could not adapt', <Section at /plone/pox-root>,
<InterfaceClass pox.controlpanel.interfaces.IImportSettings>)
```

When opening a form on an object, `z3c.form` will try to find out if each field has an appropriate adapter for the context (the `Section` object) and its interface. This test will fail and raise the above error because these fields don't have an adapter yet.

Using **Zope Component Architecture**, we can create (**Step 4**) and register (**Step 5**) an `ISection` **adapter**, capable of getting the above fields, and the problem will be solved:

  ▶   The `import` module in Step 4 provides us with the necessary data placeholders. Nevertheless, this approach doesn't persist the submitted data (we will take care of persistence in *Registering a local utility*).

  ▶   Component registration in Step 5 is for objects providing `ISection` interface: use the `ImportAdapter` class to adapt them if the `IImportSettings` interface is used.

There's more...

There is another example of a **z3c.form** with a different type of **adapter** in the code for *Using the ZCA to extend a third party product: Collage* (Chapter 12).

See also

  ▶   *Customizing Zope 3 browser templates and files*

  ▶   *Adding configuration options in Plone control panel*

  ▶   *Preparing a form to take full advantage of KSS*

  ▶   *Using i18n with paster created products*

  ▶   *Registering a local utility*

  ▶   *Registering a global utility*

  ▶   *Using the ZCA to extend a third party product: Collage*

Registering a local utility

As we have said before, using the above **adapter** for our `ISection` interface has a drawback: field values are never stored.

In this recipe, we will create a **local utility** to persist data. Like **global utilities** (covered in *Registering a global utility*) they can supply some functionality. But, unlike global utilities, they are persisted in the database, so they are generally used to store configuration settings.

How to do it...

1. Create this new `utilities` module in the `pox.controlpanel` package:

```
from persistent import Persistent
from zope.interface import implements
from pox.controlpanel.interfaces import IImportSettings

class ImportSettings(Persistent):
    implements(IImportSettings)

    url = ''
    user = ''
    password = ''
```

2. Register the utility: In the `profiles/default` folder, create this new `componentregistry.xml` file:

```
<componentregistry>
 <utilities>
  <utility
      interface="pox.controlpanel.interfaces.IImportSettings"
      factory="pox.controlpanel.utilities.ImportSettings"
      />
 </utilities>
</componentregistry>
```

3. Change the adapter: Open the `import.py` file in the `browser` sub-package, remove the `ImportAdapter` class and add this new function:

```
from zope.component import getUtility

def import_adapter(context):
    return getUtility(IImportSettings)
```

After this change, we must update the `configure.zcml` file inside the `browser` sub-package to change the `<adapter />` factory:

```
<adapter
    for="pox.banner.interfaces.ISection"
    provides="pox.controlpanel.interfaces.IImportSettings"
    factory=".import.import_adapter"
    />
```

4. Change the interface (optional step). As we are now saving the settings, we should give the user the chance of whether or not to store the password in the **ZODB**. To do that, add this `schema` field definition in `interfaces.py`:

```
class IImportSettings(Interface):
    """ Defines import form schema
    """
    ...
    store_password = schema.Bool(
        title=_(u"Store Password"),
        description=_(u"Store OpenX password in Plone site"),
        default=False,)
```

And then modify the `handleApply` method in the `import` module in the `browser` sub-package:

```
    ...


    @button.buttonAndHandler(_(u'Import'), name=import')
    def handleApply(self, action):
        data, errors = self.extractData()
        if errors:
            self.status = self.formErrorsMessage
            return
        store_password = data.pop('store_password')
        changes = self.applyChanges(data)


    ...
```

5. After the above change, we must reinstall the `pox.controlpanel` product for `GenericSetup` to process the new import step.

How it works...

Step 1 shows an extremely simple class that will become our local utility. Most remarkable is its base class: `Persistent`. The three initially empty attributes will be stored automatically in the **ZODB**.

Local utilities are not registered in **component configuration files** (`configure.zcml`) but in **GenericSetup** extension profiles, as we did in Step 2. In this way, when the product is installed, the local utility will be created directly into the database.

Once the utility is registered, we can safely change the adapter—used in *Creating a configuration form*—for a new one which, by returning the utility, will let us persist the data. This is done in Step 3. Notice that the change in the adapter factory was made just for Python naming conventions.

Since the `store_password` field added in Step 4 isn't included in the utility in Step 1, we must ensure its value isn't stored, stopping an `AttributeError` exception.

From now on, we can get the new utility with a piece of code like this:

```
>>> from zope.component import getUtility
>>> from pox.controlpanel.interfaces import IImportSettings
>>> openx_settings = getUtility(IImportSettings)
>>> openx_settings.user = 'admin'
>>> openx_settings.user
'admin'
>>> openx_settings.password = 'secret'
>>> openx_settings.password
'secret'
>>> openx_settings.url = 'http://localhost/openx'
>>> openx_settings.url
'http://localhost/openx'
```

Fortunately, **z3c.form** takes care of setting and getting the above attributes to show the latest submitted values.

See also

▸ _Creating a configuration form_
▸ _Registering a global utility_

Registering a global utility

Unlike local utilities, **global utilities** can't persist data, they are used to provide general functionality.

 Local utilities could also have their own functions and methods, but we prefer our example as it is: just to keep some useful data and make it available for other utilities.

Let's create the code we need to connect via **XML-RPC** to the remote **OpenX** server and get all the information we need.

Getting started

In this recipe, we will extend the pox.controlpanel package we started in *Adding configuration options in Plone control panel* (Chapter 9) and continued developing in *Creating a configuration form* and *Registering a local utility*. If you don't have that package, you can download it from this book's webpage.

How to do it...

1. Create the utility interface: Open the interfaces.py file in pox.controlpanel package's folder and add this new interface:

```
class IImporter(Interface):
    """ Importer utility
    """

    def import_all():
        """ Import all Sections and banners
        """
```

2. Create the utility code: Modify the utilities.py file in pox/controlpanel by adding this class and methods:

```
import xmlrpclib
from zope.component import getUtility
from zope.interface import implements
from pox.controlpanel.interfaces import IImporter
from zope.app.component.hooks import getSite

class Importer(object):
    implements(IImporter)

    def _server_proxy(self, service):
        """ Helper method to get every different OpenX service
        """
        settings = getUtility(IImportSettings)

        url = '%s/www/api/v1/xmlrpc/%sXmlRpcService.php' % \
            (settings.url, service)
        return xmlrpclib.ServerProxy(url)
```

 This Importer class should also contain the following import_all and _do_import functions, which have been outdented for legibility purposes.

```python
def import_all(self):
    """ Loop through OpenX Inventory to get publishers,
        zones and tags to be imported
    """
    # Get the OpenX server settings
    settings = getUtility(IImportSettings)

    # Try to log in as a manager
    logon_server = self._server_proxy('Logon')
    session_id = logon_server.logon(settings.user,
                                    settings.password)

    # Get all the agencies to get their publishers
    agency_server = self._server_proxy('Agency')
    agency_list = agency_server.getAgencyList(session_id)

    for agency in agency_list:
        # Get all publishers for every agency
        pub_server = self._server_proxy('Publisher')
        publisher_list = \
            pub_server.getPublisherListByAgencyId(
                        session_id,
                        agency['agencyId'])

        for publisher in publisher_list:
            # Get all zones for every publisher
            zone_server = self._server_proxy('Zone')
            zone_list = \
                zone_server.getZoneListByPublisherId(
                            session_id,
                            publisher['publisherId'])

            for zone in zone_list:
                # Get the invocation code for every zone
                # adjs = JavaScript
                tags = zone_server.generateTags(
                                    session_id,
                                    zone['zoneId'],
                                    'adjs',
                                    {})
                # Create sections and banners
                # in Plone accordingly
                self._do_import(publisher, zone, tags)
```

```python
def _do_import(self, publisher, zone, tag):
    """ Do the actual import job
    """
    # All sections will be created starting from pox-root
    site = getSite()
    context = getattr(site, 'pox-root')
    publisher_name = publisher['publisherName']

    # Create a section (if required) and get it
    if publisher_name:
        for part in publisher_name.split('_'):
            if hasattr(context, part):
                context = getattr(context, part)
            else:
                part = context.invokeFactory('Section',
                                             part)
                context = getattr(context, part)
                context.reindexObject()

        # Create a banner (if required) and get it
        banner_changed = False
        if not context is None:
            zone_name = zone['zoneName']
            if hasattr(context, zone_name):
                banner = getattr(context, zone_name)
            else:
                banner_id = context.invokeFactory(
                             'Banner', zone_name)
                banner = getattr(context, banner_id)
                banner_changed = True

        # Update banner attributes
        if not banner is None:
            if banner.title != zone_name:
                banner.title = zone_name
                banner_changed = True

            if banner.body != tag:
                banner.body = tag
                banner_changed = True

            if banner_changed:
                banner.reindexObject()
```

3. Register the global utility: Open the `configure.zcml` file in the `pox.controlpanel` package and add this directive:

```
<configure
    xmlns="http://namespaces.zope.org/zope"
    ...
    />

    ...

    <utility factory=".utilities.Importer" />

</configure>
```

4. Use the utility to import data: Now that we have the real import code, we can modify the original `import.py` file and replace the TODO comment in the `handleApply` method with this:

```
...
from pox.controlpanel.interfaces import IImporter

import logging
logger = logging.getLogger('pox.controlpanel')
...

class ImportForm(form.EditForm):
    fields = field.Fields(IImportSettings)
    label = _(u"Import sections and banners from OpenX")

    @button.buttonAndHandler(_('Import'), name='import')
    def handleApply(self, action):
        data, errors = self.extractData()
        if errors:
            self.status = self.formErrorsMessage
            return
        # store_password field won't be saved
        store_password = data.pop('store_password')
        self.applyChanges(data)
        importer = getUtility(IImporter)
        try:
            importer.import_all()
        except Exception, msg:
            self.status = msg
            logger.log(logging.ERROR, msg)
            errors = True
```

```
# blank the password if desired
if not store_password:
    password = data['password']
    data['password'] = ''
    self.applyChanges(data)
if not errors:
    self.request.response.redirect(
        self.context.absolute_url())
```

How it works...

Let's go through the code in Step 2:

▸ Communication with the OpenX server will be made through Python's native `xmlrpclib` package.

▸ `_server_proxy` is a helper method used to get the proper `ServerProxy` according to the XML-RPC methods we need in every step. OpenX API is organized in several services like `AgencyXmlRpcService.php` and `PublisherXmlRpcService.php`.

 Note how we are using the local utility created in *Registering a local utility* to get the server URL.

▸ `import_all` function will take care of logging into OpenX and looping through all publishers and their zones. With publisher, zone names, and zone invocation code, `_do_import` method will be called.

▸ The `_do_import` function creates Section and Banner objects in the Plone site. Logical groups of OpenX zones can be joined in underscore-separated named publishers, which will be translated into a hierarchical structure of Plone Section objects; for example, Economy_Headlines publisher will have a resultant matching Economy > Headlines structure in Plone. Additionally, OpenX zones will be appended to the above hierarchy as a Banner object. More explanation about this is in this chapter's introduction.

In Step 4, we have updated the `import` module to make the real work:

▸ After persisting the data in the local utility (calling `applyChanges`), we try to import all the publishers and zones using the `import_all` method of the global utility.

▸ If there is an any exception, we log it to the server's console and pass it to the user to inform about the error message.

▸ If the user preferred not to store the password, we blank the `store_password` field and `applyChanges` again. Notice that initially we stored the `password` because it was required by the `import_all` method.

▸ Finally, if everything goes well, the browser will be redirected to the default view of the `Section`.

As with the local utility before, we can now get a handler to this new global one with `getUtility` or `queryUtility` of the `zope.component` package:

```
>>> from zope.component import getUtility
>>> from pox.controlpanel.interfaces import IImporter
>>> utility = getUtility(IImporter)
>>> logon_service = utility._server_proxy('Logon')
<ServerProxy for localhost/openx/www/api/v1/xmlrpc/LogonXmlRpcService.
php>
>>> session_id = logon_service.logon('admin', 'secret')
>>> session_id
'phpads4b15ce174249c7.97856899'
```

There's more...

Changing the look of the form

It's possible to make simple changes to integrate our form into the Plone Control Panel using the same technique we used for the *Adding configuration options in Plone control panel* recipe. The example code for this chapter includes this cosmetic improvement. Have a look at the `import.py`, `controlpanel_layout.pt` file, and the `configure.zcml` file of the `browser` package to get this final result:

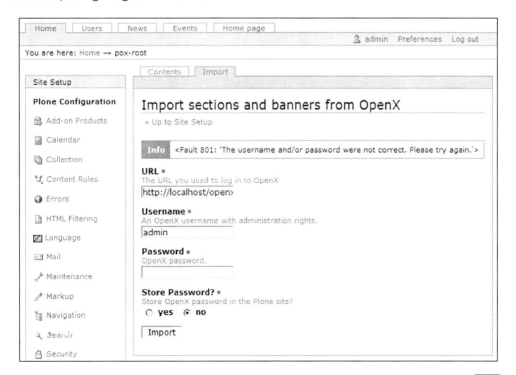

Named utilities

We didn't mention it here but there is another kind of utilities: **named utilities** (unnamed utilities are in fact named utilities with a blank name). They are used to provide the same interface but with a different implementation.

We could have registered, for instance, two global-named utilities for OpenX XML-RPC: one for version 1 and the other one for version 2. Then we could use one or the other depending on the version of the OpenX server, but both of them would share the same settings stored in the local utility.

Installing OpenX

You can find a buildout configuration file within this chapter's source code to automatically install Apache, MySQL, PHP, and OpenX in Linux.

Further reading

If you have *Professional Plone Development* by Martin Aspeli, consider reading Chapter 9, *Nine Core Concepts of Zope Programming*, especially the utilities and adapters sections.

He has also written various manuals available at Plone.org:

- http://plone.org/products/dexterity/documentation/manual/five. grok/core-components/utilities.

- http://plone.org/products/dexterity/documentation/manual/five. grok/core-components/adapters.

- http://plone.org/documentation/tutorial/borg/a-whirlwind-tour-of-zope-3.

Python 2.4 xmlrpclib documentation can be found at http://docs.python.org/release/2.4.4/lib/module-xmlrpclib.html.

You can also check the complete OpenX API at http://developer.openx.org/api, focusing on XmlRpcService classes.

14
Getting our Products ready for Production

In this chapter, we will cover:

- ▶ Installing and configuring an egg repository
- ▶ Submitting products to an egg repository
- ▶ Writing a production `buildout.cfg`

Introduction

Congratulations! If you are reading this, you have most likely finished a product. Or even better, you may be ready to make the production installation.

Having gone through a number of development techniques and tasks for different kinds of Plone products, we are all set to wrap them up and get them ready to be used in a production environment.

In this last chapter, we will create an **egg** repository to store all the Plone products (they are actually **Python packages**) we create. Of course, we can use the public Python egg repositories, like **PyPI** (formerly known as **Cheese Shop**), but sometimes, our products may only be suitable for specific requirements and submitting them to a public server may not be advisable. Anyway, we will also cover how to work with more than one egg repository, including PyPI.

Then, we will create a new **buildout configuration** set of files that will be used for the production deployment. Given that we may have development-only customizations in the original `buildout.cfg` file, it is important to separate them so that they are not included in the live site.

Installing and configuring an egg repository

PloneSoftwareCenter is a Plone add-on product which keeps track of software projects and their releases. It also offers the ability to upload eggs and fetch them automatically, providing the same support for this that PyPI offers.

 You can read more about PloneSoftwareCenter at
http://plone.org/products/plonesoftwarecenter

As Plone developers, it should be easy for us to install and maintain a Plone site with this particular product. In fact, this tool will help us by saving more time than that which it requires to be installed.

Since the egg repository we are about to create will be useful *not* just for a single project (like the one we have been working on from the very beginning of this book), it is recommended to create a new standalone Zope instance in our development server so that we will be able to use it as many times as we need—in this and in future projects (think of it as a development tool like a version control system).

Getting ready

Given that we are to build a new Zope instance, don't forget to install all the basic software you need to compile it. For both Linux and Windows requirements see *Installing Python on Linux*, *Installing Plone on Linux*, and *Installing Plone on Windows*.

How to do it...

1. Make sure you have installed the latest **ZopeSkel**:

   ```
   easy_install -U ZopeSkel
   ```

2. Create the new instance folder and buildout. In your development server, wherever you think is suitable, run the following `paster` command to create a new directory and its **buildout configuration file**. We have chosen the folder name `psc`, after PloneSoftwareCenter.

   ```
   paster create -t plone3_buildout psc
   ```

When the command is run, several options will be presented to finish the new instance environment:

Option	Value
Expert mode?	easy
Plone Version	If you have an updated version of ZopeSkel, the default value will be the latest available Plone version.
Zope2 Install Path	If you want to share this instance of the Zope installation with another existing one, enter its path. If not, just leave it blank.
Plone Products Directory	Again, if you already have a previous installation with the list of Plone products you want to use, enter its path. If you want a fresh installation, leave it blank.
Initial Zope Username	The desired Zope administrator user.
Initial User Password	Choose one. Don't leave it blank as you won't be able to log in.
HTTP Port	Pick a free port in your development server.
Debug Mode	off
Verbose Security?	off

3. Modify the new `buildout.cfg` file: Use this configuration file for a Plone 3.3.4 installation or see this chapter's source code for a Plone 4 alternative.

```
[buildout]
parts =
    zope2
    productdistros
    instance
    zopepy
    plonesite

extends =
    http://dist.plone.org/release/3.3.4/versions.cfg
    versions33.cfg

versions = versions
# Add additional egg download sources here.
# dist.plone.org contains archives of Plone packages.
find-links =
    http://dist.plone.org/release/3.3.4
    http://dist.plone.org/thirdparty

# Add additional eggs here
eggs =
    Products.PloneSoftwareCenter
```

```
            collective.psc.externalstorage
            collective.psc.mirroring
        develop =

        [versions]
        # Version pins for new style products go here
        plone.recipe.zope2instance = 3.6

        [zope2]
        recipe = plone.recipe.zope2install
        fake-zope-eggs = true
        url = ${versions:zope2-url}

        [productdistros]
        recipe = plone.recipe.distros
        urls =
        nested-packages =
        version-suffix-packages =

        [instance]
        recipe = plone.recipe.zope2instance
        zope2-location = ${zope2:location}
        user = admin:admin
        http-address = 8080
        #debug-mode = on
        #verbose-security = on
        eggs =
            Plone
            ${buildout:eggs}

        zcml =

        products =
            ${buildout:directory}/products
            ${productdistros:location}

        [zopepy]
        recipe = zc.recipe.egg
        eggs = ${instance:eggs}
        interpreter = zopepy
        extra-paths = ${zope2:location}/lib/python
        scripts = zopepy

        [plonesite]
```

```
recipe = collective.recipe.plonesite
site-id = plone
instance = instance
products =
    PloneSoftwareCenter
post-extras =
    ${buildout:directory}/psc-post-extras.py
```

4. Add a Python file to automatically create a `PloneSoftwareCenter` object in the Plone site: The `psc-post-extras.py` file in the `post-extras` parameter above is as follows:

```python
PSC_ID = 'psc'
PSC_TYPE = 'PloneSoftwareCenter'

# Is there any psc object?
if hasattr(portal, PSC_ID):
    print 'An object with id "%s" already exists' % PSC_ID
    psc = getattr(portal, PSC_ID)
    # Is psc object a PloneSoftwareCenter one?
    if psc.portal_type != PSC_TYPE:
        print 'Object with id "%s" is not %s. \
                You should fix it if you think it is wrong.' \
                % (PSC_ID, PSC_TYPE)
else:
    # Create a PloneSoftwareCenter
    try:
        id = portal.invokeFactory(PSC_TYPE, PSC_ID)
        print 'A "%s" object was successfully created \
                with the id "%s".' % (PSC_TYPE, id)
    except Exception, msg:
        print 'Couldn\'t create a %s object: %s' \
                % (PSC_TYPE, msg)
```

5. Build and run the new instance: Run buildout and then launch your new Zope instance:

```
./bin/buildout
```

```
./bin/instance start
```

How it works...

In Step 1, we make sure we have the latest version of the **ZopeSkel** package, which is always advisable.

 ZopeSkel is the name of a **Python package** with a collection of skeletons and templates which create commonly used Zope and Plone projects.

These are the meanings of every part of the `buildout.cfg` file in Step 3:

- ▶ `parts`: Unlike the `buildout` file we have been using so far in the previous chapters, we don't need extra parts here, like `omelette` or `ipzope`, because we won't be doing development tasks, like debugging, in this instance. By adding a `plonesite` part (as defined at the bottom of the file), we will create a new Plone site automatically when building our instance.

- ▶ `versions33.cfg`: You can download a `versions33.cfg` file from this book's webpage, with the **pinned** versions required by a `PloneSoftwareCenter` running on a Plone 3.3 installation. We must set these version numbers as some dependency packages are updated to work only in Plone 4.

- ▶ `eggs`: This way, we fetch the `PloneSoftwareCenter` product, which is delivered as a Python **egg**. Together with it, we also get two useful packages to store and synchronize uploaded files in an external storage.

- ▶ `plonesite`: The rest of the file has no special part to be commented (except for the `plonesite` section at the bottom). The `collective.recipe.plonesite` recipe creates (or updates) a Plone site when building our Zope instance. Additionally, we can automatically install a list of products, like `PloneSoftwareCenter` above. We have also included a Python script that will be evaluated after installing the products.

Scripts like the one in Step 4 are typically found in **policy products**. In our example, it would have been cumbersome to create one. It simply creates a `PloneSoftwareCenter` object with `PSC` ID.

Once you have finished this installation, you can launch the new instance and log in to play around with `PloneSoftwareCenter`. In *Submitting products to an egg repository*, we will see how to submit new releases of our products, so that `PloneSoftwareCenter` can store, manage, and handle them.

There's more

Learn more about `collective.recipe.plonesite` at its page at **PyPI**:
`http://pypi.python.org/pypi/collective.recipe.plonesite`.

- ▸ *Submitting products to an egg repository*
- ▸ *Installing Python on Linux*
- ▸ *Installing Plone on Linux*
- ▸ *Installing Plone on Windows*
- ▸ *Creating a Plone site*
- ▸ *Creating a policy product*

Submitting products to an egg repository

In the development phase, we used a **version control system** to help us with synchronization—among the several team developers—to keep version control, to see who did what and why and, if required, to reverse changes; and to fetch (check out) the code when installing a new development instance.

It is now time to release the first deliverable version. This might be an alpha release or a stable one. No matter how mature our product is, we can always submit it to an **egg repository** to allow testers or a third party to install it, try it, and finally use it.

In this section, we will not only upload our Python eggs into a custom egg repository but also into PyPI.

Getting ready

To complete the following example, you should register a new user in the Plone site we created in the *Installing and configuring an egg repository* section; `PloneSoftwareCenter` accepts regular members' submissions of packages.

How to do it...

1. Install `collective.dist` (required for Python 2.4):

   easy_install collective.dist

2. Create a repository configuration file (optional, but desirable). To ease the registration and upload of our products to a repository server we should create, in our home folder, a file named `.pypirc` with this configuration:

   ```
   [distutils]
   index-servers =
       pypi
       psc
   ```

```
[pypi]
username:user
password:password

[psc]
repository:http://my-devel-server/plone/psc
username:prolific
password:contributor
```

 In Windows, the user home folder is available via the `%USERPROFILE%` environment variable.

3. Register and upload your package: Go to the product's folder and run the following command to create an entry for your package in the egg repository and then upload it.

   If you are using Python 2.4 together with `collective.dist`, run:

   ```
   python setup.py mregister sdist mupload -r psc
   ```

   If you are using Python 2.6, run:

   ```
   python setup.py register sdist upload -r psc
   ```

How it works...

If your current Python version is 2.4 (the one required by Plone 3) and you don't have Python 2.6 installed (you may be using Python 2.4 with **virtualenv**), you'll need to install `collective.dist`—as shown in Step 1—to be able to submit packages to more than one server. Once installed, three new commands will be available when running `setup.py`: `mregister`, `mupload`, and `check`.

 You can read more about `collective.dist` at http://pypi.python.org/pypi/collective.dist.

The `.pypirc` file in Step 2 contains:

- ▶ The `[distutils]` section which contains a list of `index-servers`' names. You can choose whatever name you want for them.
- ▶ Next, there is a configuration section for every index-server where we must specify three parameters: `repository` URL (`pypi` server doesn't require this), `username`, and `password` (if not present it will be requested during submission).

In Step 3, we run several commands from the `setup.py` file of our package:

- ▸ `(m)register`, to connect to the server and create a distribution with all the metadata found in the development egg.

 Most of the metadata is requested on screen when creating Plone projects with **paster**. If you want to modify it later, the version number for instance, modify the `setup.py` file.

Note that registering distributions in `PloneSoftwareCenter` with regular members will create the corresponding projects (`PSCProject` content type) in the **Pending approval** state and a manager should manually publish them.

- ▸ `sidst`, to create a `zip` file in a `dist` directory of the package.

If you prefer `egg` files to `zip` files, replace `sdist` with the `bdist_egg` command.

- ▸ `(m)upload`, to upload the code (the `zip` or `egg` file) to the server.

Again, when uploading files in `PloneSoftwareCenter`, regular members will create the matching releases (`PSCRelease` content type) in the **Unreleased** state and a manager should manually change them to the **Final** state, as you can see in the following screenshot:

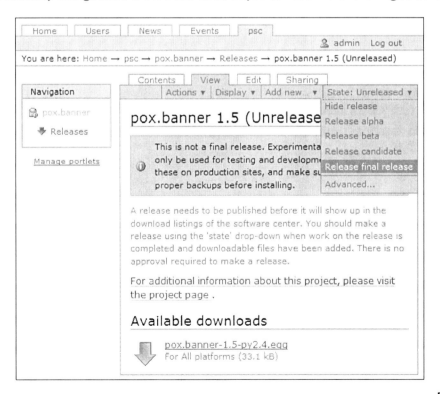

> ▸ The `-r` parameter specifies the **index-server** we want to connect to. In the command line above, we are using `[psc]` information from the `.pypirc` file. If you omit the `-r` parameter, the **PyPI** server will be used.

In *Writing a production buildout*, we will see how to use submitted packages in `PloneSoftwareCenter`. For the time being, check available releases by going to `http://my-devel-server/plone/psc/simple` and compare it to `http://pypi.python.org/simple`.

There's more

Changing the package version number

Initially, all paster created eggs are marked as in the development stage. Consequently, when uploading files, their version numbers will be something like this: `1.5dev-r1640`, which is composed of:

> ▸ `1.5`: the version number taken from the `setup.py` file
>
> ▸ `dev` part showing that the package is in the development state
>
> ▸ `r1640`: the last revision of the current package according to the SVN repository

If you want to change this, modify these lines in the `setup.cfg` file (or just remove them):

```
[egg_info]
tag_build = dev
tag_svn_revision = true
```

An alternative method to submit your package

You can also register and upload the code in different consecutive steps; however, this option only works for **PyPI**:

```
python setup.py (m) register
python setup.py sdist
python setup.py (m) upload
```

Submitting packages to `PloneSoftwareCenter` up to version 1.5.5 is only possible in one step, as shown in the explained procedure.

See also

> ▸ *Installing and configuring an egg repository*
>
> ▸ *Writing a production buildout*

Writing a production buildout

Production systems are essentially different from development environments, so they require separate configurations. Nevertheless, they do share lots of settings, so, it not necessary to write a whole new **buildout** configuration file for each of them.

Fortunately, several buildout files can be merged easily with an **extension** mechanism. This is what we are going to cover in this recipe.

Getting ready

Throughout this book, we have been updating the `buildout.cfg` file for our in-development instance. If you don't have it or you are not sure if it is correct (you can apply this example to any buildout file, actually), you can get a copy of it from this chapter's source files.

How to do it...

1. Identify the common settings between development and production systems: The first step we must take in the creation of separate buildout files is to spot the parts and sections that are shared with the different kinds of environments we will have— environment and production typically, but we could also have a staging instance.

   Let's put all these settings together in a new `base.cfg` file:

```
[buildout]
parts =
    zope2
    productdistros
    zeoserver
    instance
    zopepy
    ipzope

extends =
    http://dist.plone.org/release/3.3.4/versions.cfg
    http://good-py.appspot.com/release/dexterity/1.0a2
    versions.cfg
versions = versions

find-links =
    http://dist.plone.org/release/3.3.4
    http://download.zope.org/ppix/
    http://download.zope.org/distribution/
    http://effbot.org/downloads
```

```
# Add additional eggs here
eggs =
    Products.poxContentTypes
    pox.banner
    pox.video
    pox.policy
    pox.controlpanel
    pox.portlet.banner
    pox.customs

[versions]
zc.buildout = 1.4.2

[zope2]
recipe = plone.recipe.zope2install
fake-zope-eggs = true
skip-fake-eggs =
    zope.i18n
    docutils
additional-fake-eggs =
    ZODB3
    Testing
url = ${versions:zope2-url}

[productdistros]
recipe = plone.recipe.distros
urls =
nested-packages =
version-suffix-packages =

[zeoserver]
recipe = plone.recipe.zope2zeoserver
zope2-location = ${zope2:location}
zeo-address = ${hosts:zeoserver}:${ports:zeoserver}
eggs =
    ZODB3

[instance]
zope2-location = ${zope2:location}
user = admin:admin
http-address = ${hosts:instance}:${ports:instance}
```

```
eggs =
    Plone
    ${buildout:eggs}

zcml =

products =
    ${buildout:directory}/products
    ${productdistros:location}

[zopepy]
recipe = zc.recipe.egg
eggs = ${instance:eggs}
interpreter = zopepy
extra-paths = ${zope2:location}/lib/python
scripts = zopepy

[plonesite]
recipe = collective.recipe.plonesite
site-id = plone
instance = instance
products =
    poxContentTypes
    pox.video
    pox.banner
    pox.policy
    pox.controlpanel
    pox.portlet.banner
    pox.customs

[ipzope]
recipe = zc.recipe.egg:scripts
eggs =
    ipython
    ${instance:eggs}
initialization =
    import sys, os
    os.environ["SOFTWARE_HOME"] = "${zope2:location}/lib/python"
    os.environ["INSTANCE_HOME"] = "${instance:location}"
    sys.argv[1:1] = "-p zope".split()
entry-points = ipython=IPython.ipapi:launch_new_instance
extra-paths = ${zope2:location}/lib/python
scripts = ipython=ipzope
```

2. Separate development-only settings: Create a new `devel.cfg` with this configuration:

```
[buildout]
extends = base.cfg
unzip = true
parts +=
    omelette
    seleniumenv
    roadrunner

eggs +=
    iw.debug
    Products.DocFinderTab
    Products.Clouseau
    Products.PDBDebugMode
    zope.testrecorder

# Reference any eggs you are developing here, one per line
# e.g.: develop = src/my.package
develop =
    src/pox.*

[hosts]
instance = 127.0.0.1
zeoserver = 127.0.0.1

[ports]
instance = 8080
zeoserver = 8090

[instance]
recipe = plone.recipe.zope2instance
debug-mode = on
verbose-security = on
zeo-client = True
zeo-address = ${hosts:zeoserver}:${ports:zeoserver}
http-address = ${hosts:instance}:${ports:instance}
zcml +=
    iw.debug
    zope.testrecorder

[plonesite]
products +=
    Clouseau

[omelette]
recipe = collective.recipe.omelette
eggs =
    ${instance:eggs}
```

```
products =
    ${instance:products}
packages =
    ${zope2:location}/lib/python ./
```

[seleniumenv]
```
recipe = rcom.recipe.seleniumenv
seleniumversion = 1.0.1
eggs = ${instance:eggs}
```

[roadrunner]
```
recipe = roadrunner:plone
packages-under-test =
    pox.*
```

3. Set aside the production environment-specific configuration: In a new
   `production.cfg` file, we will include all the settings required for the final
   production deployment.

 The following settings (cronjobs, Pound server, and so on)
only work in a Linux system. For Windows alternatives, you
can check the links mentioned in the *There's more* section.

```
[buildout]
extends =
    base.cfg
    versions.cfg

versions = versions

extensions += buildout.dumppickedversions

parts =
    zope2
    zeoserver
    instance1
    instance2
    instance-debug
    productdistros
    pound-build
    pound
    varnish-build
    varnish
```

```
        logrotate
        supervisor
        backup
        zopepy
        ipzope
#       start-supervisor
#       logrotate-cronjob
#       backup-cronjob
#       zeopack-cronjob

find-links +=
        http://my-devel-server/plone/psc

develop =

[settings]
instances-user = admin
instances-password = admin
supervisor-user = admin
supervisor-password = admin

[hosts]
instance1 = 127.0.0.1
instance2 = 127.0.0.1
instance-debug = 127.0.0.1
zeoserver = 127.0.0.1
pound = 127.0.0.1
varnish = 127.0.0.1
supervisor = 127.0.0.1

[ports]
instance1 = 8080
instance2 = 8081
instance-debug = 8089
zeoserver = 8090
pound = 8091
varnish = 8092
supervisor = 8093

[instance1]
recipe = plone.recipe.zope2instance
zope2-location = ${zope2:location}
debug-mode = off
verbose-security = off
```

```
zeo-client = True
zeo-address = ${hosts:zeoserver}:${ports:zeoserver}
user = ${settings:instances-user}:${settings:instances-password}
http-address = ${hosts:instance1}:${ports:instance1}
eggs =
    ${instance:eggs}
zcml =
    ${instance:zcml}
products =
    ${instance:products}


[instance2]
recipe = plone.recipe.zope2instance
zope2-location = ${zope2:location}
debug-mode = off
verbose-security = off
zeo-client = True
zeo-address = ${hosts:zeoserver}:${ports:zeoserver}
user = ${settings:instances-user}:${settings:instances-password}
http-address = ${hosts:instance2}:${ports:instance2}
eggs =
    ${instance:eggs}
zcml =
    ${instance:zcml}
products =
    ${instance:products}


[instance-debug]
recipe = plone.recipe.zope2instance
zope2-location = ${zope2:location}
debug-mode = on
verbose-security = on
zeo-client = True
zeo-address = ${hosts:zeoserver}:${ports:zeoserver}
user = ${settings:instances-user}:${settings:instances-password}
http-address = ${hosts:instance-debug}:${ports:instance-debug}
eggs =
    ${instance:eggs}
zcml =
    ${instance:zcml}
products =
    ${instance:products}
```

```
[pound-build]
recipe = plone.recipe.pound:build
url = http://www.apsis.ch/pound/Pound-2.4.3.tgz

[pound]
recipe = plone.recipe.pound:config
balancers =
     main ${hosts:pound}:${ports:pound} ${hosts:
     instance1}:${ports:instance1} ${hosts:instance2}:${ports:
     instance2}
alive = 10
timeout = 90
daemon = 0

[varnish-build]
recipe = zc.recipe.cmmi
url = http://downloads.sourceforge.net/varnish/
varnish-2.0.4.tar.gz

[varnish]
recipe = plone.recipe.varnish:instance
backends =
        ${hosts:pound}:${ports:pound}
bind = ${hosts:varnish}:${ports:varnish}
cache-size = 1G
verbose-headers = on
mode = foreground
daemon = ${buildout:directory}/parts/varnish-build/sbin/varnishd

[logrotate]
recipe = collective.recipe.template
input = templates/logrotate.conf
output = ${buildout:directory}/etc/logrotate.conf

[supervisor]
recipe = collective.recipe.supervisor
port = ${ports:supervisor}
user = ${settings:supervisor-user}
password = ${settings:supervisor-password}
serverurl = http://${hosts:supervisor}:${ports:supervisor}
programs =
        10 zeo ${zeoserver:location}/bin/runzeo ${
        zeoserver:location}
```

```
          20 instance1 ${instance1:location}/bin/runzope ${
          instance1:location} true
          30 instance2 ${instance2:location}/bin/runzope ${
          instance2:location} true
          40 pound ${buildout:bin-directory}/poundrun true
          50 varnish ${buildout:bin-directory}/varnish true

[backup]
recipe = collective.recipe.backup

[start-supervisor]
recipe = z3c.recipe.usercrontab
times = @reboot
command = ${buildout:directory}/bin/supervisord

[logrotate-cronjob]
recipe = z3c.recipe.usercrontab
times = 0 0 * * 7
commandb = logrotate -s ${buildout:directory}/var/logrotate.status
${buildout:directory}/etc/logrotate.conf

[zeopack-cronjob]
recipe = z3c.recipe.usercrontab
times = 0 3 * * 7
command = ${buildout:directory}/bin/zeopack

[backup-cronjob]
recipe = z3c.recipe.usercrontab
times = 0 1 * * *
command = ${buildout:directory}/bin/backup
```

4. Build your instance: After having created the three buildout configuration files as above, we can now build different environments depending on the file we use.

   To build and run the development system, run:

```
./bin/buildout -c devel.cfg
./bin/instance start
```

   On the other hand, if you are going to build the production environment, run:

```
./bin/buildout -c production.cfg
```

   If you want to start the production system, you can use the `supervisor`:

```
./bin/supervisord
```

How it works...

Let's go through the **first buildout configuration file**: `base.cfg`:

- `parts`: For a base configuration, we don't need a development-specific part like `omelette`.

- `extends`: We included several extensions to **pin** the version numbers of the packages to be downloaded and installed.

- `find-links`: URLs of the Python packages index servers.

- `eggs`: All the **eggs** we want to fetch during the buildout process that will be available in our Zope instance.

- `versions`: More version **pins**.

- `zope2`: To download and install Zope2. The `url` parameter is defined in `http://dist.plone.org/release/3.3.4/versions.cfg`, included in its `[versions]` part.

- `productdistros`: In this particular instance, we won't use any old style product. But you might need it.

- `zeoserver`: We will install a **ZEO server** not only in the production environment, but also in development. This will allow us to start instances faster and run `ipzope` while the instance is running.

- `instance`: This part is to configure the Zope instance. It has no associated `recipe` parameter so it won't install any code at all. It is just a configuration section to be used in the `devel.cfg` and `production.cfg` files later.

> Note that there is no `hosts` or `ports` section in this `base.cfg` file, they will be defined in other configuration files. If we tried to run a buildout process based on this particular file, it wouldn't work at all because of these undefined data.

- `zopepy` and `plonesite`: After defining the `zopepy` script—very useful to check if every package is available as expected—we automatically create a Plone site with several products pre-installed.

- `ipzope`: During development, `ipzope` is extremely useful. In the production system, it can help us find problems.

Let's look at the **second configuration file** we created: `devel.cfg`:

- ▶ `extends`: This is the key concept we want to show here (although we already saw this in previous **buildout** files). When using this `devel.cfg` file to create a new Zope instance, all the settings found in `base.cfg` will also be considered. By using the `+=` (plus equal) operand, we literally *add* values or options to already defined parameters. However, if we use the `=` (equal) operand, we will simply override those configurations.

- ▶ `parts`: We will process three other development-specific parts, including **omelette**, which need all eggs to be unzipped (`unzip = true` in `base.cfg`).

 More about `omelette` at `http://pypi.python.org/pypi/collective.recipe.omelette`.

- ▶ `eggs`: Besides the eggs created by us, included in `base.cfg`, we want to install other helpful **eggs** into the development environment.

- ▶ `develop`: During the development stage, we require our products to be fetched from the `src` folder in our instance instead of from a package index.

 Read *Checking out code from a Version Control System* for a development intended buildout extension named `mr.developer`.

- ▶ `hosts` and `ports`: As mentioned in the previous step, we add two custom sections to set host names (or IP addresses) and their ports. They are used in the `[instance]` part in `base.cfg` to configure the Zope instance.

- ▶ `instance`: This `[instance]` part has settings here (`debug-mode`, `verbose-security`, and extra `zcml` slugs) and other settings (admin user, `eggs`, etc.) in `base.cfg`. This is a good example of how to use the extension mechanism to configure just what is needed.

- ▶ `plonesite`: We would like **Clouseau** also to be installed automatically when creating the Plone site.

- ▶ `omelette`, `seleniumenv`, and `roadrunner`: These last three sections are to define the development-only `parts` we added at the beginning of this file, in the `[buildout]` section.

Before going through the highlights of the **third configuration file**—production.cfg—consider the following screenshot to easily understand the proposed schema of a services and their port numbers:

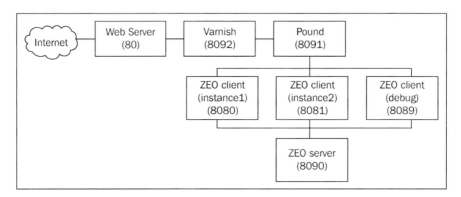

- ▶ versions.cfg: This buildout file is an extension of the base.cfg file and also of a new version-pin-specific one.

- ▶ extensions: We include a very important extension to dump all the eggs fetched during buildout in a versions.cfg file. This will make sure that, if required, a subsequent installation will have the exact same configuration. You can read more about it at http://pypi.python.org/pypi/buildout.dumppickedversions.

- ▶ parts: Unlike in devel.cfg in the previous step, instead of *adding* new parts to the ones defined in base.cfg, we re-define the whole parts parameter of [buildout] given the number of differences between the two of them. In this file, there is no zope2, zeoserver, zopepy, or ipzope parts configuration, they are *inherited* from base.cfg.

If you see the list of parts above, you can get an idea of the many other things—apart from installing Zope—we are going to install when building the production system:

- ▶ A Varnish proxy server, to improve the performance of our website by serving cached versions of the pages.
- ▶ A Pound load balancer, to deal with clients' (usually web browser) requests.
- ▶ Two separate ZEO clients (Zope instances), to run against the ZEO server defined in base.cfg.
- ▶ A special ZEO client (Zope instance), for debugging purposes only.
- ▶ A supervisor, to take care of managing the above services.
- ▶ A logrotate configuration, to rotate the logs of our Zope instances.
- ▶ Several crontab jobs, to auto-start supervisor when the system is booted, to perform the rotation of logs, to compact (pack) the database weekly, and to make daily backups of the ZODB.

The last four parts have been commented out so that they will be installed and run only when you are sure you want to run them:

- `find-links` and `develop`: Given that we are going to use the released versions of our custom packages, we must add the new index server into the `find-links` parameter: the index server we created in the previous recipe based on **PloneSoftwareCenter**. Besides, there are no more packages at development stage, so we clean the `develop` parameter.

- `settings`, `hosts`, and `ports`: These three sections set general settings for all the services we are going to install. Although you might think unwise to set all the same settings (user, password, and host) for every one, it will help in case you are forced to install the services into separated servers (computers).

- `instance1` and `instance2`: Configuration settings for these two instances are identical except for the `http-address`. Besides, they are a copy of the one in `base.cfg` with some extra settings:

    - It is a `zeo-client`, so, it has a `zeo-address`.

    - The lists of `eggs`, `zcml` slugs and `products` are copied from the original `base.cfg` file.

- `instance-debug`: This is a debugging instance that should be launched manually only when required.

- `pound-build` and `pound`: Two separate sections to fetch and build a **Pound** load balancer server and to set its configuration: one `balancer` (`main`) listening to port 8091 (in our example) with two backend servers—`instance1` and `instance2`.

>
> For information about other parameters—like `alive`, `timeout`, and `daemon`—visit `http://pypi.python.org/pypi/plone.recipe.pound` and `http://www.apsis.ch/pound`.
>
> If you are interested in HAProxy, another load balancer, you can use `plone.recipe.haproxy` recipe instead. There is more information about HAProxy at `http://haproxy.1wt.eu`.

- `varnish-build` and `varnish`: Two other parts to build a **Varnish** HTTP accelerator (or proxy cache server) and to set its configuration options.

>
> For information about these parameters, visit `http://pypi.python.org/pypi/plone.recipe.varnish` and `http://varnish.projects.linpro.no`.

- ▶ `logrotate`: This configuration is to automatically rotate all the logs generated by these servers. Check the `templates/logrotate.conf` file in this chapter's source code to see this configuration.

- ▶ `supervisor`: The required settings to install a `supervisor` to control all the installed servers.

- ▶ `backup`: A short section to install and configure several scripts to create incremental and full backups, snapshot backups, and restore **ZODBs**.

- ▶ `start-supervisor`: The `z3c.recipe.usercrontab` recipe creates a new job in the `crontab` of the user running the buildout. In this case, every time the system is rebooted, the supervisor command—the one that controls all the services above—will be run.

- ▶ `logrotate-cronjob`: Another `crontab` job to rotate all the logs every Sunday at midnight.

- ▶ `zeopack-cronjob`: A `crontab` job to pack the database every Sunday at 3 a.m.

- ▶ `backup-cronjob`: The last `crontab` job to make an incremental (default) backup every day at 1 a.m. After detecting a ZODB pack on Sundays, a new full backup will be automatically run on Mondays.

These last four recipes won't be run unless you manually uncomment them in the `parts` parameter at the top of `production.cfg`.

Alternatively, you can run:

```
./bin/buildout -c production.cfg install <partname>
```

to install just the `<partname>` specified.

In Step 4, we introduced the use of `supervisor` to manage the services we installed with **buildout**: `supervisor`, this when launched, will automatically start every attached service. We are then able to use `supervisorctl` to start, stop, or interact with these services:

```
./bin/supervisorctl status instance1
./bin/supervisorctl stop all
```

There's more

Configuring a web server

As depicted in the previous diagram, a web server will be at the front of this chain of servers. We didn't mention any reference about installing or configuring Apache or other servers because we assume that a production environment would already have one installed (one web server can be used for multiple backend application servers, like Zope).

If you are using **Apache**, this is the only rule you should include in your configuration to redirect all requests to **Varnish** (the second server in the chain):

```
<IfModule mod_rewrite.c>
    RewriteEngine On
    RewriteRule ^/(.*) \
http://127.0.0.1:8092/VirtualHostBase/http/%{SERVER_NAME}:80/plone/
VirtualHostRoot/$1 [L,P]
</IfModule>
```

Where `8092` is the Varnish port number and `plone` is the name of the Plone site.

Using or not using buildout.cfg

Note that in this recipe we have consciously omitted any reference to the original `buildout.cfg` file we have been using so far. Regarding this, there are five scenarios that we would like to consider:

1. Use the `buildout.cfg` file name for the development-only configuration file (`devel.cfg`, above).

    This might be particularly useful for developers who have to create a new development instance several times. Instead of running:

    ```
    ./bin/buildout -c devel.cfg
    ```

    they would just run:

    ```
    ./bin/buildout
    ```

    without worrying about which of those many configuration files they have to use.

    This is useful, yes. But what if we have to apply changes to the production system and forgot to add the `-c production.cfg` parameter? Our whole live site would probably crash.

2. Use the `buildout.cfg` file name for the production configuration file (`production.cfg`).

    This is the opposite situation to the previous and has the pros and cons that we mentioned but the other way round.

3. Use the `buildout.cfg` file name for the basic shared configuration settings (`base.cfg`).

    This alternative has the same problem as the first one: we could smash a live production system if we forgot the `-c` parameter.

4. Do not use a `buildout.cfg` file.

   This is certainly an option. If we started the buildout process, we would immediately get this error, without any further damage:

   ```
   While:
     Initializing.
   Error: Couldn't open ./buildout.cfg
   ```

5. Use a special `buildout.cfg` file for every different environment.

   This is to say, create this `buildout.cfg` file in your development environment:

   ```
   [buildout]
   extends = devel.cfg
   ```

   And another `buildout.cfg` in your production system:

   ```
   [buildout]
   extends = production.cfg
   ```

   With the above files, you will be always free to run:

   `./bin/buildout`

   without any risk to your current system.

   You could also add a `-c` parameter with whatever configuration file you like but you must choose whichever option deliberately.

   Of course, you should also exclude these files from your **version control system** to prevent overwriting it in other environments.

Production buildouts for Windows

Martin Aspeli has published several production buildouts that you might find interesting and, most likely, useful. Find them all at `http://svn.plone.org/svn/collective/buildout/uber`.

See also

- ▶ *Installing Python 2.4 on Linux*
- ▶ *Installing Plone on Linux*
- ▶ *Installing Plone on Windows*

Creating a Policy Product

In every Plone undertaking, there are several configuration steps we must take to make sure our project meets the customer's (the project owner's actually) requirements. We shouldn't leave these actions to a manual—likely to be forgotten—procedure, even if we document them.

Creating a policy product

A **policy product** is a regular product that can be installed as other Plone add-ons and will take care of general customizations to meet project needs.

How to do it...

1. Create a package boilerplate with **paster**: We have already created several product packages with the `paster` command. This time it won't be anything special.

   To create the `pox.policy` product, run the following command inside the `src` folder of your buildout:

   ```
   paster create -t plone
   ```

Provide these values at the options `paster` prompts:

Option	Value
Enter project name	pox.policy
Expert Mode?	easy
Version	1.0
Description	Policy product for PloneOpenX website
Register Profile	True

2. Add the policy product to your instance. In the main `[buildout]` section, modify the `eggs` and `develop` parameters:

```
[buildout]
...
eggs =
...
    pox.policy
...
develop =
    src/pox.policy
```

Optionally, if you want the product to be installed at building time, modify the `[plonesite]` section:

```
[plonesite]
recipe = collective.recipe.plonesite
...
products =
...
    pox.policy
```

3. Create an extension profiles folder: In the package's folder, create this folder structure:

```
mkdir -p ./profiles/default
```

 In Windows, change the above command to this:
`mkdir ./profiles/default`.

4. Build your instance up again by running:

```
./bin/buildout
```

How it works...

Policy products are regular products with a special meaning, they configure the website with characteristics the project has and, sometimes, no other project has. Examples of these are the title and description of the site, the initial folders' structure (displayed most of the time on navigation bars), and installation of required products, among others.

 The `<genericsetup:registerProfile />` directive (found at configure.zcml file) makes Plone aware of this product and turns it installable.

To understand how and when GenericSetup runs special installation scripts, you may find it useful to continue reading until *There's more...* or have a look at *Installing CacheFu with a policy product*. The key actions to keep in mind are:

* Drop **extension profiles** (special XML files) you need in the `profiles/default` folder to let GenericSetup automatically install and configure anything you need.

* If there's no XML-based import step for a specific customization, update `configure.zcml` with a `<genericsetup:importStep />` directive as explained in *There's more...*

There's more...

In several recipes of this book, we trusted Plone's GenericSetup process to work as we needed: we dropped some special XML files in the `profiles/default` folder and everything worked as expected.

However, there might be times when we need special steps or actions to be taken when installing a product. For example, we may need to create folders or content inside the portal.

GenericSetup is aware of this requirement many developers have and it supplies a special procedure to get a hook at installation time.

1. Modify `configure.zcml` in your `pox.policy` package:

```
<configure
  ...
    xmlns:genericsetup=
                    "http://namespaces.zope.org/genericsetup"
  >
  ...
    <genericsetup:importStep
        name="various"
        title="pox Policy: miscellaneous import steps"
        description=" "
        handler="pox.policy.setuphandlers.setupVarious"
```

```
    >
<!--       <depends name="other step's name"/>   -->
  </genericsetup:importStep>
  ...
</configure>
```

This will make GenericSetup call the specified `handler` after all of the dependent import steps (none in our example, that's why we have commented it) had run.

2. Create a `setupVarious` method (the above `handler`) in the `setuphandlers.py` file inside the `pox.policy` package:

```
from zope.app.component.hooks import getSite
from Products.CMFCore.utils import getToolByName

def setupVarious(context):

    if context.readDataFile('pox.policy_various.txt') is None:
        return

    portal = getSite()

    # perform custom operations
```

3. Create an empty **flag file** for the setup handler: In the `profiles/default` folder, add the `pox.policy_various.txt` file (read by the `setupVarious` method) to tell GenericSetup whether to run this step or not.

When an import step has been run once, it will be run every time GenericSetup is called, even from other products. As the `readDataFile` method is called in the installing product *context*, if the flag file is not found, the step handler won't be run. That's why it is important to use unique names for these flag files.

4. Reinstall the policy product if needed.

See also

▸ *Changing base class in paster content types*

▸ *Creating a folderish content type*

▸ *Installing CacheFu with a policy product*

Index

Thank you for buying
Plone 3 Products Development Cookbook

About Packt Publishing

Packt, pronounced 'packed', published its first book "*Mastering phpMyAdmin for Effective MySQL Management*" in April 2004 and subsequently continued to specialize in publishing highly focused books on specific technologies and solutions.

Our books and publications share the experiences of your fellow IT professionals in adapting and customizing today's systems, applications, and frameworks. Our solution based books give you the knowledge and power to customize the software and technologies you're using to get the job done. Packt books are more specific and less general than the IT books you have seen in the past. Our unique business model allows us to bring you more focused information, giving you more of what you need to know, and less of what you don't.

Packt is a modern, yet unique publishing company, which focuses on producing quality, cutting-edge books for communities of developers, administrators, and newbies alike. For more information, please visit our website: www.packtpub.com.

About Packt Open Source

In 2010, Packt launched two new brands, Packt Open Source and Packt Enterprise, in order to continue its focus on specialization. This book is part of the Packt Open Source brand, home to books published on software built around Open Source licences, and offering information to anybody from advanced developers to budding web designers. The Open Source brand also runs Packt's Open Source Royalty Scheme, by which Packt gives a royalty to each Open Source project about whose software a book is sold.

Writing for Packt

We welcome all inquiries from people who are interested in authoring. Book proposals should be sent to author@packtpub.com. If your book idea is still at an early stage and you would like to discuss it first before writing a formal book proposal, contact us; one of our commissioning editors will get in touch with you.

We're not just looking for published authors; if you have strong technical skills but no writing experience, our experienced editors can help you develop a writing career, or simply get some additional reward for your expertise.

Practical Plone 3

ISBN: 978-1-847191-78-6   Paperback: 592 pages

A Beginner's Guide to Building Powerful Websites

1. Get a Plone-based website up and running quickly without dealing with code

2. Beginner's guide with easy-to-follow instructions and screenshots

3. Learn how to make the best use of Plone's out-of-the-box features

4. Customize security, look-and-feel, and many other aspects of Plone

Plone 3 Theming

ISBN: 978-1-847193-87-2   Paperback: 324 pages

Create flexible, powerful, and professional themes for your web site with Plone and basic CSS

1. Best practices for creating a flexible and powerful Plone themes

2. Build new templates and refactor existing ones by using Plone's templating system, Zope Page Templates (ZPT) system, Template Attribute Language (TAL) tricks and tips for skinning your Plone site

3. Create a fully functional theme to ensure proper understanding of all the concepts

4. A step-by- step approach to ensure proper understanding of all the concepts

Please check **www.PacktPub.com** for information on our titles

LaVergne, TN USA
29 November 2010
206676LV00006BA/3/P

9 781847 196729